How Schools Change

How Schools Change

Lessons from Three Communities Revisited
Second Edition

Tony Wagner

RoutledgeFalmer
New York and London

First RoutledgeFalmer paperback edition published in 2000.
RoutledgeFalmer
29 West 35th Street
New York, NY 10001
www.routledge-ny.com

Published in hardcover and paperback in 1994 by Beacon Press

RoutledgeFalmer is an imprint of the Taylor & Francis Group.

Printed in the United States of America on acid-free paper.
Text design by Diane Levy
Composition by Wilsted & Taylor

Library of Congress Cataloging-in-Publication Data

Wagner, Tony.
How schools change: lessons from three communities revisited/ Tony Wagner.--2nd ed.
p. cm.
Includes bibliographical references and index.
ISBN 0-415-92763-3 (pbk. : alk. paper)
1. High schools—United States—Case studies. 2. Educational change—United States—Case studies. 3. Hull Junior-Senior High School. 4. Academy at Cambridge Rindge and Latin. 5. Brimmer and May School. I. Title.
LA222.W25 2000
373.73—dc21 00-047021
CIP

10 9 8 7 6 5 4 3 2 1

For my three wonderful children—Dan, Sarah, and Eliza—who have taught me much about how schools are, how they might be made better, and why improving schools is the most critical issue of our time.

Contents

Foreword by Theodore R. Sizer ix
Acknowledgments xv
Introduction to the Second Edition xvii
- Introduction: A Nation at Risk 1
- One: The Hull Junior-Senior High School 15
- Two: The Academy at Cambridge Rindge and Latin 81
- Three: The Brimmer and May School 171
- Four: Some Lessons Learned 233
- Five: Reflections at the Dawn of the Millenium 271

Notes 311
Bibliography 321
Index 325

Foreword

In *How Schools Change*, Tony Wagner summarizes his findings about schooling with three observations that may strike the reader as but elementary common sense. He tells us that to be good a school must have *clear academic goals*, it must live as a community by explicitly articulated *core values*, and it must foster *collaboration* among its several key constituencies—students, faculty, parents, and community members. Even as these statements beg definition, they seem obvious. Who could be against them? Of course a school must be clear about where it is going. Of course it must be a place of consistent and worthy values. Of course all those with something at stake must be gathered together to the task.

Yet in the reality of American secondary schools the obvious is often smothered. The routines of schoolkeeping—the rushed schedules, the fragmented curriculum, the notion that people learn primarily by being told things and display their knowledge simply by talking it all back—have a stubborn hold. "Mindless" is a word long used by critics of the schools. Many generous places for children's learning continue to do things that seem to defy common sense, mostly because they have "always" done them and conventional wisdom is that in some past day their doing "worked."

But not all schools. In recent years the restlessness always found at the grassroots, in the classrooms of thoughtful teachers, has in some places coalesced into broader action. Schoolpeople and parents have started questioning. They have gone back to the beginning, and in so doing have re-illuminated the obvious.

Tony Wagner lived in the midst of three such interesting schools during the late 1980s and early 1990s. He listened and watched and helped out and tried to understand. He found and chronicled constructive movement in all of them, and he has endeavored in this book to extract from that chronicle some generalizations which might help others. He has given a voice to those who are going beyond slogans, back to common sense.

In pondering Wagner's message, one is struck by how difficult change is, how impenetrable institutional habits are, how irrational politics and the school marketplace can be. One is also impressed by the need for skillful leadership. Nothing happens without a nice mix of direction and persuasion.

For example, the (obvious) need for clear academic goals can be addressed only when people have the courage to go back, to look again, to try to understand what they really care about in students' work and how they will know it when they see it. It takes leaders to give permission for and to energize such reflection.

Core values are played out in the minutiae of the school day: the mood of the morning assembly, coping with the perpetrator and the recipient of cruel remarks or physical violence, the struggle to define the boundary between taste and tastelessness and the arbitration of that line. Jollying a community first into recognizing the need for explicitly defining its values (What does justice mean here?) and then into finding the ways and means of living them—especially when these explicit values don't jibe with the values of the street—takes sustained leadership.

A willingness to let members of the community into the school as necessary partners entails time, patience, and tolerance on all sides, and such work requires stubborn persistence on the part of all those who care. Keeping at the commonsensical notion that all of the key adult figures in a child's life need to be part of his or her education takes extraordinary persistence.

Tony Wagner tells us the stories of people who are struggling with these matters. We marvel at how difficult change is even when the objectives are so obviously sensible. Understanding the nature of these difficulties is the beginning of wisdom for those people who would reform our schools. Sadly, common sense alone cannot do it at all.

How does one know a school?

Most Americans depend on hearsay because that is all that there is. How did your daughter do there? Who are the best teachers? Is it really safe, and will my son run with a good crowd of kids?

Most scholars and policymakers depend on "objective" measures: attendance rates, per-pupil expenditures, library book counts, course-taking counts on transcripts, test scores, college admissions, student and teacher absentee rates. From these data they construct profiles. Sometimes they use these profiles to praise or blame. Realtors use them to sell houses in particular communities, ones with "good schools."

Tony Wagner took a different, riskier tack. He showed up and listened and watched, for months. He ran his tape recorder. He questioned school folk, asking them to explain why they did what they did. He took their time, and to repay their generosity he offered them ideas arising from his work and from similar efforts elsewhere. He ran workshops. Simply put, he joined their communities.

Was he "objective"? If this means was he an invisible, omniscient, and removed analyst—no. His very presence must have distorted what he heard and saw. All of us inevitably act a bit differently when we know we are being observed, and we often dream up reasons for what we do only when we are asked to have reasons. Those of us who read this book must depend on Wagner's judgment and discretion. He is an actor, albeit in a bit role, upon his own stage.

However, can one deeply plumb matters such as academic goals and core values and collaboration in any other way? We can read schools' "statements of purpose." We can examine course lists and rule books. We can inquire about "times parents met with teachers," and so forth. Such inquiries tell us something, but not much.

The only meaningful academic goals are those played out, usually implicitly, almost by habit, in classroom after classroom, and it is here we must patiently look. Course titles and texts assigned are not the essence of it. One truly learns about standards and academic performance only by looking at that real performance itself, over and over again, not at its tokens, course syllabi and amassed test scores. One knows the feel of the "core values" of a school by being there, by watching carefully when the rich variety of issues found in any group of adolescents unfolds and by observing how the school reacts. One understands the commitment of parents only by watching carefully what happens to a particular adolescent and his or her parents over many months.

One listens patiently over time. One engages in order to earn people's confidence and thus the privilege to question and eventually to understand deeply. This sort of inquiry draws as much from the disciplines of the humanities as from the traditional social sciences. It requires an extraordinary commitment of time and an attitude of respect and willingness to listen closely. When it is all done, of course, one ends with conclusions in which the scholar himself—in this case, Tony Wagner—is intertwined.

It is from such risky and dogged and creative inquiries that the subtle and most important natures of individual schools and of "school change" will emerge. The crux of schooling is found in the details, in the usually routine dailinesses of keeping school, in the acts of the people involved. It is there that goals are realized, that values are absorbed, that collaboration is employed. Wagner has found these qualities to be at the heart of school reform, and we must—through books such as this one—learn to understand and value them well. From them one can move confidently toward reform, toward common sense in the schooling of American children.

Theodore R. Sizer
Brown University

Acknowledgments

First, I wish to acknowledge all of the help I received from the participants in my study. This work would not have been possible without the strong support of superintendent Claire Sheff and principal Bob McIntyre of Hull, housemaster Ruben Cabral, assistant headmaster Diane Tabor, and headmaster Ed Sarasin of Cambridge Rindge and Latin, and headmistress Anne Reenstierna and assistant head Judy Guild of Brimmer and May. They gave generously of their time for numerous interviews and permitted me unrestricted access to meetings, classes, and documents within their schools. I admire the intellectual curiosity and courage they demonstrated by giving me the freedom to pursue this research, without preconditions of any kind.

I am also most grateful for the active cooperation of many students, parents, teachers, administrators, trustees, and school committee members at the three schools I studied—especially the ninth-grade teachers from Hull, the Academy at Cambridge Rindge and Latin, and Brimmer and May, all of whom welcomed me into their classrooms and spent many hours talking with me about their work.

Second, I want to express appreciation for all of the assistance and support that I received from several individuals while I was at Harvard. The three faculty members at the Graduate School of Education who were readers for the two studies that were the origins for this book—professors Sara Lawrence Lightfoot, Harold Howe II, and Vito Perrone—gave my various proposals, drafts, and completed manuscripts very careful reading and thoughtful criticisms. I also benefited from editorial suggestions and the careful copyediting of my dissertation by Susan Alexander, who has been a sympathetic critic and a helpful colleague in many educational ventures during the past decade. Additionally, Howard Gardner and Theodore Sizer read my dissertation after it was completed and suggested revisions for a book that might be of more general interest.

Third, I wish to thank PJ Blankenhorn, who has consistently encouraged me and made many helpful comments on my writings, and Susan Worst, my editor at Beacon Press. Susan has kept the faith with this project and made most helpful substantive and stylistic suggestions. I also wish to acknowledge the fine copyediting work of Chris Kochansky on this manuscript.

Finally, some of the key findings and recommendations from the last chapter of this book are described in a different form in two previously published articles of mine: "Improving High Schools: The Case for New Goals and Strategies," *Phi Delta Kappan*, May 1993, and "Systemic Change: Rethinking the Purpose of School," *Educational Leadership*, September 1993.

Introduction to the Second Edition

It is hard to imagine a time in which there has been more change in our society than the decade between 1990 and 2000. Ten years ago the Internet was virtually unknown outside of academia. E-commerce hadn't been invented. Now the rapid spread of high-speed information technologies is creating a "new" and increasingly globalized economy. The implications for fundamental economic and social change may be as profound as those associated with the transition from an agrarian economy to what is now called the "old" industrial economy. Living in the midst of this transformation, it is hard for us to understand the impact.

What is clear, however, is that the pressure on our public education system to improve has intensified dramatically. On the one hand, business leaders are increasingly strident in their calls for fundamental change and increased accountability in public education, as they've seen the pool of skilled workers shrink drastically in an expanding, skill-based economy. And on the other, growing numbers of students and their parents are also beginning to understand that further learning beyond high school is essential in order to earn more than a minimum wage in both the new and old economy.

According to the numbers, this is truer than they may realize. In an address on the New American High School,

Patricia McNeil, the assistant secretary for vocational and adult education at the U.S. Department of Education, said, "The high school diploma has lost its economic value. The median earnings of young men ages 25 to 34 years old with only a high school diploma fell by $14,000 from 1973 to 1993."[1]

More and more students are attempting to go to college, in order to have a shot at earning a decent living. According to McNeil, 62 percent of all high school students went on to college in 1994. However, only 30 percent end up completing their associates or bachelors degree.[2] Most are neither prepared nor motivated to do the work required.

In response to the growing chorus of dissatisfaction with our education system, the last seven years (since the first publication date of this book) have seen state legislatures pass sweeping reforms aimed at pressuring public education to improve. The two most widely adopted reforms are the introduction of "choice" into the public school system, primarily through the establishment of publicly funded "charter schools," and the so-called standards movement. I discussed these two reform strategies briefly in chapter 4, primarily from a policy perspective, because in 1992–93 they were merely blips on the education horizon that had no real impact then on the process of change in the schools I studied. Now these two forces have combined to challenge the educational status quo, in the same way that e-commerce has drastically altered the business landscape.

The printing of a second edition of this book has afforded me an opportunity to revisit the three communities I first studied in the early 1990s. In the winter of 2000 I spent time reviewing the history of the past decade of educational reform in Massachusetts and studying the impact of these policy revolutions on the three communities I first visited more than ten years ago. Chapter 5, which is new to this second edition of the book, is a case study of how one state—Massachusetts—has ushered in the "brave new educational world" of choice, charters, standards, and high stakes tests. It is also an account of how school choice and high stakes tests are affecting these three schools.

I believe a close look at how these policies are actually working in real communities raises fundamental questions about what it will take to fulfill our promise to give all students adequate preparation for work and citizenship in the twenty-first century. I explore both the possibilities and limitations of the school choice and high stakes tests strategies in conclusion of Chapter 5.

Meanwhile, back in classrooms, while the world changes, most schools—especially high schools—still do not. In the decade since I completed my research for this book, I have spent the majority of my time in schools—consulting to districts, schools, and educational foundations around the country (and internationally) on strategies for systemic change. Despite the increased pressures associated with the trend toward more testing and school accountability, I find that the daily routine in most classrooms remains substantially unchanged. And so the descriptions of the three communities in this book are still surprisingly current studies of the student and teacher experience of high school and of how schools try to change—what stands in the way, what they need to do to be successful, and how we as citizens can and must be involved.

Introduction: A Nation at Risk

In 1983, the U.S. government issued a dramatic report, entitled *A Nation at Risk*, telling Americans that our country was imperiled—not from an external threat, but from one of our own making. American schools were in shambles, the report said, threatened by a "rising tide of mediocrity," and as a result the country's economic survival was endangered. Unless Americans acted immediately, the report argued, we would not "win" the international economic "wars" being waged with the Japanese, the Germans, and others; the country lacked a sufficiently skilled labor force.[1] A growing chorus of employers agreed that high school graduates lacked even basic skills—like the ability to read software manuals, do simple computations, or write clear paragraphs—as well as "higher order" skills such as critical thinking and problem solving. During the first few years of the ensuing "school wars," the battleground was frequently state legislatures, where new state laws and policy guidelines were passed that required students to take more rigorous academic courses for a high school diploma, and teachers to meet new and higher standards for certification.

Highly respected academics like Theodore Sizer, John Goodlad, Ernest Boyer, and others agreed with the call for higher academic standards, but argued that much of the real problem with schools was the result of outdated teaching methods and curricula—things you can't fix with new state laws and more central-office memoranda. They advocated treating teachers more like professionals and giving the task of improving schools to them. The highly influential 1986 Carnegie Commission report *A Nation Prepared: Teachers for the 21st Century* pushed this argument further, and visionary union leaders like American Federation of Teachers president Albert Shanker also actively supported new efforts to give teachers more authority and responsibility for school reform.[2] As a result, beginning in the late 1980s, school systems like Dade County, Florida, and Rochester, New York, began "school-based management" or "total quality improvement" programs that gave teacher-administrator management teams greater autonomy to make improvements in their own schools.

In the 1990s, despite these reforms, test scores have remained the same or have continued to decline in most school systems, and high school graduates appear no better prepared for productive work than they were a decade ago. Increasingly impatient with the pace of change, a growing number of business leaders, policymakers, and academics have begun to argue that new weapons are needed in the battle to improve schools: national standards and tests, and so-called school choice.

Competition and choice of products work to stimulate rapid improvements in the marketplace—why not in schools? Get rid of the educational monopolies and make schools compete by giving parents the right to send their children anywhere they wish, even perhaps to private schools, some now argue. Improving schools is simply a matter of creating new incentives, with quality guaranteed by nationally or state mandated standards. The new strategy has broad appeal because it fits the American free market ideology and promises a quick, cheap fix. It is almost elegant in its simplicity.

And therefore dangerous. With the exception of the work of academics like those mentioned above, school reform efforts to date have been long on slogans and rhetoric (some of it hysterical, such as the allusions to the threat to national security) and short on careful analysis. School reform has also been largely "business-driven"—propelled by the undeniable need for a more highly skilled labor force and inspired by examples of "restructuring" in the corporate world.

The Unanswered Questions

Before the country embarks on yet another new strategy to win the "school wars," we need to step back and consider what the war is really about—besides the need for better-educated employees—and what has actually taken place in schools that have attempted significant changes. As a country, we continue to lurch from one educational fad to another without answers to some basic questions:

Why haven't schools changed? What's really wrong with them, and whose fault is it? Is it an aging teacher force, waiting to retire and reluctant to change? Parents who aren't home much anymore? Kids who watch too much TV? Community members who don't respect teachers or spend the money needed to make schools better? Business leaders who push only for vocational education?

How can we really know if a school is good or bad? What do standardized test scores tell us about students' abilities to reason, communicate clearly, and solve problems—the competencies business leaders now say we need most for a changing workplace? What else do students need to know and be able to do for the twenty-first century? Do we have to teach new subjects, teach in new ways?

And why do so many students seem unhappy and hard to motivate in school—and at home, too? Rarely consulted, students have been hostage to the "school wars" for more than a decade, but they have much to tell us.

Will more school choice and national tests and standards finally do the job? What are the risks in such a bold new set of strategies? What do we do if these, too, fail to transform our schools?

What actually happens when a school engages in a process of systemic change? Why do some teachers and administrators choose to work together to change schools? What do they hope to accomplish? And what do the students and parents in these schools think? Are there some lessons being learned about how to create better schools?

What more might concerned business leaders, parents, community members, teachers, and even students be doing to help improve schools?

This book explores some new answers to these questions. By looking at three representative but very different high schools, we see the process of school change as it actually occurs. At the Hull Junior-Senior High School, a small public school in a small, predominantly white, blue-collar town; the Academy at Cambridge Rindge and Latin High School, a program within a large multiethnic, urban school; and Brimmer and May, an elite private school in a wealthy suburb, we will observe classes, listen in on meetings, talk at length to community leaders, administrators and teachers, parents and students—all in order to understand how schools change and what lessons we can learn from the struggle for school reform in three American communities.

Superficially, these schools do not look very different from schools in comparable communities around the country. They teach all the usual subjects that make up the American high school curriculum—English, math, social studies, science, and foreign languages—and students and teachers alike have their share of disappointments and boredom, as well as perhaps a few moments of joy and inspiration, along the way. What is special about these schools is that groups of people in each are working together, consciously and deliberately, to rethink and reshape what a high school education should be. Their goals, strategies, and reasons for seeking change differ. But the concern—for some even the passion—for finding better ways to engage adolescents and prepare them for adulthood unifies them.

None of these schools represents a casual academic exercise or a precious pilot project with lots of extra money and special attention from foundations, universities, or the central office. All are struggling, seat-of-the-pants efforts. Any or all may fail, either partially or wholly. They represent a new kind of social "R & D"—research and development to reinvent high schools—and are kin to the best of similar efforts launched around the country in response to the growing chorus of school critics.

Perhaps because they are driven in part by outsiders' increasingly impatient demands for fundamental school reform, there is at times a gritty, determined, even desperate-seeming quality to these efforts—almost as if people were trying to reinvent the airplane in mid-flight. The sense of urgency, of mission, is something that many adults in these three schools share and sets them apart from some of their more complacent colleagues elsewhere.

The Schools Studied

My choice of schools for this study was influenced by several factors. First, I wanted to study schools that were undertaking what are now called systemic reforms. In the past, schools have attempted to introduce many different kinds of separate innovations—such as team teaching or community control or a thematic approach to curriculum—but it has not been common practice to attempt a series of more fundamental changes all at once. A growing number of school systems now claim to be undertaking "systemic change," but these efforts are comparatively new and have not been studied. I wanted to explore what happens in a school that attempts sweeping changes in teaching methods, curriculum, and the ways in which decisions are made, all at once.

Second, I wanted to consider a diverse mix of schools. Hull interested me because it is a comparatively small school—400 students—in a town that might be characterized as blue-collar. This is the kind of school and town one might find in many parts of suburban or rural America. Cambridge Rindge and Latin, on the other hand, with its 2,100 students and 54-percent minority population, is the kind of large urban school that one might find in any number of cities. Many parents and teachers will find one or the other of these schools in some way familiar.

The choice of Brimmer and May as the third school for my study was influenced by several factors. Brimmer and May is a private school, and at a time when the public policy called "school choice" is being widely debated, I was interested in looking at a school that was "chosen" by parents and students, and largely free of the kinds of regulation and constraints that most public schools face. Its teachers are not unionized, and the "central office" is down the hall rather than across town. I wondered how much freer this kind of school might be to undertake changes.

Another reason for choosing Brimmer and May was because of its membership in an organization called the Coalition of Essential Schools (CES), a school-university partnership to promote high school reform that was organized by Theodore Sizer in 1984 at Brown University. The Coalition's work and Sizer's critiques of American high schools have become nationally prominent forces for change in American education today, and there are now more than 550 affiliated schools around the country.[3] (While several studies of CES schools are now under way, none have been published to date.)[4] The key leadership, including many teachers, in all three of our schools had read Sizer's books, heard him speak, and often referred to his work to help explain or justify changes they were seeking. Administrators at both Cambridge Rindge and Latin High School and Hull High School have explored the possibility of joining the Coalition of Essential Schools, but only Brimmer and May was a formal member.

Choice of Methodologies

In addition to choosing what schools to study, I had to decide *how* to study a whole-school change process. Traditional quantitative sociological research methods—looking at changes in average test scores, dropout rates, and college acceptance rates—

are useful for certain purposes, but they tell us nothing about how schools change. To answer this question, I needed to study a school's culture, and so I searched for more qualitative research techniques—those that are closer to what anthropologists do.

The mix of qualitative methodologies that I ultimately used for this study was influenced by my experiences with several outstanding individuals in the field. As a research assistant to Dr. Michael Maccoby for two studies of character and work in corporations, I learned many valuable lessons about studying a workplace culture and administering and interpreting open-ended questions in one-on-one interviews.[5] I also learned a great deal about the use of focused group interviews, or focus groups, from Daniel Yankelovich, John Doble, and my colleagues at the Public Agenda Foundation, where I worked for two years. Finally, while a doctoral student at Harvard from 1988 to 1992, I studied with Sara Lawrence Lightfoot and discovered a research methodology she calls portraiture.

Portraiture is a comparatively new approach to qualitative research—and one that is hard to describe. Lightfoot sees the methodology of portraiture as part art, part science. She believes that the nature of the inquiry must be sensitive as well as skillful, and sympathetic and critical at the same time. Portraiture requires listening in a different way—with the heart as well as the head. In her landmark study, *The Good High School*, Lightfoot describes portraiture as "a genre whose methods are shaped by empirical and aesthetic dimensions, whose descriptions are often penetrating and personal, whose goals include generous and tough scrutiny. It is a sensitive kind of work that requires the perceptivity and skill of a practiced observer and the empathy and care of a clinician."[6]

And so I set out to create a series of in-depth portraits of three schools in the process of change. I recorded extensive observations of classes and of small and large group meetings over a period of several years. I conducted analysis of numerous documents—official publications, meeting notes, memoranda, and so on—in all three schools. And I interviewed teachers, community leaders, parents, and students—both individually and in groups. I arrived at several working hypotheses about the change process only after comparing and analyzing data from all of these sources—a process anthropologists refer to as triangulation. These portraits, then, represent a compilation, distillation, and synthesis of data from many different sources.

Duration and Focus of Study

Most of my research was done during the 1990–91 school year. However, since completing my initial study, I have periodically returned to look at how the change process has evolved, and I have added recent updates for all three schools.

I spent varying amounts of time observing in each school. My association with Brimmer and May was the longest, spanning two and a half years, from January 1989 to June 1991, for reasons explained below. My time spent observing at both Hull and the Academy began informally in the spring of 1990 and then spanned the full 1990–91 academic year. On average, I spent between one half and one full day a week in each school during that year. My time was divided among many different kinds of observations—classes, team meetings, faculty meetings, school improvement meetings—as well as extensive interviewing and document analysis. The choice of what to observe and which issues to explore in greater depth at Cambridge Rindge and Latin was particularly difficult because of the size of the school.

I focused my observations on ninth-grade classes because in all three schools this is where the change process began. While Brimmer and May has now pushed curriculum and teaching changes up to include all four high school grades—and in fact graduated its first "Coalition class" in June 1991—I limited my study there to ninth grade so as to have more points of comparison between the three schools.

There were four ninth-grade English/social studies teams

teaching in the Academy. I observed them all, but chose to narrow the focus of my observations, and thus the data I present, to just one team. I picked the pair of teachers that Ruben Cabral, the housemaster, felt were the leaders in the change process—the ones whose teaching practices were the most successful and most likely to be emulated by colleagues. While I was not able to corroborate his judgment about colleagues' emulation, I found this pair to be the most effective in engaging students actively—one of Sizer's essential concerns. Thus, I chose to look at illustrations of "best practice," reasoning that we might all have the most to learn from such examples.

In all three schools I observed classes in all subject areas—math, science, English, history, and foreign languages. While I am well aware of the concerns of many about the poor quality of teaching in math and science, I chose to focus most of my critical analysis of teaching and curriculum on the English and social studies classes for two reasons. Having been a ninth-grade English and social studies teacher for a number of years, I felt most qualified to analyze teaching and curriculum in these classes, and I thought descriptions of these classes would be more accessible to most readers.

Research and Participation: The "Critical Friend"

Complicating my methodology for this study was the fact that at different times and to varying degrees in each school I have had more than one role. At all three schools I have been both a researcher and a paid consultant and/or seminar leader.

I first came to know Brimmer and May's headmistress, Anne Reenstierna, and assistant head Judy Guild through my initial research at the school in the spring of 1989. In September of that year, there was a last-minute resignation from the faculty, and so they asked me to take over the job of teacher of twelfth-grade English. I happily accepted the offer to be a part of a CES school and taught there part-time for two years. During this period, I was also hired by the school as a consultant to work on several different projects. First, I was asked to lead the faculty in a series of workshops on improving the moral climate of the school (this conversation continued with students and parents as well, and is described in the Brimmer and May chapter). Later that year, I also consulted with Anne and Judy about developing a process for shared decision making. Finally, I was asked in the second year to be a peer supervisor and mentor for new faculty, and to help assess the work of their faculty-administrative committee for shared decision making.

My association with the Hull public schools also extended over several years and a number of capacities. In January 1990, I was hired to do a series of introductory workshops on school-based management, first for the system's administrators, and then for teams of teachers and administrators from each of the three schools. During the school year 1990–91, I continued to provide technical assistance to the school-based management teams and also assisted the team of ninth-grade teachers. During 1991–92, I provided additional training and technical assistance for school-based management and leadership workshops for administrators, and consulted with the superintendent about new approaches to defining and assessing student outcomes.

My involvement at Cambridge Rindge and Latin has been more limited. In the spring of 1990, I was hired to teach a mini-course to interested faculty on the principles and practices of the Coalition of Essential Schools.

Was my work as a consultant and researcher in some way at cross purposes? I think the answer is no. As a consultant for school improvement, I have prior experiences and explicit values that inform my work, but I do not go into a superintendent's office or a faculty meeting with a set of workshops or prepackaged solutions to sell. Rather, I see my role as that of a problem-solver, working with others toward goals which *they* define. My first job as a consultant is to collect data, to do research. Before teaching workshops at any of these three schools, I spent time observing in classrooms and talking to teachers, students, and administrators.

Far from creating a possible conflict of interest, my work as a consultant in these schools was completely consistent with my stance as a researcher. My role was one which Theodore Sizer calls that of "critical friend"—a sympathetic outsider who can see things with a fresh set of eyes, ask the tough questions, and make unencumbered recommendations. (I describe the role of critical friend further in the last chapter.)

This is not to suggest that I approach either consulting or research completely neutral or value-free—I am skeptical of any such claims to total neutrality. When it comes to thinking about education, I have a clear point of view, informed by my graduate studies, by fifteen-plus years of experience in schools—variously as a teacher at many grade levels, a school head, trustee, researcher, and the father of three children—and by my six years of experience as a CEO in nonprofit organizations, where I have worked with business and community leaders, academics, and policymakers.

I take seriously the thoughts and feelings of everyone concerned with schools—educators and students, parents and community members, academics, employers, and policymakers. I am not an advocate for any one group, and so all of these different voices are in some way heard in this study. When I observe in a school, I have certain fundamental questions in mind—things I look for first. Do all students feel stimulated and challenged? Do they feel that adults in their school care about all students equally, and that things besides just being smart and getting good grades also matter? What are the working conditions like for teachers in the building? Is there a spirit of professionalism and collegiality? Finally, are outsiders—parents, community leaders, researchers—welcome? Is there a willingness to consider a range of points of view and to learn?

It has been my experience that better schools typically have *clear academic goals* which apply to all students, *core values* that attend to the needs of the heart as well as the head, and a high degree of *collaboration* within and beyond the school walls. How these elements are dealt with in our three schools, and the changing educational needs of both students and our society, are key themes in this study.

In all three schools studied, I shared this explicit set of values and commitments with the leaders and many of the teachers. The people who hired me to help them in these schools knew their practices were new and therefore imperfect. They were not afraid of criticism; they actively sought it. And they trusted that my criticism would be constructive.

Trust comes with time. Because I spent so much time in these three schools, people had a sense of who I was and what I stood for beyond labels like "consultant," "teacher," or "academic." Though we might have disagreed on strategies or in our assessments of the success of certain endeavors, most knew that my commitment—whether in the role of researcher, consultant, or teacher—was consistent: to help make schools more challenging and nurturing for students, more professional and collegial for teachers, and more open to the concerns of "outside" adults. These were values that all respected and in most cases actively shared.

To guard the trust that so many in these schools gave me, I promised to keep certain negative comments made by teachers, students, and parents completely confidential. You will notice that in this study I give credit where it's due to real schools and real people, but without permission I do not attribute negative comments given in confidence to named individuals. (Pseudonyms are used occasionally in long passages, for clarity.)

It is you, the reader, who must decide whether any or several of the factors discussed above may have in some way distorted my findings. Consistent with the best traditions of qualitative research, I present raw data from classes, meetings, conversations, documents, and so on—either prior to or after giving my own analysis—in order to allow the reader to draw his or her own conclusions.

This study, then, attempts to bring you into each of these schools as an active observer. By looking and listening with a caring yet critical eye, and then reflecting on the lessons learned, we will better understand some of the crucial issues related to how schools change: what's working, what's not, some of the reasons why, and what else is needed—what more each of us as citizens can and must do.

ONE

The Hull Junior-Senior High School

The rules of the game have changed. It's not just that schools haven't been doing their job; the job is fundamentally different. Kids are different; community structures are different; global impact is different. We can't just do business the way we have traditionally. We're still doing things as if we had "Leave It to Beaver." But June, Ward, Wally, and the Beaver no longer exist! We have to stop acting like that's who's out there in the way we teach and interact with families.

—Claire Sheff
Superintendent of Schools, Hull

A Struggling Community with a Heart

The small town of Hull, Massachusetts—population 10,000—sits at the end of a long thin peninsula that points into the Atlantic Ocean. Visible from the high school, Boston's glass skyscrapers glitter in the afternoon sunlight across the bay. Although this multicultural high-tech capital of the East lies only an hour's car or boat ride away, it is a world apart from the nearly all-white (98 percent Caucasian) working-class town of Hull.

Driving through the two-block-long center of town is a trip back in time. No malls or chain stores here. Few neon signs, even. Just a handful of small, locally owned stores: a pizza shop, drug store, hardware, market, insurance agency, gift shop. Except for a few large homes on the hill outside of town, the houses of Hull's residents are equally modest—mostly small cape-style cottages packed close together with tiny yards in front. In front of every fourth or so house, there is a wooden work boat of some kind up on blocks. Waiting for a new engine, or some caulking and a can of paint, perhaps. Waiting for better times. Even the marine repair yard at the end of town seems more like a graveyard for abandoned boats than a working concern.

Despite the fact that the town's population swells by nearly 50 percent in the warm months, as many come to enjoy one of the best beaches in the region, Hull is a poor town. A 1989 background publication of the Hull Council for Business and Cultural

Development states, "Because of its relatively small size, isolation, and population density, the town is more characteristic of a low-income urban area than a suburb. According to the 1980 U.S. Census, the proportion of low and moderate income is much higher than the surrounding region. Estimates place this figure at about fifty percent."[1]

The town lost its only "industry" when an amusement park closed about twelve years ago, shortly after the great blizzard of 1978. In fact, many attribute the town's continuing financial woes to the irreparable devastation caused by that storm. Now, according to the 1990 census data, 20 percent of the town's adult population are homemakers, 18 percent clerical workers, 18 percent professionals, 11 percent skilled workers; 11 percent work in service occupations, 6 percent in managerial positions, and 15 percent in miscellaneous jobs.[2] About a third of the families with children in the public schools receive some form of public assistance. Many in the town try to make ends meet by lobstering in the evenings and on weekends. Unlike those of most New England coastal towns, Hull's small harbor shelters many more work than pleasure boats.

"Hull is known as a welfare community," Bob McIntyre, Hull High School's principal, explained when I first interviewed him in October 1989. "There's a lot of unemployment and single-parent families. People keep putting their hopes into the town becoming an ocean-front resort again, but it hasn't happened." A modern condominium development, which had been deliberately planned to draw middle-class professionals to the town as year-round residents, went bankrupt in 1989.

Hull's only high school, a long, low, brick structure built in 1957, was a source of pride to the then-thriving town when it first opened. It was a brand-new, first-class facility with a young and highly committed staff. For years, the school's marching band won awards and was considered one of the best in New England. By 1976, the high school's enrollment had grown to more than 1,000 students.

According to veteran teachers, the school was then a relaxed, pleasant place to work. Bill Hurst, who has taught English at Hull High for twenty-one years, explains: "When I first started teaching here in 1969, there was a lot more money for education. We had an excellent staff, and it was a great place to work. I taught only four classes—one was an honors class with only six kids. My total load was only about seventy-five students. I had three planning periods three days a week, and I only had to supervise one or two study halls a week."

But the high school has not been a happy place to work or learn for some time. Because of its dwindling population and thin economic base (most of the town's revenues come from residential property taxes), the school system was one of the first in the northeast to suffer from severe financial cutbacks. The 1992 per-pupil expenditure for schooling in Hull was $4,642—about $400 below the state average. Three separate efforts to override a state-mandated 2.5-percent cap on property taxes failed in 1988. (The tax cap was the result of a statewide voter initiative, "Proposition Two-and-a-Half," which was passed by referendum in the early 1980s.)

Enrollment has declined steadily. In 1990–91, there were fewer than 400 students in grades 9–12, and 1,500 students in the entire school system, K–12. As a result of both financial cutbacks and reduced enrollments, faculty and staff at the high school have been reduced by nearly 40 percent over the last five years. Average class size in 1990–91 had crept up to about 27 students. With all teachers teaching five periods a day, their average student load is more than 120. Most teachers are also required to monitor study halls one period every day, leaving only one period for class preparation and conferences.

To save money, the town's three small schools—Jacobs Elementary, Memorial Middle, and Hull High—were reorganized in 1989, and all seventh- and eighth-grade students now attend the high school, where many of the high school teachers claim the younger students receive less supervision from their teachers and administrators and are disruptive. The marching band and many other extracurricular and sports programs were additional victims of budget cuts.

Worsening student achievement is perhaps both a reflection of and further cause for the dispiritedness of the school. Hull High School's average SAT scores declined every year from 1986 to 1990, with the 1990 combined average of 796 (out of a possible 1600) being the worst ever. Until a new dropout prevention program was put into place in 1989, the cumulative four-year high school dropout rate had been nearly 30 percent, while only about 40 percent of the remaining students went on to four-year colleges. These statistics are all only too well known by the teachers, many of whom share the sentiments of a colleague who observed, "The only way out of town for most of these kids is the army."

Nevertheless, this is a town that many love still. Surrounded by ocean on two sides, Hull residents cherish their long, thin beach, with the dark green sea beyond and the ever-changing sky above. Locals wryly observe, "There aren't any jobs in Hull, but it doesn't much matter because everyone would rather be at the beach anyway."

Hull is also a place where people care about one another. A computer consultant who recently moved his family from a wealthy Boston suburb told me, "The thing I like about Hull is that it's a town where people help each other out, instead of pushing one another aside to get something. There's not a lot of pretense here. You can live simply and quite well."

Finally, Hull is a community with a core of teachers, administrators, and community members who care very deeply about young people. When asked what she liked most about teaching, ninth-grade Spanish teacher Mary Lou Galluzzo, who is also a longtime resident of the town, answered with a depth of feeling that many involved in the town's school improvement effort seemed to share. "I really love these kids," she said. "Hull kids are really special. They're very needy emotionally, but they are down-to-earth, funny, very open kids. They don't put on airs."

A New Superintendent with a Passion

The efforts to reform Hull's schools began late in 1987, when Richard Charleton, superintendent of schools for seventeen years, resigned unexpectedly to take a job as a superintendent in Rhode Island. According to several people, in and out of the school, whom I interviewed, Richard had been a traditional, somewhat autocratic but effective superintendent for many years. However, he had become increasingly impatient and demoralized by the steady cuts to school programs that were the result of Proposition Two-and-a-Half. "Because Hull's major industry is people who own second homes, we were one of the three most adversely affected communities in the state," explained Richard Cochran, who has served on the school committee since shortly before Richard Charleton left.

Rather than quickly appointing a replacement for the departing superintendent, the school committee decided to hire a seasoned person as interim superintendent to give the town some time to determine its educational needs and priorities. Eugene Crowell, who had been superintendent in neighboring Cohasset for many years, was persuaded to come out of retirement and serve as acting superintendent for five months while the town conducted a search for a permanent successor.

Claire Sheff, their eventual choice, was an unlikely candidate for the Hull superintendency. True, she had grown up in a community outside of Boston not very different from Hull. Born the second child of six in an Irish-Catholic family, the daughter of a fireman, Claire had to put herself through Stonehill College in Easton, Massachusetts. She graduated with honors in 1970. Claire also had eleven years of experience in public high schools—as an English teacher, guidance counselor, and assistant principal—and an additional six years' experience as assistant superintendent in the neighboring middle-class suburb of Norwell. But Claire was young, a little over forty when she took the job in Hull, and she had never been a superintendent before.

And Hull, like most American towns, was accustomed to having older men in the leadership positions in its schools. (In fact, Claire was one of the first women to be appointed superintendent in the state.)

Rick Cochran explained some of the factors that led to the school committee's three-to-two vote to hire Claire in June 1988. "We had another candidate who was tried and true, but I felt that after two failed efforts to override Proposition Two-and-a-Half in town, we needed someone who would be proactive, dynamic, strong in community relations, and an innovator. We needed someone to keep kids from abandoning ship and going to private schools, to establish a campaign that this was a good school system to send kids to. Claire had a reputation as a take-charge go-getter—an active person who would go out and do things, deal with change. We were at the point that if we played by the old rules and stayed where we were, we would be dead. We had to change the rules, break the mold."

At first glance, Claire's appearance belies the notion of a "take-charge" administrator. Youthful in manner, Claire is more inclined to wear floral-print dresses than dark and dour business suits. But Claire's steady, alert, and confident gaze tells another tale. Her eyes often spark with a kind of passion-infused intellect. In a recent interview for an *Executive Educator* article that highlighted her accomplishments as Hull's superintendent, Claire hinted at her profoundly moral sense of purpose. "I'm a product of the sixties," she said. "I want to feel I am making a difference."

When I asked Claire about leaders who'd served as role models for her and for her own educational vision, it became more clear what she had meant by "making a difference." "I really admire this black woman principal in Harlem—Lorraine Monroe. I heard her speak and read about her, and what I admire most is her single-minded insistence that schools are for kids, and that kids can and will learn! She's a real taskmaster. . . . I want to create schools where learning is uppermost in the culture. Right now, athletics and everything else is of more importance. I say 'learning' rather than 'teaching' because that puts the focus on kids and what they get from the whole process. When you put teaching first and focus on teachers, you never get to kids except in a peripheral way."

In an unusually candid and philosophical memo entitled "Hull Public Schools—Now and in the Future," which was sent to all faculty in the school system early in 1990, Claire described some of her priorities and strategies:

> I became superintendent twenty months ago. Most times it feels much longer than that. When I took over, it became clear that I had inherited a school system in chaos, a system that had suffered the loss of public confidence. . . . My first goals as superintendent became apparent: to restore public confidence in the Hull Schools; to establish trust and credibility with the community; and, through the first two goals, to secure enough financial support to operate the schools.
>
> In an article entitled "Navigating the 90's," Rosabeth Moss Kanter talks first about the challenge of developing a focus, concentrating on core strengths. She says that less is more. [Theodore Sizer's] Essential Schools principles and the themes can be seen as our focus. She says the second critical challenge is moving fast. "In a highly competitive market, the innovator has an edge . . ." As other school districts face what we have they will be competing for the shrinking pool of resources. We need to maintain our "leg up" position in our ability to attract supplemental resources. Third, she says that a staff that adapts is absolutely essential because flexibility in and use of personnel is a major factor in success. Rapid change and competition for resources mean that all of a school system's staff must be more flexible. Teaming, interdisciplinary curricula, cooperative learning, etc., all take flexibility on the part of staff. Collaboration is the fourth challenge with collaboration inside a system being matched by collaboration outside. Kanter says an organiza-

> tion needs "to be friendly—to count on external partners in order to gain the reach of a giant without adding new capacity." Our efforts to link ourselves to businesses, colleges/universities, foundations, and other resources are an attempt to increase our reach. She ends by talking about the new business hero as someone who can "do more with less, who can both conserve resources and pursue growth." That certainly sounds like our task!

A clear focus on students rather than teachers, aggressively pursuing educational and management innovations, a strong public relations effort, pushing hard for new forms of collaboration both in and out of the schools, and moving quickly on every front—these qualities have defined Claire Sheff's very assertive style of leadership. She is smart, tough-minded, pragmatic—and an educational revolutionary. For reasons both idealistic and practical, she has taken the tiny town of Hull's school system by storm and is trying to pull students and faculty alike (kicking and screaming if necessary) out of their doldrums and into the future—from almost dead last to being, as Claire puts it, "out on the edge—because that's where you're usually going to be, if you have a vision."

A Plan for Change

Claire's first step was to choose a small advisory committee of parents, teachers, and administrators to develop a mission and "core values" statement and to generate some broad goals for school improvement. The following statement was written during the summer and fall of 1988 and is prominently posted in the main offices of all three school buildings:

> *Mission:* To provide an education program of the highest quality that prepares each student to develop as an individual, to be a moral person, a socially responsible citizen and a productive member of society.

Core Values:

1. Respect for individual students, staff and community members;
2. Highest quality education based on research, high standards and expectations;
3. Equal access to educational opportunity for all students;
4. Shared ownership of the schools with the community; and
5. Ongoing professional development as an essential ingredient for continued improvement.

For the remainder of 1988, Claire was too busy with the schools' mounting financial woes to pay much more attention to issues of educational change. After the failure of a third effort to override Proposition Two-and-a-Half shortly after she took over in June, Claire was forced to cut about $1 million from her already lean $7-million school budget; it took most of the fall to figure out how to reduce the budget with the least effect on students' learning, her number-one priority. She cut administrative staff, sports programs, and extracurricular activities, and she deferred maintenance and the purchase of badly needed new texts, but few instructional programs were cut.

By early 1989, Claire was again on the educational offensive. A list of the actions she spearheaded in the school system in 1989 alone reflects more change than many superintendents attempt in a decade:

1. In order to allow for a reduction in the number of administrative positions the school system was restructured. The junior high was eliminated as a separate building, and seventh- and eighth-grade students began coming to the high school for classes.
2. The positions of all high school department heads were eliminated and replaced by a smaller number (three) of

systemwide interdisciplinary curriculum coordinator positions.

3. A high school dropout prevention program, called STRIDE, was introduced. A young teacher was given permission to work with a dozen or so of the most at-risk high school students outside of the school building for most of the day. He put them to work in an experiential, outdoor learning program that involved competitive rowing, renovating an old boathouse and dories, and learning about the islands in the bay.
4. As a first step toward implementing school-based management, all teachers were invited to be part of the budget planning process. A lengthy working budget document was distributed, with background information, so that teachers could help select spending priorities.
5. A parent and community committee was established in the summer of 1989 to formulate broad goals for systemic change throughout the school system. These efforts led to the creation of the school system's "Strategic Plan—A Blueprint for Becoming Competitive with Private Schools," in the fall of 1989. Eleven advisory committees, consisting of parents, community members, and teachers, were put in place for all the different new programs to be introduced.
6. Plans were made to develop themes for interdisciplinary studies for each of the four grade levels in the school system: art for the Jacobs Elementary School, technology for the Memorial Middle School, great people/great works for junior-high students, and the environment for the high school. The faculty at each school voted their approval of the themes early in 1990.
7. Finally, groups of teachers and parents set to work writing grant proposals to gather outside support for the schools' new programs.

This flurry of activity created a great deal of positive public attention in the town of Hull and in the surrounding area. In 1989–90, the town voted to increase both the superintendent's salary and the school budget for the first time in a number of years, while the town budget for other departments and services remained the same. That year, Claire became the first rookie superintendent to be honored with the President's Award of the Massachusetts Association of School Superintendents. Area newspapers began to run very positive, upbeat stories about changes in the school system. By 1990, headlines like "The Sky's the Limit," "Town Officials Upbeat on State of Hull Schools," and "Optimism Prevails with Resumption of Classes" were commonplace in the local papers. In November 1990, the *Boston Sunday Globe* ran a long feature story on Claire, titled "Troubled Schools Revived: Hull Superintendent Brings New Life to the System."

School committee member Richard Cochran observed that Claire took a good deal of time in her first year to begin to develop a vision for the Hull public schools, but it was one that few people knew or understood; by year two, "people began to hear about her vision and even to see some examples."

Not everyone was pleased by Claire's efforts, however. As early as 1989, some teachers were becoming uneasy about all the changes, which they felt were being imposed upon them by a young, upstart superintendent. Some complained about the process for creating the advisory committees, expressing the concern that Claire had chosen only her favorite teachers for the committee work. Other teachers felt that their voting on different themes for their schools was pro forma, that Claire had picked the themes and merely used the advisory committees to make it seem as though teachers had participated. Finally, a number of teachers were upset by the way in which Claire tried to involve them in the budget planning process. They felt they had no training and too little time in which to make sense of the budget materials and planning documents they were given.

Claire publicly acknowledged her mistakes in initial efforts to involve faculty in setting budget priorities, and she worked with a group of teachers to revise the process the following year. She also made faculty training programs her number-one priority in seeking outside grant money for the school system; it was an essential part of her strategy for school change. For these reasons, Claire sometimes found it difficult to understand why teachers did not perceive her as on their side. She felt they gave her little credit for at least trying to involve them more in decisions or for having secured for them a variety of new training opportunities.

A perceptive veteran teacher who remains a strong supporter of Claire's shed further light on the problem in an interview. This teacher felt that the most serious erosion of trust occurred in 1989 when, as mentioned above, Claire unilaterally eliminated all high school department heads and appointed the three new curriculum coordinators and a new assistant principal. "A lot of people didn't agree with the way she picked the people for the new positions," according to this teacher. "We all said, 'You have to post the jobs and let anyone apply.' She said, 'Fine, we'll do that, and then I'll put the same people in.' Up until then, I had Claire on a pedestal. She kind of lost everyone after that. They felt she had no respect for the [union] contract."

While Claire tried to involve faculty more in decision making and moved quickly to implement school-based management, as we will see, her continuing difficulty with some faculty led to a certain ambivalence about sharing power. In discussing her strategies for change in July 1991, Claire talked about both the importance of the concept of shared decision making and her uneasiness with the actual practice: "Over time, you have to increase people's participation in decision making. But it's a tough one because initially you have to have some vision and set some goals, and people can feel angry and resentful about that. So that when you talk about inclusive decision making, they want to use it as a bludgeon on you. There's also a lot of testing of limits. Initially people want to use their new-found decision making to resist change, to go back to the status quo. It's a real challenge of my belief in including people. The more you include them, the greater the chance that you won't be able to accomplish your original goals."

In spite of the tensions and the resistance of some teachers, Claire continued to move forward in 1990 with far-reaching plans for systemic change in the Hull schools. Early in the year, Theodore Sizer was invited to Hull to talk to a meeting of all teachers about the principles of the Coalition of Essential Schools, and a new advisory committee was formed to explore Hull's joining the Coalition. By the spring of 1990, Claire had identified teams of "volunteer" teachers (many claim they were conscripted) in each of the four schools to begin developing curricula for the proposed interdisciplinary study themes. She had also been very successful in securing a number of professional development grants—to train teachers in strategies for cooperative learning, to secure released time for a ninth-grade team of teachers to work over the spring and summer on an interdisciplinary environmental curriculum, and, finally, to train first administrators and then teams of teachers for each school in the processes of school-based management. (My formal and continuing involvement with the Hull school system began when I was hired in January 1990 to teach this series of workshops on school-based management.)

Claire's initiatives were neither random nor haphazard. They were all a part of the "strategic plan" first developed in late 1989 and refined over the next year (largely by Claire herself). By the fall of 1990, it was a forty-plus-page document that contained both an analysis of preexisting problems and a detailed outline of three broad goals, with dozens of objectives, and an administrative and advisory committee assigned for each. The first of the three goals was described as follows in the text of the plan:

> *Goal A: Improved teaching and learning through restructured schools that adapt to societal changes.*
>
> - Full Inclusion of Teachers
> - Interdisciplinary Teams

- Greater Parent and PTO Role
- Strong Assessment
- Optimum Use of Cable TV
- Improved Special Education
- 9 Coalition of Essential Schools Principles
- School-Based Management
- Professional Development
- Elimination of Tracking
- Inter-Town Programs
- Community Service

This list (only a third of the three-goal outline) may strike the reader as confusing at best, and perhaps even overwhelming. Unfortunately, as we will see, many of Hull's teachers had the same response. The scope and ambition of what Claire planned and attempted to implement in her first few years was, in retrospect, both a prod and an impediment to change.

Claire's great strength as a leader was that she had a clear understanding—or diagnosis—of what the community needed and a bold and comprehensive vision of what schools ought to be. However, in this case it was a vision that few teachers, parents, or students understood. Most of the ideas listed in the plan came from Claire, and only she really knew all that they might mean. Some of those that were broadly understood by many teachers—like the elimination of tracking—were vehemently resisted. Claire recognized that she had to have "buy-in," but beyond creating a few advisory committees she didn't know what more to do to achieve it. (Not only in Hull, but in school systems around the country, the lack of teacher and community understanding and support for change is a major contributing factor to the failure of many local school reform efforts. This is one of the problems we will return to in the concluding chapter.)

Claire's goal setting and strategic planning did, in fact, jump-start substantive changes in the school. By September 1990, several new initiatives were in place at the Hull High School. First, a team of five teachers (of math, English, history, science, and Spanish) who had worked together over the summer on an environmental studies curriculum began teaching all ninth-graders together and meeting daily in an additional common planning period to work on curricula and discuss students. Second, the school's faculty had voted the previous June to begin a trial school-based management effort, and so as the school year started a group of eight teachers and two administrators began meeting monthly to discuss schoolwide issues. Finally, many upper-level courses had been eliminated throughout the high school. Most classes, including all of those for the ninth grade except for two levels of Spanish and math, were grouped heterogeneously for the first time.

What did these changes look like? What happened in the classrooms and teachers' meetings? And what did these events mean for the participants? To begin to answer these questions, we'll look more closely at some representative ninth-grade classes and teacher team meetings. Then we'll consider the work of the schoolwide, school-based management committee.

Days in the Life

Hull students, like their counterparts in almost all American high schools, attend classes in five academic subjects each day: math, English, history, a foreign language, and science. They also take an assortment of other classes as well: physical education, health, industrial arts, economics, and so on. Students are assigned to a study hall in any period they do not have class. A few are also involved in the usual sorts of extracurricular activities, like yearbook, student government, and the media club. Each class or activity period lasts forty-two minutes, with half an hour in the middle of the day for lunch.

In the spring of 1991, after the teachers had been working together for more than seven months, as well as for several weeks of curriculum planning the previous summer, this is what a typical day of ninth-grade academic classes was like:

It's 8:15, second period: Algebra I, the more advanced of the two ninth-grade math sections. Twenty-six students are seated in four straight rows, almost equally boys and girls. The plain, green-walled room feels cramped and airless.

Students carry on a lively social chatter for the first fifteen minutes of class, while the teacher goes from desk to desk checking their homework papers. Almost half do not appear to have their homework sheets with them.

The teacher now goes to the front of the room and writes several of the homework problems on the board. Three or four kids, almost all sitting in the front row, routinely shout out the answers.

One boy suddenly asks in a loud voice, "Hey Ms. R——, can we have another quiz before the end of the marking period, so we can bring our averages up?"

The proposal is greeted with a loud chorus of about an equal number of yesses and nos. The teacher's mumbled reply cannot be heard above the din.

Another boy shouts across the room from the back, "Hey, Paul! How much time do we have left?"

As the teacher again turns to the board, the steady drone of conversation continues unabated. A few kids rest their heads on their desks. But most appear to be chatting with friends, with only an occasional glance at the board.

Third period: General Science. Students sit on uncomfortable metal chairs behind rows of smooth-surfaced lab tables. The wall at the back of the room has several colorful charts of plants and animals. An empty aquarium sits on a table beneath.

The teacher stands at the front of the room and begins to review the "overview questions" at the beginning of the new chapter on chemistry in the text. Fewer than a third of the students have the book open in front of them.

"What is a chemical?" The teacher asks a series of questions in a staccato fashion. "How are chemicals and matter related? What are properties of matter? Of a stapler? Of Carlos?" Blank stares greet her assertive questioning. She continues, "We can talk about size, shape, weight, volume, area—these are some of the ways in which we determine properties of matter."

The teacher passes around a small piece of copper pipe and asks each student to write down his observations. Perhaps half the class appears to scribble on a piece of paper. The teacher points at each student around the room in turn and asks him or her to say one word that describes the pipe, not repeating words that have already been used. "Round . . . cold . . . heavy . . . hollow . . . heavy [again]," come the replies. Now she weighs and measures the pipe, using several methods and instruments arranged on her lab table at the head of the room. As she performs each measurement, she reports her findings to the class.

Next, the teacher reviews key vocabulary words from the chapter in the textbook, asking students to recite definitions from their homework papers. More than half the class does not have homework.

"Density is a key attribute of property. What is density?" No reply. "Okay, everybody up—out of your seats. I want everyone to crowd into the corner by the door." Nervous laughter greets her request, but nevertheless the students all get up and shuffle slowly toward the door. The teacher joins them. "Closer," she urges. "Now, this is density."

Students take their seats and move on down the list of vocabulary. The PA speaker suddenly blares forth from the wall announcing variously a canned-food drive, a walk for freedom, tickets for Mystery Night, a meeting of the senior banquet committee, and a reading of the names of students who are to report to the main office after school for detention (there are more than twenty). Students chat on through the announcements, seemingly oblivious to the voice in the box, which can only be half heard.

Fourth period: English. With about twenty students in the room five minutes into the period, the teacher still hasn't started class. She is apparently waiting for stragglers. Student bantering and even roughhousing—guys grabbing baseball-style hats from one another—is loud and incessant.

Several minutes pass and two more boys straggle in. The teacher asks why they are late. They shrug and take seats in the back of the room as she tells them not to be late again.

The teacher now stands in front of the room. Behind her, one boy sits in a chair at her desk, twirling his cap while she explains a new project to the class. Students will be divided into small groups. Each group will be given one character from Romeo and Juliet, *which the class has just finished reading. Their first task will be to write a description of their character, based on what they've learned in the play. Then they will write a scene to act out that will be based on a contemporary scenario that the teacher will give them for their character. She gives several examples: Tybalt has to confront his son, who has just come home drunk from a party; Juliet has to find a date for the prom, and so on.*

Students are reasonably quiet and attentive as the teacher gives her explanation. She asks them to move into their groups to begin discussing the traits of the characters they are assigned. There are loud screeches as students drag and slide their occupied chairs around the room so they can sit with friends. Once in the groupings of four or so, a few students in a couple of the groups open a copy of the play and appear to make a halfhearted effort to begin talking about the assignment, but within a couple of minutes the conversation has turned to social topics in all five groups. When the teacher periodically stops by to check on progress, usually only one student in each group makes even a monosyllabic effort to answer the teacher's proddings, the rest keep on chatting.

Fifth period: Spanish I. Twenty-four students face the front of the room, sitting in four straight rows. The class begins with a vocabulary review, with the teacher asking students questions in Spanish: "How many churches are there in Hull? How many restaurants? How many schools?" She calls on different students to answer in turn. When the students aren't being called on to answer, a number are talking quietly to neighbors. Several appear to be doing homework for another class.

A tall, muscular young man in the middle of the class continues to talk after the teacher has told him several times to be quiet and listen up. She asks him to take a seat close to her at the front of the room. He moves slowly, with a somewhat cross, defiant look. She continues the review. He whispers once more to a neighbor. She tells him to see her after class. He picks up a stack of vocabulary cards from the teacher's desk and starts to thumb through them without taking off the rubber band in the middle. The teacher tells him to leave the room. She does not appear angry—in fact has a kind of half smile. He stands up slowly with a wry smile of his own, shakes a mock fist at her, and mumbles something about her son better not be caught in any dark alleys alone. Both her expelling him and his threats have an unreal quality, more like ritualistic role playing than a genuinely angry confrontation. It's as if they are acting out parts and both know it's more farce than tragedy.

"Bet you he doesn't go to the office," mutters a boy near me, to his neighbor. "He's probably just standing out there in the hall."

For the rest of the period, students work through a two-page ditto in pairs, asking and answering each other questions similar to the ones the teacher had begun the class with. She moves among the groups, correcting pronunciation and encouraging.

Sixth period: History. Twenty-one students are seated in rows in a room that somehow appears cleaner and better organized than the others. There are several colorful posters on the walls and books arranged neatly on shelves. A large TV monitor and a VCR stand on a cart at the back of the room.

"Okay, we're going to do a review of the Congress of Vienna today. What was the overall goal of the Congress?" The teacher's voice is loud, authoritative, very male. The whispered replies from two boys sitting at the head of rows in the front of the room cannot be heard at the back.

"Okay, . . . good. Now, two basic principles governed the actions of the delegates. What were they?" No answers.

"Legitimacy—which means what?" No reply. The teacher gives a definition.

"And compensation. What does that mean?" One boy mumbles something about money. "That's part of it. But compensation doesn't always have to be with money, does it? Compensation can be in the form of territory." He goes on to explain.

"Now, which two 'isms' would upset the balance of power in Europe?"

Two students can be heard whispering near the back of the room. "Okay, quiet down you two," the teacher insists. The students do not talk again.

"The first is liberalism. Why would that upset the balance of power?" No reply. The teacher explains.

"And what was the second 'ism'—nationalism. What does nationalism mean?"

"Countries wanting more for themselves?" Yet another

boy at the front of the room hazards a guess. So far, not one girl has attempted a reply to a question.

"Well, yes, but 'more' in what ways?" The teacher goes on to answer his own question.

Now he hands out a paperback text down the rows, gives a page number, and asks for four volunteers to read. Three hands go up—the three boys at the front of the room. The teacher picks the fourth reader—a girl. Each student reads a part from a script of a discussion between delegates from the Quadruple Alliance countries. At the end of the two pages of mock dialogue, they are asked to take turns reading aloud another several pages of explanatory text and the study questions at the end of the chapter. The teacher hands out a ditto with about twenty true-false questions from the chapter, and students work on circling their answers for the rest of the period.

An analysis of these classes reveals a few moments in which real thinking and active learning took place. The science teacher attempted a hands-on way of introducing properties of matter as she passed materials around and asked students to observe carefully. The Spanish teacher used a conversation-based model for foreign language instruction in her choices of dialogue and vocabulary for her lesson. The English teacher tried to relate Shakespeare to the students' lives by asking them to write about how the play's characters might deal with current adolescent dilemmas. These were times when students were asked to hypothesize, interpret, or connect pieces of information—all of which develops what Howard Gardner refers to as "education for understanding," what Ted Sizer calls "habits of mind."[3]

However, such moments were few and far between, and they were not the dominant experience for most students. Except for the efforts noted above, this day is sadly typical of what passes for learning in most American high schools today.

Very little actual work was being asked of students. Except for the three or four students sitting in the front row of each room, most students appeared to make no effort to respond to the teacher in any of the classes. The real activity seemed more social than academic (indeed, if you ask high school students today why they go to school, many will tell you that it's to be with friends). Fewer than half the students came to class with books, and about the same percentage appeared to have done the minimal homework that had been assigned. Hull students, like their counterparts in most American high schools, spend many more hours a day watching television than doing homework.[4]

Not only was very little work being done, but the work consisted almost entirely of rote tasks that did little or nothing to develop thinking or communication skills. Most of the testing going on was not of students' minds, but of the teachers' authority. The final exams in the ninth-grade English and modern European history classes reflect how little students were expected to think or write. For history, students had to answer a hundred true-false questions on a scantron form, answer about twenty-five fill-in-the-blank identification questions, label countries on two maps, and find terms in a "hidden word puzzle." They also had to write answers to eight "essay" questions, like "Why were the Balkans prior to World War I called 'the powder keg of Europe'?", but the amount of space allotted on the exam form for answers to these questions was about three lines each—in other words, only enough space for a two- or three-sentence answer.

Similarly, three quarters of the English exam consisted of fill-in-the-blank vocabulary questions, one-sentence-answer literature identification questions, and a *Romeo and Juliet* crossword puzzle. Two drafts of a one-page essay on the topic "Why is it important to study the environment?" counted for the remaining twenty-five percent. But how much could students be expected to say on this subject when, by all accounts, their yearlong environmental studies program consisted of a two-day ropes course at the beginning of the year, a one-day introduction to the ecosystems of Paddock's Island in Boston Harbor, taught by Park Service staff and for which there was no follow-up in classrooms, and, finally, an overnight camping trip where students made T-shirts and sang songs with environmental themes?

In-depth interviews I conducted with two ninth-graders revealed how unchallenging and unmotivating the students themselves felt most of their classes to be. One was a bright girl whom I will call Alice. She had recently moved from a "good" suburban school system, and this was her first year in the Hull system. She had strong opinions, nevertheless:

"What do you like most about Hull High?" I ask.

"Media club. It gets me out of class. Did you see the photo exhibit they had a couple of weeks ago? I did almost that whole thing by myself!"

"Could you briefly describe your classes and tell me what you think of them?"

"Spanish is my favorite. I like speaking a language. . . . We just had to write and perform job interviews. I dressed up as a waitress, and the person I was interviewing was a stewardess—it was sort of goofy, but good. Gym is a farce. I didn't feel like playing kickball today so I just sort of stood on the side. I flunked it first term. Home Ec is okay. I just made a pillow.

"Math—I don't do well. I'm not sure why. I can't concentrate in her class. Sometimes I think she goes through it real fast, just so she can get it over with. History is the easiest part of my day. All we do is word searches, sort of like crossword puzzles—like for the name of a German submarine commander. I'm not learning that much. We have to answer questions at the end of the chapter for a test every two weeks, but I can wait till the night before. Science is okay, I guess. But I don't like science, so I don't do very well.

"In English we read Romeo and Juliet *and then had to*

do mini-plays based on one of the characters. Mine had Count Paris going on a date with Juliet. I wrote our group's script because all the others were goofing off."

"What about the environmental theme?"

"The ropes course at the beginning of the year was a lot of fun. We've done a couple of field trips; we've got boxes for recycling paper in the classroom, but that's about it. Nothing's much different."

"What about the trip to Paddock's Island?"

"I fell asleep. But we learned some stuff. About the fish, the plants—the island as an ecosystem."

"How much homework do you usually have a night?"

"I usually get it done in class."

Precocious in her opinions and getting mostly A's and B's in school, except for an occasional C in math or science, Alice is one of the more academically able students in her class. Would a student who was closer to the "average" feel better served by the ninth-grade classes, I wondered? My second interview was with a "C student." Tom, as I will call him, is a shy boy who has attended Hull schools all his life.

"What do you like most about Hull High?"

"My industrial arts class. You can make what you want within reason, but they also teach you things related to the outside world. We made these CO_2*-powered cars out of wood that we raced around a track. It taught us about aerodynamics, but also about safety, because we had to put eggs in the cars."*

"Could you briefly describe your classes and tell me what you think of them?"

"Science is my favorite. We do a lot of busy work like vocabulary, check-point questions and stuff, but I like doing

experiments in labs. It's not boring. Algebra is hard. I don't know what's going on most of the time. The class is so big—twenty-eight. A kid was absent, so I moved up to the front of the room a couple of weeks before the end of school, and I did better.

"English is slow-paced. Not really a lot of work. We had one lengthy assignment on Romeo and Juliet, *but the rest of the time we did small assignments—like reading stories and doing vocabulary. Spanish. I learned enough this year so I could talk to somebody from Spain. The teacher is pretty good. She doesn't make it all straight, boring work. You have to keep up with work at home if you want a good grade. She doesn't give you a lot of time to do homework in class.*

"History is a fun class. You get together with other people to figure out answers to worksheets. When you finish, he tells you the answers. By the time there's a test every two weeks, you know all the answers."

"What about the environmental theme?"

"We had a couple of trips related to the environment, but they didn't go as planned. We didn't actually get into environmental things in classes, it was more something separate. I worked on building and doing a report on a bat house for the environmental exhibit, part of the Spring Curriculum Fair, but it added to my work. I would rather have had the study halls, so I wouldn't have to do as much work at home."

"How much time do you spend on homework a night?"

"About an hour."

Findings from the student interviews are both consistent with my observations and sadly revealing. For both Alice and Tom, there are moments in some classes where they feel challenged and stimulated. But they are few and far between. For both students, the most challenging and interesting part of their day has nothing whatever to do with any of their five academic subjects. For Alice, it was her involvement in the media club, and for Tom, the industrial arts class.

Teacher Team Planning

These ninth-grade classes and students' criticisms reflect a situation substantially the same as the one Sizer and other education critics like John Goodlad and Ernest Boyer saw, heard, and lamented in high schools all over the country during the 1980s.[5] How is this academic program any different from what has taken place in previous years? What has changed?

Very little, according to the five teachers working on the program. They say they simply have not had the time to plan interdisciplinary units in the way that they would like. Nor have they had time to really consider how to implement newer strategies like cooperative learning for dealing with heterogeneously grouped classes. Their common planning time has been used in other ways.

It's 7:45 A.M. Monday, the first period of the day, and all five ninth-grade teachers—whom I'll call Angela, Lois, Marilyn, Steve, and Sandra—are meeting together around a cafeteria-style table. Bob Burwood, the district's math/science curriculum coordinator, has been invited to the meeting to help the group plan the overnight trip to Paddock's Island.

For the first twenty minutes of the meeting, the teachers discuss details for an upcoming field trip to the town dump, the last half of the day on Friday. Angela seems to be more or less running the meeting; she's the one who raises topics and keeps people on task. She asks Bob if he thinks there'll be a problem with getting a bus, and he thinks not. Half of the group of 119 ninth-graders will go to the dump. The half of the class who remain behind will clean up the litter around the school building in preparation for the New England Association for Schools and Colleges (NEASC) accreditation committee's three-day visit next week. Steve raises a question about what to do if kids misbehave on the trip to the dump. One woman shrugs her shoulders, another looks out the window.

Angela moves on to the question of whether and when the other half of the class should also go to the dump. "I think they'll definitely learn something. It's a good thing for them to see," Sandra, the science teacher, says. No one disagrees, and a date is set.

Next is the topic of when to give the weekly SAT vocabulary quiz. A common period is quickly agreed upon.

For the remainder of the forty-minute period, the teachers talk about planning for the overnight trip to Paddock's Island. The idea is to have boys and girls go on separate nights, with teacher chaperons, in early May.

"Will someone call the Coast Guard to see if, with the Gulf War and all, they're still going to be able to take us out?" Angela asks. No one volunteers. "Okay, I guess I can call them."

"Since we've had so many class disruptions this spring, I wonder if it's worth all the time and trouble?" Sandra asks in a tentative voice.

"It's very innovative and a nice way to end the year," Angela says with feeling. "Besides, the kids have their hearts set on it."

"Hearts were made to be broken," Steve quips.

"But by lovers, not by teachers," rejoins Bob, with a tight smile.

Angela tries to make peace and move both the planning and the meeting forward. "Maybe we can divide responsibilities, so everybody doesn't have to plan everything. Sandra, you can do River Crossing—"

"I was told *to do River Crossing. I have no choice," Sandra quietly interjects.*

[River Crossing is a vacant condominium building by the side of a river estuary at the other end of town, part of the development project that went bankrupt. The bank foreclosed and then was persuaded to give the school system a no-cost lease on one building. Claire Sheff's idea was to turn it into a field site for studying freshwater ecosystems, as a part of the environmental theme at the high school, and Sandra has been "asked" to develop a program for the facility.]

"So you can do that," Angela continues, ignoring the momentary flash of resentment. "And Steve can plan the environmental exhibit for the Curriculum Fair, and the rest of us can plan the island overnight."

They talk for awhile about the logistics of planning, buying, and cooking meals, and getting kids to bring drinks. Everyone begins to look tired all at once.

"Maybe you can get the PTA to do some of the organizing of meals and even to cook," Bob suggests.

"Now, what about the exhibits?" Angela asks. "Marilyn, can you help Steve with that?"

Marilyn frowns. "I'm worried. I haven't done any environmental projects in my classes, except a few posters." She is in her early twenties, probably twenty years younger than anyone else in the room. She has only been teaching three months, having been hired mid-year.

"It doesn't have to be about the environment. It can be anything interdisciplinary. The long-range goal is to have students exhibit what they've learned." Bob's low-key, one-sentence explanation does not seem to diminish Marilyn's or the others' anxiety and resentment.

I sense the teachers all feel under some pressure to have something to show for their year. There is a long uncomfortable moment of silence.

"Are we going to let all the kids go on the camping trip?" Angela suddenly wonders. "What will we do if a kid screws up?"

"You have to tell them what you expect and then follow through—no booze, no personal boats. You have to check their bags and make sure they bring only sodas that are sealed closed—" Steve is interrupted mid-sentence by the ringing of the bell. Their daily team planning period is over.

As teachers stand up wordlessly with their piles of books, Angela quickly hands out the SAT vocabulary quiz for the week.

Judging from the blank stares, followed by looks of apprehension that greeted Bob's comment about "the long-range goal," the teachers apparently had not heard of or discussed such "authentic" assessment methods as Sizer's idea of student "exhibitions of mastery," wherein students are asked to present orally what they have learned in the consideration of problems or exploration of "essential questions."[6] Nor was it clear whether Bob himself understood or supported the idea of such exhibitions. But all the ninth-grade teachers knew that they were supposed to be doing stuff related to the environment in their classes—that's what they'd been paid to work on over the summer. Interdisciplinary teaching around the environmental studies theme was the centerpiece for Claire Sheff's plan to reform the curriculum of the high school.

Three weeks later, at eight o'clock on a cool and rainy Wednesday morning, the same five teachers sat around the same table in the faculty lounge, without the curriculum coordinator this time. They were very quiet, subdued.

The teachers review logistics for the upcoming first overnight to Paddock's Island once more. Everything seems taken care of, except for how one of the teachers will get a tent before Friday. Finally, that too is figured out.

The discussion turns to the Curriculum Fair. No one

seems to know how the event will be organized, or what they are required to do for it. Sandra says some of her kids are supposed to be doing environmental projects for extra credit, but only one group, so far as she knows, is likely to have anything done in time.

I can no longer ignore the palpable sense of dispiritedness among the group and ask what the matter is.

"Last Monday, the town approved the budget for next year, with a $400,000 cut to the schools. That probably means we'll lose two of our team. If we lose half the team, I think I'll go be a bum for the rest of my life," Angela states in a flat voice.

I ask when they're likely to hear something more definite. "The day before school starts in the fall," one replies.

Then Angela tells me that's not all the bad news. Last week, they'd given a pop quiz on the accumulated list of one hundred SAT vocabulary words they'd been giving students weekly all winter long. "Most of the kids got less than half right, so we have to figure something else out. . . . Maybe we should try playing charades with the kids next time." No one responds.

After a period of silence, the discussion turns to individual students who are having trouble in their classes. They talk about a boy who's been coming to some teachers' classes but not others. Angela asks Lois—whose class he's missed a total of thirty-five days this semester—if she has called the boy's parents. She says she's pretty sure they were notified by the school when his absences totaled twenty-eight, the cutoff for receiving credit.

"It's such a shame because he's coming to some classes now and doing the work, but because of the days he's missed he won't get credit, no matter what." Angela shakes her head. "These kids don't connect what they do to the future, from one day to the next."

Her comment leads the group to the topic of the large number of seniors who missed deadlines for applying for college scholarships. When teachers asked them about it, some said they had no idea you had to apply for scholarships, they thought you were just given them; others said they couldn't figure out how to fill in the forms.

"Where are the parents? Why don't they help these kids?" Angela asks with exasperation.

Steve replies, "They don't know how to fill them out either."

Despite Claire Sheff's dynamic leadership and bold plans for systemic change, after nearly two years of planning and implementation, ninth-grade students and teachers alike seem disengaged and deeply demoralized. Why this gap between the rhetoric of change and the reality of an unremitting status quo? What has gone wrong?

Reading this portrait, some business and community leaders, or even parents, might argue that lack of professionalism, even teacher incompetence, is the problem. While I did see some examples of poor teaching, the majority of teachers at Hull were competent, committed professionals. The ninth-grade teachers, in particular, had worked very hard all year long to make the new program a success.

In fact, these teachers were their own most severe critics. When I asked how they assessed their efforts at the end of the year, one replied, "As far as changing dynamics which allow for more effective learning in the classroom, I'm sad to say I don't see any real change. . . . And nothing measurable took place this year in terms of environmental learning, either. Coming up on year two, we have to rethink things." Another replied, "Teaching a heterogeneous group, I feel I failed miserably. I tried to teach to the middle, and there is no middle." "Interdisciplinary team teaching has failed," declared a third.

Tools for Change

As I see it, there are three essential reasons for the failure of ninth-grade teaching and curriculum reform efforts in the first year at Hull (and in most other schools where I have observed the change process). First, there was a lack of clarity and consensus around a few clearly stated educational goals or outcomes. Second, there were no core values that might create more of a sense of community, as well as address students' emotional needs and inappropriate behaviors. Finally, most faculty were not committed to collaboration and change.

A deeper understanding of these three vital factors suggests some powerful lessons for other school systems initiating change. It will also give us some criteria or benchmarks for analyzing change efforts at the other two schools in this study—Cambridge Rindge and Latin, and Brimmer and May.

Academic Goals to Focus the Change Process

Both observational and interview data suggest that trying to undertake too many changes at once was the first obstacle the ninth-grade teachers encountered. Consider the number of issues the teachers were dealing with in just the two forty-minute team planning meetings described above. They were planning for two major field trips, carrying out and assessing the results of weekly SAT vocabulary testing, responding to a request for environmental exhibits for the Spring Curriculum Fair as well as requests for a new program (River Crossing) and for help with an all-school cleanup, and dealing with the attendance problems of individual students—all while also trying to cope with a collective sense of dispiritedness about possible staff cuts for the following year.

When asked what had been hardest about the year, one teacher said, "Everything's been too fragmented. There have been too many things initiated: cooperative learning, heterogeneous grouping, interdisciplinary teaching, school-based management are all being attempted in a short period of time. It was frustrating as hell when we started trying to apply all this to the agenda of our team. . . . It would have been far better to have devoted time and energy to a few things, instead of trying to do so much." Another replied, "There's too much going on. I don't like doing things I don't feel I'm good at. I know change is necessary and I welcome it, but I would prefer to do a few things at a time and really figure them out before going on to other things." "I think changes are necessary," agreed a third, "but I think they need to come more gradually. There have been so many changes this year. Trying to deal with each one is overwhelming."

Not only were there too many innovations, there was also real disagreement about some of the strategies for change—such as heterogeneously grouped classes with more cooperative, small-group approaches to learning—which had not been resolved. One teacher repeatedly expressed the view in team meetings that so-called cooperative learning benefited the slow learner but held the more advanced students back. Another had concerns about the effect of heterogeneous grouping on both high and low ability students: "My concern is that we're really harming kids. I've tried a number of things to get the brighter students to work to their ability, not just to get an A. . . . And I still feel the lower achieving kids get left out. They'll never receive an academic achievement award no matter how hard they work. They have no way of seeing if they're working to the best of their ability in a heterogeneously grouped class, where if they were homogeneously grouped, I could give the hardest workers an A."

In part, the teachers' difficulty resulted from their inexperience with teaching techniques new to them. While several had attended workshops related to environmental education, as well as programs on cooperative learning, none had been in classrooms where these new strategies were being used. They wanted lesson plans. They wanted to see teachers successfully doing some of the things they were being asked to try. They wanted models for change and more training.

"If you're going to have reform, you're going to have to seek out the best people and come up with good models that your staff will feel comfortable with," said one. Another observed, "I've never worked so hard in my life as I have this year. What's been so hard is that we had no models. We had to start from scratch."

If the ninth-grade teachers had had opportunities to visit other schools, they might have learned some new techniques, which would have enabled them both to feel more confident and to eliminate a lot of trial and error. But I believe their efforts would still have remained diffused at best. The most serious problem with the ninth-grade program, as well as many of the other changes superintendent Sheff was trying to implement system-wide, was the lack of a clear sense of purpose or goals. There was no coherent focus.

What were the real problems that innovations like an environmental studies curriculum, team planning, cooperative learning, heterogeneous grouping, and so on were supposed to solve? And what were the goals, other than to get students to achieve more? What is meant by the term "high quality education"? And how is it measured? Low achievement on standardized tests was an inadequate definition of the problems these teachers were supposed to fix. If SAT scores go up, do teachers feel they've succeeded? Do parents?

There was no real discussion—let alone a consensus—about the goals of school improvement efforts, neither among ninth-grade teachers, nor in the system as a whole. Heterogeneous or ability grouping, cooperative learning, environmental studies, team teaching—none of these are goals. There are only strategies, means to ends—ends that remained undefined in the first year at Hull.

Deciding what most needs improving in a school or curriculum takes a great deal of thoughtful, collaborative discussion, as well as knowledge of alternative models that suggest better ways to do things. These ninth-grade teachers did not have the benefit of either. They all felt that they lacked sufficient time to plan, let alone discuss deeper issues. "I wish they could pay us to work all summer," one said. "I would like to sit here and develop curriculum on how to teach with cooperative learning and heterogeneous grouping."

Simply giving the teachers more time to meet would not necessarily have produced clear goals. In fact, thanks to a number of grants for the new ninth-grade program which Claire Sheff had secured, the amount of time these teachers had to plan was generous by some standards: released days in the spring, several weeks of paid time over the summer, two planning periods every day—one common for the five teachers together, plus one for individual planning and preparation. Some money for additional training and consultant help was also available. However, because they did know how to discuss or decide the larger questions of what was most important to learn, and had no help in doing so, the teachers understandably focused on smaller changes they were confident they might accomplish. The ninth-grade team spent most of their summer time planning for the September ropes course program and deciding which environmental themes to focus upon. Once the school year began, the common planning period was used mostly for discussion of individual students' problems and for trip planning.

Some of the teachers saw the problem clearly. "It's good to have that common planning time," one acknowledged, "but too often it breaks down to talking about the strengths and deficiencies of individual students, or procedural details, like who's going to call the Coast Guard. We didn't spend enough time talking about why we're doing out-of-school activities. And we didn't spend our time talking about goals."

Late in the spring of 1991, I observed the same pattern in an all-morning meeting for a new team of tenth-grade teachers who were planning the second phase of an environmental curriculum for their group, to begin in September 1991. One of the ninth-grade teachers met with them to help. The questions they asked her all had to do with what the students were like and what field trips they had taken. Armed with this information, they then proceeded to spend the next three hours of paid released time discussing whether to focus on energy or pollution, local or regional environmental problems, and what sorts of field trips they might take. Again, there was no discussion of the goals of the program.

Without clear goals, there is no clear focus for change, no way to measure results, and no criteria for selecting curricula, teaching strategies, other schools to observe, or training options for teachers. But teachers cannot be expected to make decisions on final curriculum goals on their own in a vacuum. I saw this more clearly when I asked the tenth-grade teachers to clarify what they expected of students—what they wanted them to learn by the end of the year. One veteran tenth-grade teacher immediately responded by saying that the curriculum was set by what colleges expected, so there was no point in discussing such questions. Several nodded in agreement. No one thought it was their job to discuss or decide what students should know and be able to do by the end of the year—that's what textbooks and district curriculum guides were for.

What is extraordinary about the ninth-grade teachers described in this chapter is that in spite of feeling coerced and/or cajoled into working together as a team, in spite of the many demands on them, and in spite of all the frustrations of year one, all five remained committed to working together to improve the program. If their efforts are to be more effective, though, they will need a great deal of help from their colleagues, from parents, and from others in the community—as well as some kinds of institutional guidance and assistance. They—like their colleagues in all school systems attempting reforms—need help and support in defining the goals of change.

We will return to this problem of community support for clear goals in succeeding chapters and in our conclusion, but back at Hull, even had there been a few well-chosen, broadly supported, and clearly defined goals, two other serious obstacles to change remained: passive, dispirited students and teachers who hadn't yet learned to collaborate. An understanding of these problems will make more clear the importance of core values and collaboration as the other two essential components of the change process.

Core Values for a Caring School Community

As we stated in the Introduction, much of the school reform debate over the last decade has focused on the need for higher standards, more teacher training, and greater autonomy for schools. But what about the students? What are their needs and perceptions, and how have these changed over time? Except in the aftermath of some incident of blatant school violence, these questions are rarely addressed in discussions of school reform. Yet most teachers will tell you that student behaviors and attitudes, of course, profoundly affect learning—for better or for worse.

No one can recall any violent incidents at Hull High School—no shootings, rarely even a fight. In nearly two years spent at the school, I did not see any students acting in a dangerous or threatening manner—either in classes, in hallways, or outside the school. As schools go, it was a pretty quiet, orderly place. But, as we saw in our classroom portraits, students were constantly misbehaving in small ways. They talked loudly and interrupted frequently, even after being asked not to. They made disrespectful remarks to one another and sometimes to teachers as well. Even those who were not overtly rebellious did not come to class prepared to learn, but rather to socialize—or to nap. Defying authority was like a game in most classes, almost as if students were daring the teacher to *make* them learn.

We heard that a strong and continuing underlying concern of the ninth-grade teachers in their planning sessions was how they would control student behavior on field trips. Yet I never heard the recurring, systemic problem of inappropriate student behavior openly discussed in any of the team meetings. Why not?

Part of the problem with poor student behavior was the fact

many students saw little point to the work they were asked to do. Students found a great deal of their class work to be boring, as we learned through interviews, so why should they pay attention or behave? There was nothing of substance to pay attention *to*.

Just giving kids more challenging and interesting work won't magically make kids behave better, though, as many teachers who try to give tougher assignments will attest. Most teachers know that the problem is far more complex. If you ask, they will tell you that students who go to high school today are much harder to teach and to motivate because of "the changes in our society," but these are changes that individual teachers feel powerless to counteract and so rarely discuss, even among themselves.

When I asked the veteran Hull ninth-grade teachers whether they felt they had seen significant changes in the students over the years they have taught, all acknowledged that students today were different. But there was an interesting split between the answers given by the men and those given by women, for reasons about which I can only speculate.[7]

The two male teachers were not very interested in the question, responded only very briefly, and tended to downplay its importance. "I don't know that students have changed all that much," one replied. "The stimuli have changed. Some behavior is different—lack of respect for peers and adults, but it isn't that overwhelming." These were also the teachers who felt most strongly that student misbehavior should be dealt with preemptively. In sharp contrast, the three women with whom I discussed this question all saw many more differences over time and were deeply troubled by what they observed.

One woman, who had taken fifteen years out of the profession to raise her own children and returned to teaching only six years ago, saw profound changes: "What really struck me was that kids were so much more cynical and less receptive to learning. They have less respect for themselves, for each other, and for teachers. But in other ways, they're more mature—they all use vulgar language, and talk about sex, drugs, alcohol, and parties like it was all a game or a joke. The values of society are so different." Even a new teacher who had herself graduated from Hull only five years earlier saw changes. "I'm shocked at some of the things kids say to parents and to teachers—all the sexual innuendoes. I thought I was in a hurry to grow up, but these kids are in super fast-forward."

"The biggest problem with kids today is that they have no self-esteem," another woman commented. "They're less responsible, attentive, motivated—more confused about life and what school is all about. They're also very passive—that's the worst thing. Technology has a lot to do with it—plus the messages they get from the media are all so bad, so hopeless. So they don't think long range. They live from day to day, hour to hour. They have no goals. With families breaking up and mothers out working, everybody is so busy just trying to cope. Parents don't spend time with their kids anymore. They don't know how to make their children feel valuable. . . . [Students] come in crying, talking about suicide. . . . It's made me stop thinking of myself as primarily an academic teacher. It's made me look at them as people first. If you can't connect with them emotionally, then you can't teach them anything."

These teachers are describing fundamental changes in student behavior over the past decade or two which obviously are not unique to Hull. Others whom I interviewed in the other two schools in this study—and many of their colleagues around the country with whom I have had discussions—report that their students seem less motivated, more passive, and more emotionally needy every year. Both their capacities and their incentives for learning seem diminished when compared to those of previous generations.

Is the problem simply too much TV? Tired, tradition-bound teachers who don't know how to motivate kids? Parents who don't care? Bad kids? I hear these ready answers all too often when I discuss the changing student population with parents, community members, and teachers. It's always someone else's fault and a problem that we can't do anything about.

Such misunderstanding and indifference will condemn future generations of adolescents to ever-increasing rates of substance abuse and suicide, as well as less drastic symptoms of chronic boredom and depression. As adults, we *all* need to take more responsibility for what the world we have created is doing to young people and how we can respond more helpfully. So immersed are we in our own individual lives and in our culture that it is very difficult to clearly see and understand some of the broad social changes that have taken place since many of us went to high school. Let me suggest two observations as starting points for what must become a serious national and community dialogue about the interrelated social changes which most affect students' learning. While these may seem somewhat speculative or not sufficiently substantiated by data cited here and elsewhere, I invite you to consider them as working hypotheses to be developed or disproved with further research.

First, students' capacities for learning—their abilities to concentrate and to work on a project over a period of time—have been eroded by the pervasive influence of our passive consumer culture.

Increasingly, consumption of goods and entertainment is a dominant attribute of our lifestyle. Instant gratification—with little or no concentration or effort—is only as far away as the telephone, TV remote, or shopping mall. Students are growing up in a world where it's become almost a virtue to want it all and want it now! Why read a novel when there's MTV? Why work at something over a period of time when you could be playing Nintendo? In such a world, students' capacities for sustained concentration atrophy, like unused muscles. Often, when they are asked to do harder but more challenging work, they don't know how to begin.

To get students' attention, many teachers respond to this problem with the use of audiovisual media: TV, slides, and movies. Others—as we saw in the English and history final exams at Hull—use puzzles and games. However, these gimmicks have little real effect on improving learning. In fact, they make the problem of teaching still more difficult as students come to expect all learning to be a multimedia show or an entertaining game. Students are increasingly addicted to passive consumption as a way of being.

Second, the traditional incentives for student learning—fear and respect for teacher and parental authority, and a belief that hard work will lead to success—are much less effective than they were for previous generations.

In the 1950s, most students rarely challenged or questioned authority. "Do this assignment because I tell you to" was usually sufficient. But after the civil rights and women's movements, the Vietnam War, the Watergate and Iran-Contra scandals, traditional paternalistic authority no longer holds sway. The positive side of this change is obvious: we are all learning to look to a wider range of individuals for leadership, to question authority, to think more critically, and to decide things for ourselves. But what is going to replace those once-effective commands in classrooms?

Not parents' cajoling. Not only do kids think less about their parents' school pronouncements, they hear them less frequently. A recent analysis of census data by the Center for the Study of Social Policy revealed that only 26 percent of American children lived in a two-parent family with a breadwinner and a homemaker in 1990. The study also revealed that in 1990, for the first time, a majority of women (more than 60 percent) with children under six were in the work force and that 64 percent of all children living with one or two parents did not have any parent at home full-time.[8] Not only are more parents working full-time, they are also working more hours—about a 15-percent increase over the last twenty years—according to a recent study by Juliet

Schor.[9] The simple consequence of these changes is that parents have less and less time to spend with their children or to supervise their school work. Many teachers believe the "absent parent syndrome" also contributes to what they see as young people's increasing emotional neediness, as well as to their ambivalence toward adult authority.

Many adolescents may feel abandoned by society as well—caught in the nether world between the increased wants and expectations of a consumer society and the diminished opportunities of a no- or slow-growth economy. Most adolescents today have what I call TV dreams—fantasies of being rich, having a high-powered career, fancy cars, and so on—but the majority believe that they will not, in fact, do as well economically as their parents have done. They see a shrinking economic pie, with more people than ever scrambling for a piece. The majority of adults apparently agree. According to a 1993 Gallup survey, 80 percent said it would be harder for the next generation to achieve "the American dream."[10]

One of the most tragic side effects of the American system of secondary schooling is that by the age of fifteen or so, almost all students now feel they have been categorized as likely "winners" or "losers." Only a small percentage of students in most public high schools believe they have a real chance at a good college and career—and thus of achieving their dreams. These are the kids whom everyone in school recognizes by ninth grade as the "good" students. They sit in the front rows of all their classes, memorize what they have to for the A's, and participate in those sports and extracurricular activities which they know will look good on their transcripts—while the rest of the students look on.

Up until about the 1970s, the majority of non–college bound students still had opportunities for blue-collar work which promised a sense of dignity and security, as well as an income that would enable them to be part of the middle class. Now—with the American economy increasingly dominated by white-collar service and technology industries—most of these industrial jobs have disappeared, and the ones that are left pay less, and have less status, than ever before. And so students who would have dropped out in the past to work on an assembly line now remain in school, in faint hope of being able to get something other than what writer Douglas Coupland calls "McJobs—low-pay, low-prestige, low-benefit, no-future jobs in the service industry."[11]

Many of these young people now believe that doing well is more a matter of luck than hard work. They've seen too many examples of some hard-working relative or older sibling being laid off, while the media touts all the stars, lottery winners, and drug dealers who seem to have it all without any work whatsoever. What is the virtue in working hard in school if what you have to do all day won't necessarily pay off?

The result is that a majority of students in the average American high school feel like "losers" and do very little in school except hang out with friends. They feel they have no real chance of a future, and so their classes have no meaning. School seems boring and irrelevant to their lives—just something to sit through for four years in order to get a ticket (a high school diploma) to stand in line for an entry-level job or go to a community college. And with the "good" students getting most of teachers' time and attention, these students also feel that no one in school knows, respects, or cares for them. They simply have no reasons—no incentives—to invest any effort or to behave or to show any respect for others.

But you don't have to take my word for it—or the teachers'. Let the students tell you in their own words:

When I asked Alice, the successful Hull ninth-grader whom I interviewed earlier, what could be done to improve the school, she said, "There's no school spirit here. No one shows up for the student council meetings. It's not like, 'Wow, how can we improve our school.' It's, 'Let's get our names in the yearbook.' . . . If the work is too easy, there should be some place you could go for extra projects. . . . Our ninth-grade teachers are pretty good, but a lot of older kids complain that their teachers just don't care."

More stimulating classes and teachers who care were also the dominant themes of a conversation Hull High School principal Bob McIntyre had with members of the Student Senate in the spring of 1991. He asked them why they thought there were fewer students on the honor roll and more students failing classes that year. "Classes are boring, the faculty are old, and most of them just don't care," was the reply.

While some of the problems described in this chapter were more acute at Hull because it had a higher percentage of non–college bound students than many suburban school systems, student disaffection from school is hardly unique to Hull. In one of the few studies that I have found of *students'* perceptions of what needs to change in schools, researchers working with the Institute for Education in Transformation at the Claremont Graduate School administered 1,776 questionnaires, plus selected follow-up interviews, in four California public schools—two elementary, one middle school, and one high school—to study student attitudes toward their education. Their conclusion: "Our data strongly suggest that the heretofore identified *problems* of schooling (lowered achievement, high dropout rates and problems in the teaching profession) are rather *consequences* of much deeper and more fundamental problems . . . best summed up in the words of the high school student who when asked, 'What is the problem of schooling?' replied, 'This place hurts my spirit.'" They found that even in these four decent public schools, many students felt classes were boring and irrelevant to their lives and that the adults seemed cold and uncaring.[12]

Yale psychologist James Comer has described the disappearance since World War II of the systems that supported black student achievement—family, role models, church, and community.[13] In a recent speech, he quoted an old African proverb, "It takes an entire village to raise a child," to introduce a discussion of the needs of minority children today.[14]

It is becoming more and more clear that it is not only the children of minorities who have lost their villages. The data presented here from teacher and student interviews at Hull and in the four California schools confirms my own observations in schools all over the United States. The majority of American students in high schools today suffer from the same deprivation. The capacities and motivations that many adults possessed in simpler times and in a more traditional culture, and so took for granted growing up—such as the ability to concentrate and the desire to do well—are simply absent in many adolescents today. Most teachers and parents find it extremely difficult to recognize, sympathize, and respond to this unraveling of such an essential part of our social fabric.

Of course, schools cannot undo all the social changes described here. A careful public consideration of the destructive psychological side effects of a culture (and an economy) based on passive consumption is long overdue.[15] Creating decent-paying, meaningful work for every American is also a serious economic and social problem that demands, and is receiving, national attention. Even if schools were suddenly to turn out a much better prepared labor force, it is not at all clear that there would be more and better jobs for better-educated students.

However, all schools can and must become places where people—adults as well as students—care for and respect one another and value learning as a means of personal growth. Clear academic goals or outcomes are not enough. Educational reform must address what psychoanalyst Michael Maccoby described as the needs of the heart, as well as those of the head.[16] This is an issue that is often a concern of teachers and parents in good elementary schools, but it is rarely discussed as a need of high school–age students.

What, more precisely, might it mean for high schools to take seriously the education of the heart?

First, high schools must have clear core values which affirm the worth and attend to the intellectual and emotional needs of each individual. *Every* student needs to feel known, respected, and cared for by adults. *Every* student needs to feel that he or she can be a "winner"—can succeed at something worth doing. And *every* student needs to know that learning is not merely a means to the ends of giving the teacher what's expected, passing a test, or getting into a good college, but rather intrinsically interesting and rewarding for itself. For *all* students, learning must be clearly connected to their developing competence as adults, as well as to personal growth and satisfaction. Self-esteem cannot be taught, but it can best be encouraged through the development of real individual interests and competencies—and the more realistic dreams and hopes that come from a developing self.

Second, high schools must have clear core values which also nurture a greater sense of mutual respect and responsibility in a caring community. Attending to students' individual needs and interests can help build self-respect and nurture hope, but creating a more caring whole school community, one which affirms respect for and responsibility toward others, is an essential counterbalance to excessive individualism. Schools must nurture the *social values* that are vital for life in a democratic society; they must teach intellectual competencies while also becoming intentional communities with explicit core values that support individual dignity, caring relationships, active, individualized learning, and personal and social growth.

But *which* particular core values? Who should decide? And how are they "taught" or caught? Do the "winner" and "loser" categories of students have different emotional needs? Can there be universal core values? These questions are complex, and we will explore them further as we look at our other two schools and in the final chapter. For now, though, it is enough to recognize that what these Hull teachers saw, heard, felt, and observed among their students—as well as the other data we have considered here—has profound implications for what must be done differently in order to develop students' capacities and motivation to learn.

Collaboration: Problems and Possibilities

It seems clear that the ninth-grade teachers at Hull could not possibly have solved all the underlying problems that prevented learning—low expectations, student passivity, and lack of respect and desire to learn—by themselves, even if they had this focus and more time to plan. Individual or even team efforts by teachers to create a moral community in their classrooms are essential, but insufficient by themselves. The work of Theodore Sizer, James Comer, Sara Lawrence Lightfoot, and many others reveals schools to be distinct cultures where values must be discussed, agreed upon by the majority of adults (and students, I will argue), and then modeled widely—schoolwide—if they are to have any effect.[17] In short, teachers, parents, and students must *collaborate* in order to agree on and implement both clear goals and core values.

Sadly, in these first two years of the change process at Hull, and in many other schools I have observed, large numbers of teachers appeared too weighed down by their own professional malaise to consider how to respond to the increased emotional needs and demands of students. When I asked ninth-grade teachers to what extent they felt other teachers in the building shared some of their educational goals and values, the replies of several revealed deep concerns about their colleagues.

"My classes are under control," one said (and, indeed, this person was one of the few who did not tolerate students' side conversations), "but building-wide what goes on in some classes is terrible and impacts what goes on in the rest of the building. Teachers too easily say it's a bad group of kids, instead of saying after a month or two, 'Things aren't going well, what should we be doing differently?' . . . Probably a third of the faculty couldn't care less what's going on."

Two other teachers thought the number of colleagues who were solely focused on course content was at least 50 percent. One commented, "Maybe half the teachers share my goals in this school. But then I look at the other teachers, and I get the feeling that they're just stuck on subject matter." "All the teachers here care about kids, but only about half try to reach kids at other than an academic level," observed another. "It's an aging faculty who just want to pay their dues and get out. . . . A lot don't want to change. Others are very contract oriented. They will not spend one extra minute in the building."

Hull High School principal Bob McIntyre was deeply concerned about the attitudes of many of his teachers. When I interviewed him in July 1991, Bob observed, "The more I think about it, the more I realize what an enormous task change is. We think we can just change a philosophy or an idea, but we're talking about mind-sets that have been here for twenty-plus years—we're still teaching the way we taught in the early 1900s. . . . I'm beginning to think that unions and public education can't coexist. Unions have a place and a service to provide, but they've missed the point in education. We're tied to contracts and to schedules—classes just so many minutes long, so many free periods a day—those things have to change."

"Just do the job and get out," is the attitude of many older teachers at Hull High School and in many other public schools around the country. From discussions I've had with teachers in dozens of schools over the past ten years, I observe that public school teachers are demoralized by a number of changes: increasing disrespect from students and their parents, the low status of their profession, years of marginal salary increases, larger class sizes, staff cutbacks and involuntary reassignments—to name only a few. At Hull, the pace and intensity of all the changes envisioned by the new superintendent has further contributed to this sense of demoralization of the entire staff. Their low morale was almost palpable.

In the spring of 1991, a three-person visiting committee from the New England Association of Schools and Colleges spent several days in Hull High School as a part of the reaccreditation process that member schools must go through every ten years. Their report, submitted to Claire Sheff in the summer of 1991, commented at length and in several places on the morale problem at the high school:

> In an attempt to revive the school system, the superintendent, with the strong support of the school committee, has initiated a complex, large-scale strategic plan, thus providing, for the first time in a long time, measurable direction for the school system. The changes include serious curriculum and personnel initiatives which have been presented and implemented somewhat rapidly in order to jump start a flagging program. . . . There is a sense, however, that at Hull Junior-Senior High School, the staff has not yet accepted that change will make a difference. Although the superintendent has empowered the faculty to be leaders by affording them the opportunity to participate in decision making, there is a clear absence of enterprise among them. Although the faculty expresses its concerns that changes are happening too rapidly, few alternatives, other than to have nothing happen at all, have been productively suggested. . . . It is obvious that the conditions of the past few years have caused many people associated with the school to feel helpless and abandoned.
>
> . . . there is an undercurrent of displeasure and discontent which, if not checked, may very well prove to be detrimental to the school and community. Teachers seem to be very upset about the number of changes going on around them. They question the degree to which faculty input has been sought in the decision making process. . . . At the same time there appears to be little desire to work cooperatively to meet the goals set by the superintendent and the school committee. The visiting committee saw a sense of "fait accompli" blended with a "laissez faire" attitude, neither of which, individually or together will make a school better.[18]

As the report suggests, because many of the Hull faculty were both angry and resistant to the changes going on all around them, important educational issues were not being discussed.

The report also points to a paradox: "The superintendent has empowered faculty by affording them the opportunity to participate in decision making," yet "teachers . . . question the degree to which faculty input has been sought in the decision making process." What were these efforts to involve teachers in decisions? How can the faculty be "empowered," yet continue to feel powerless?

An Experiment in School-Based Management

From the very beginning of her tenure as superintendent, Claire Sheff stressed the importance of greater participation of faculty (and parents) in school governance. In one of our first conversations, she talked about having a vision of a school system run by teachers. The idea of "school-based management" is mentioned frequently in the system's various strategic planning documents, and, as we saw, early in her first year she attempted to get faculty input in the budget-setting process. Claire has said that "faculty involvement in decision-making is a key part of an overall strategy for change"; if the teachers do not "own" changes by helping to shape and implement them, Claire believes, then what happens will be superficial and of short duration.

However, Claire's interest in shared decision making is "student-centered," as is much of her thinking about approaches to educational reform. Excerpts of a memo she circulated to all staff in March 1990 make it clear that for Claire the primary purpose and value of school-based management is to find more effective ways to meet the needs of students:

> We have begun to explore the possibility of School-Based Management (SBM). This is not really a new concept. Many of you have heard about quality circles and other practices which are being used in the corporate world. Schools are beginning to think about ways to increase the involvement of faculty, parents and students (high school) in decision-making.

> The purpose of SBM is to improve our services to students. Because we are ultimately accountable for and to our students, they are our priority and focus. Other benefits of SBM can be an improved working environment for staff and increased understanding of and support for what we do by parents and students.
>
> The kinds of decisions that might be made by those involved in SBM include the following: curriculum, staffing, scheduling, and budget. SBM is a means by which teachers can take risks, try out new ideas for new opportunities and practices, get involved in budgeting.

The memo went on to spell out the various initial steps Claire had taken to implement "SBM" in the Hull schools: first, a presentation to the Hull Teachers Association's executive board and a training workshop for the three school principals, then workshops for teachers from each school who had volunteered to be a part of an initial steering committee. The memo also explained that informational sessions would be held at each school for all faculty to learn more about school-based management. (I planned and facilitated all these workshops and meetings as a paid consultant to the school.)

The informational sessions were held at each of the three schools in early June of 1990. Most faculty attended the meetings, and there were very few questions. Afterward, faculty were asked to vote on whether they wanted their school to be involved in a one-year trial effort. All three school faculties voted in favor. The vote at the high school was the closest, with about 60 percent in favor.

School-based management teams finally had their first meetings in the three schools in the late fall of 1990. The process was slow in starting for several reasons. It was very difficult to identify meeting times, because the union contract specified that teachers could not be required to work after school except on a limited number of days. Also, there was a feeling in all the schools that with so much going on it was very hard to add even one more new thing. Finally, despite the workshops we had held, I sensed that neither the principals nor the faculties were really sure what school-based management was all about—what they were actually supposed to do.

The high school team consisted of the principal, assistant principal, guidance counselor, and the eight teachers who'd volunteered the previous spring. Two of the teachers were also on the ninth-grade team. Initially, the group met every four to six weeks, usually during a common planning period. For the first several meetings, the focus of discussion was the school's low SAT scores; that year they were the worst in the school's history. The group agreed to take an SAT vocabulary list, divide it by four, and teach it to students over four years, in grades 9–12. It was their first decision as a team. (And, as we've seen, the ninth-grade team began giving weekly vocabulary quizzes to all their students early in 1991.) The discussion also led to the realization that the group knew little about what was taught in lower grades—when and how grammar was taught, and so on. The high school team expressed some interest in learning more about what was being taught in the other schools, but there was no follow-up.

After these initial discussions, topics varied from meeting to meeting, with little carry-over from one meeting to the next. In one week in early March, there was a presentation by two teachers, one from the elementary school and one from the high school, who were working on ways to improve the school system's public relations. They were soliciting ideas for ways to show the community some of the school system's strengths before the town meeting—scheduled in less than four weeks—at which the system's budget for the next year would be decided; the schools were facing at least $300,000 in cuts to an already lean $6-million budget. The March meeting became a lively brainstorming session; possible actions mentioned included everything from teachers demonstrating to organizing to call parents, trying to get community members to attend awards assemblies, and holding faculty benefit basketball games. But no one at the meeting took either notes or responsibility for any kind of follow-up.

At the next meeting, five weeks later, no mention was made of the topic of the March discussion or what ensued:

Five minutes into the period, teachers are still drifting in for the meeting. As they sit down, several look around and wonder where the absentees are. Four teachers, the assistant principal, and the guidance counselor are present. Someone wonders where Bob, the principal, is. He's been seen in the building; he knows there's a meeting.

The group begins to talk, without an apparent agenda or someone in charge. A teacher wonders whether or not there's a need to have both written and PA announcements every day. He says that many of the PA announcements are specific to grades and should not have to be heard by everyone—teachers can just read the relevant announcements. There is general agreement, but then another teacher suggests that this group shouldn't make any decisions by themselves without asking other teachers. Someone suggests the idea of a questionnaire.

The conversation then drifts on to the topic of whether and when in the day there should be homerooms [when attendance is taken] versus just taking attendance at each student's first-period class. Someone wonders whether there should be study hall periods as well.

"They provide a recess for kids," one teacher says by way of explanation. [No one seems to question the notion of study hall as recess.]

"What about an activity period instead?" another teacher wonders. "It would be a chance to schedule clubs and other extracurricular activities into the school day, instead of after school. It would also give kids who don't have an activity a chance to do homework."

Conversation goes on for five or so minutes about kids not doing homework. All seem to agree that it's the number-one problem in their classes. There's also some talk about how fewer and fewer kids bother to get involved with extracurricular offerings. After school they just seem to want to go home. One teacher wonders whether part of the problem is that too few faculty are themselves interested in doing out-of-class activities with kids.

The conversation comes back to how you might schedule an activity period—shortening homeroom, lengthening the school day a bit, starting a few minutes earlier, shortening the periods in order to add another. One wonders what neighboring schools' schedules are like.

"How come we don't have assemblies any more?" a teacher suddenly asks.

" 'Cause kids are too unruly," someone replies.

Getting back to the scheduling issues, one teacher begins to list some of the topics or questions they might want to put on a questionnaire for teachers.

"Who's going to make this up? I sure don't have time," another teacher interjects.

One of the ninth-grade teachers volunteers to bring a draft of a questionnaire to their next meeting. Then she wonders about the overlap between the SBM group and the Faculty Senate, which she also serves on. Bob McIntyre comes in at this point, apologizing for being late. He'd been tied up with an "emergency" meeting with a parent about a low grade a student had received in a course.

Bob speaks to the question of the difference between the two committees. "[The] Faculty Senate is more for teacher and student problems, where this group deals more with curriculum issues."

A teacher suggests that what's also needed is a group that meets regularly with the superintendent. There used to be one, and she doesn't know what happened to it. Murmurs of agreement around the room are interrupted by the period bell.

After another meeting to consider a draft of the faculty questionnaire (as well as other, unrelated topics), the following questionnaire was distributed in early May. It went without an explanatory memo and was the first communication from the school-based management team to the full faculty:

1. How do you prefer to have the morning announcements done?
   a. To continue the present system?
   b. To have them just read over the PA and not delivered?
   c. To have them just delivered and not read over the PA?
   d. Other suggestions?
2. Are you content with homeroom in its current time slot?
3. If not, how would you change it?
4. Should students be allowed to receive 1 academic credit for 25 hours of community service performed on their own time?
5. Do you see a necessity for an activity period during the existing school day?
6. If so, how much time should be allotted to it?
7. Do you have any suggestions on how to find the time within the school day to do this?
8. Should perfect attendance on the part of the students be rewarded?
9. If you agree, should it be rewarded on a quarterly basis or on a yearly basis?
10. Should students be exempted from final exams for either of the following reasons?
    a. Perfect attendance?

b. Inclusion on the honor roll?

11. Would you be interested in serving on the School-based Management Team next year?

Forty-four questionnaires were returned, which represented more than three quarters of the faculty and many more than the team expected. Faculty opinions were divided on most of the topics, except for the idea of giving credit for community service, an idea widely supported. Significantly, and again much to the surprise of the current members of the school-based management team, nineteen teachers expressed interest in serving on the team the following year.

In May 1991, the Hull Teachers Association—the local union—insisted that there be another vote in each school on whether to continue with school-based management teams. The union had never officially voted to cosponsor the school-based management experiment, its leadership explained, and some of the issues that the teams were dealing with had to do with working conditions and were therefore union issues. Many felt, however, that the union's real concern was a loss of power and that the intention was to try to get a vote of no confidence against one of the superintendent's initiatives. (Earlier in the spring the union had circulated a questionnaire to members, asking questions like "Do you feel confident in the direction Hull Public Schools is heading?" "Do you feel confident that the Leadership of the Hull Public Schools is steering the system in what you would consider to be the right direction?" "What role should the Hull Teachers Association play in determining the future direction of the Hull Public Schools?" The results were not released to teachers.)

On June 5, 1991, just prior to the faculty vote, there was a meeting at the high school to provide teachers with an opportunity to hear members of the school-based management team talk about their efforts and to ask questions. (It was one of the very few full faculty meetings all year that wasn't taken up with just reading announcements.) The session revealed what both team members and others thought about what the school-based management team was for, what it had accomplished, and how it might be made more effective. The following is based on excerpts of my notes from that meeting:

The leader of the school-based management team, whom I'll call Bill, begins the meeting by explaining the purpose of the team as he sees it: "It's a group that can be a visionary change agent for the school—to think about how things could be better. This is what we've done this year: approved giving one credit for community service, moved homeroom to the beginning of the day to allow time for grade-team meetings next year, created a proposal for a twenty-minute activity/reading period every day. Next year, we want to talk about final exams. . . . We're trying to get away from the traditional decision making by administrators to move it to shared decision making with teachers who know best what needs doing." Bill then asks if anyone has questions.

"Do you make recommendations or decisions?" one faculty member wants to know.

"Well, the school committee has to decide about giving credit for community service. As far as homeroom goes, Bob [the principal] has reservations, but will go with it."

Bob McIntyre speaks: "I think the activity period is maybe something worthwhile, but I have reservations about how it will be used. It needs more thinking through."

In response to another question, one of the teachers on the team explains more about the decision to move homeroom to first period.

One of the school system's K–12 curriculum coordinators then observes, "It seems that most of the decisions that were made were administrative. What about academic concerns?"

Bill replies, "A lot of what we've done this year has been sort of cleanup and reactive. Taking care of preexisting problems. In the future, we'd deal more with a plan."

One of the ninth-grade team members adds, "We also decided to wait for the results of the NEASC [New England Association of Schools and Colleges] evaluation to decide what we need to work on."

The Hull Teachers Association president now speaks: "We're concerned because school-based management deals with working conditions. We're also concerned that every-one *on the staff be trained so that they know what's going on."*

Few seem stirred by the union representative's comments. Another faculty member asks a question: "Does the team make decisions for faculty?"

A team member answers, "We need to communicate more with faculty, have meetings to discuss things."

"Will the team be elected next year?" asks a teacher.

The answer is yes, the team had recently been talking about how and when to hold elections and decided to do it at the beginning of the new school year.

"What about the overlap with the Faculty Senate?"

Team members look to each other and shrug. "To be honest, we're not sure. It's one of the things that has to be talked about."

The curriculum coordinator speaks once more: "School-based management will only work if there's frequent communication and meetings with faculty, rather than a committee that makes decisions and hands them down."

A team member replies, "You're right. We need to talk about things more as a full faculty. I'm wondering if the faculty would be willing to come to meetings after school two or three times a month to air things?"

Her question hangs in the air, unanswered. People shift uncomfortably in their chairs. There are no further questions. The meeting, which lasted about twenty minutes, is over.

The faculty fill out ballots to vote on whether or not to continue school-based management and drop them in a box on their way out the door. Later in the day, a member of the administration and a union representative will count the votes together.

The results of the vote were significant. Despite the fact that the team apparently had not helped to bridge the gap between a proactive superintendent and a reluctant faculty, and despite the union's lack of support, the full faculty voted by a substantial margin to continue the school-based management experiment. The vote was thirty-six for continuing, twenty-one opposed.

But the question remained, What must this team do to become more effective themselves and to promote greater collaboration within the school?

When, in the spring of 1991, I had asked the school-based management team members as a group for their assessment of their year's work together, all who spoke expressed the view that they had taken some important first steps by beginning to talk about serious issues and to trust one another. However, most also seemed well aware that they had some distance to go before realizing the full potential of shared decision making and collaboration. A number of suggestions were made for making their work together more productive, including meeting for more than forty minutes at a time so as to better focus on issues, clarifying for the full faculty the respective roles of their team and the Faculty Senate, seeking more input from all the faculty, and getting a broader representation of teachers on the team itself.

I also interviewed several team members individually. Some of their comments suggested a kind of cautious optimism. "Right now, the whole idea of school-based management is kind of cloudy, but I think it'll get more clear as we go along," said one. "It's been sort of imposed on us—like heterogeneous grouping. We're working on small matters right now. As people get more used to power and find that they really can do it, I think we'll begin to tackle the more important issues." Another said, "I got involved because I'm tired of people telling me this is what I'm going to have to do, and I think there's things that need changing—like student discipline. As a team, we've made a start. We haven't done a whole lot, but it's too soon to actually change the climate. As long as we strive to make it more effective, I think it can work."

Regular communication with the full faculty, greater clarity about the role and authority of the team, more time to meet—all of these are necessary but insufficient steps toward making the school-based management team more effective. Collaboration is both a core value to which both "management" and "labor" must be committed, and an individual competency that takes initial confidence, skill, and regular practice.

Local unions have a role to play in helping to establish collaborative rather than adversarial relations as a systemwide value. As we saw, the union leadership in Hull did not encourage change, and certain provisions of the contract made finding meeting time difficult. There were similar difficulties with the local union at Cambridge Rindge and Latin, as we will learn in the next chapter. By contrast, there are some stunning success stories about what happens when district administrators and union leaders work together for school change. The pioneering partnerships of the late 1980s between then-superintendent Joseph Fernandez and union president Pat Tornillo in Dade County, Florida; David Dickson and Patrick O'Rourke in Hammond, Indiana; and Peter McWalters and Adam Urbanski in Rochester, New York, are three notable examples of local union-management collaboration for school reform. At the national level, American Federation of Teachers president Albert Shanker has been a leading proponent of greater union-management collaboration for school reform for the past decade, enabling the local union officials mentioned above and many others to take greater risks.[19]

But even such institutional cooperation won't necessarily change behaviors in individual schools. Susan Moore Johnson's important study *Teachers at Work* documents how most teachers' work is structured in ways that inhibit collaboration.[20] Individual teachers spend their days—indeed, their careers—each working alone in a room with students, isolated from other adults. In traditional schools, there are neither opportunities nor incentives to work together. Most teachers don't know how to collaborate; they lack practice.

In my own study of seven schools attempting restructuring, conducted for the Massachusetts State Department of Education in 1991, I found that it was the business partners assigned by the state to each of the seven school-based management committees who taught administrators and teachers the skills of collaboration: how to run effective meetings, determine priorities, set and keep to agendas, delegate responsibility, and so on. School people were deeply grateful for the help—in part, perhaps, because these businesspeople acknowledged learning a great deal from them, as well, about the reality versus the rhetoric of changing schools. After a year of working together, both the educators and businesspeople in these seven communities came away with a deepened appreciation for each other's different skills.[21]

The findings of this small pilot study suggest some important new roles that business leaders can play in the school improvement process. But before teachers can comfortably work with outsiders, they must first do some preliminary work together. The teachers in the seven schools I studied had all spent some time talking about what changes they wanted to make before inviting parents and business leaders to participate. Perhaps it was a matter of professional pride, or of simply gaining confidence as a faculty through greater cooperation. Whatever the reason, the faculty in these schools—and in dozens of others with whom I have worked as a consultant—all needed to talk at length about the important issues before they felt comfortable inviting "outsiders into the kitchen."

So we are back to the question of goals—and who sets them. As of 1991, what the Hull school-based management team needed to do above all to facilitate the change process at Hull was involve the full faculty in discussions of the school's strengths, weaknesses, and priorities for change. It is the first—and most important—step toward greater collaboration.

The Limits of Top-Down Change

For a few, the change process at Hull had been empowering and energizing. One of the ninth-grade teachers said, "I remember what it was like under the old people. One couldn't be creative. There was none of this openness. That's what's been lacking in education—teachers have never been allowed to be creative or to think. Claire's been totally supportive of what we've done."

However, in 1991 most Hull teachers, as the NEASC report stated, seemed to be sitting on the sidelines—perhaps waiting for what they saw as the latest school reform fad to blow over, or waiting for a new superintendent. One had the sense that this split among the faculty prevented an honest dialogue about what went on in the building. Another of the ninth-grade teachers flagged this lack of honesty and attributed it to the way in which change was introduced into the system. "About twenty of us [faculty from the high school] were paid to go to this curriculum planning workshop all week, but most people were there because they felt they had to go along, not because they wanted to be there. If you have intellectual dishonesty, you're not going to have school reform—whether it's a workshop or a pilot for ninth grade. The issue is what is the motivation [of teachers] for involvement."

"How would you do it differently?" I asked this teacher.

"I would have tried to create a genuine consensus among staff for the need to develop a theme approach at the high school level. I would have spent at least a year or two trying to create consensus and develop ownership. I'd allow staff to decide, Hey, this is the direction we're going in because it's crucial. Then I would have proceeded with a pilot for ninth grade about year three."

Indeed, teachers must be actively involved in the process of educational change *from the beginning*. Systemic change imposed from the top simply cannot create lasting changes in classrooms—in teaching or learning. "Bottom-up" change is the only kind that lasts, but it takes much more time to evolve.

Few superintendents are given such time. The superintendency in most school districts is essentially a political appointment and highly subject to shifts in local opinion. Perhaps due to our relatively quick turnover of presidents and other political leaders every few years, or because of our "instant" culture, wherein most needs can be satisfied at a moment's notice, the American public expects instant change in schools. Rarely are superintendents given more than a two- or three-year contract. (Claire's initial contract, like most, was for three years.) Like many CEOs, superintendents are under tremendous pressure to produce short-term results. Many feel they must undertake everything all at once in every school in order to prove their worth. "There's a real pressure that if you don't show some changes overnight, then people will say the reforms aren't working," Claire explained.

For two years after the study this book is based on was completed, and after her contract was renewed, Claire spent much time trying to establish clear academic outcomes, promoting respect as a schoolwide value, and balancing her strength as a "student-centered," visionary educator with greater patience and concern for the process of faculty coming to their own conclusions about change. She rightfully points to the spring 1993 union contract and accompanying memorandum of understanding as a landmark in this effort, a collaborative negotiation which resulted in the local union becoming a full and equal partner in all aspects of the change process, in each school and at the district level.

"With the benefit of twenty-twenty hindsight, there's a lot I would do differently," she said in conversation. "I underestimated the degree to which teachers would resist the changes I saw as needed. But I begin to see signs of teacher ownership of curricular change—like when the eleventh-grade team had students do exhibitions on what they'd learned about the environment this fall. So we're continuing, and I feel hopeful."

I, too, am still hopeful about the possibilities for change at Hull. Although Claire accepted a new position as superintendent in a larger New Jersey school system in July of 1993, she left behind a solid foundation for continuing reforms: five years of steady progress—albeit through trial and error—as well as a core group of teachers and administrators who are deeply committed to finding better ways to meet the needs of young people. So long as teams of Hull teachers, parents, and community members continue to collaborate to further refine goals and core values, and regularly monitor progress, there is real hope that the process will evolve and become both top-down and bottom-up systemic change.

But what happens when the impetus for educational change begins in the way the teacher last quoted recommended—from teachers sitting down and talking together about what's right and wrong in their school, and what *they* want to improve? What are the problems and possibilities with this kind of collaboration, and how does it affect the development of educational goals and core values? And how do school boards and central office bureaucracies affect the school reform process in a larger school system? The next portrait, of the Academy, a program within the Cambridge Rindge and Latin High School, provides us with some answers to these questions.

TWO

The Academy at Cambridge Rindge and Latin

Kids and the world have changed. The issue is whether education is to transmit knowledge or to foster learning. As Sizer says, we have to have students as workers and teachers as coaches to foster learning. We should agree on the skills that kids need to learn, not just the texts they should study. Doing away with textbooks is not so that teachers can shoot from the hip, but so that we can get back to research. New programs help teachers to rethink everything they do.

—Ruben Cabral
Housemaster of the Academy,
Cambridge Rindge and Latin High School

A Cosmopolitan City of Contrasts

From the public housing projects in Cambridgeport to the colonial mansions along Brattle Street, from the ivied campuses of Harvard and MIT to the scruffy bargain stores in Central Square, Cambridge, Massachusetts, is a city of contrasts. Its population of nearly 100,000 includes both black and white, rich and poor—often coexisting within a few blocks of one another, or even in the same neighborhoods, yet living largely separate lives. The Harvard/Brattle Street end of the city is mostly white and upper-middle-class, while the Central Square stores and neighborhoods just a mile or so away are populated predominately by minorities with noticeably darker skin and less money.

The thirteen K–8 schools and single high school, serving a total student population of about 7,600, are one of the few common meeting grounds for the city's diverse population. The percentage of minorities attending Cambridge public schools has risen steadily over the past decade from 34 percent in 1980 to 54 percent in 1990—33 percent black, 14 percent Hispanic, and 7 percent Asian. Harvard professors' progeny (those who don't go to private schools) rub shoulders with the children of newly arrived Haitian immigrants who can speak only a few words of English. Forty-two percent of the students are eligible for federally subsidized lunches. And white, black, and Hispanic parents all appear at parent meetings and before the school committee to demand, with varying degrees of success, education programs to meet the needs of their children.

Because the city's chief "industry" is education, many of its most vocal taxpayers are associated with educational institutions and have been generally supportive of efforts to improve the public schools. In sharp contrast to Hull, where the impact of the passage of Proposition Two-and-a-Half in 1982 has had a continuing devastating effect on the school budget (by capping property-tax increases), the Cambridge school budget has continued to rise, from $52,272,963 in 1987 to $68,783,465 in 1991. In 1991, the system spent more than $8,500 per student—the fourth highest per-student expenditure in the state. That same year Hull spent about $4,600 per pupil—yet another example of a "savage inequality" in education, as reformer Jonathan Kozol has put it, albeit one that is related to economic class rather than race.[1]

These dramatic differences in levels of funding have had their greatest impact on average class size. While some Cambridge Rindge and Latin High School (CRLS) programs have been reduced or cut altogether in recent years as student enrollment has declined from 2,619 in 1986 to 2,069 in 1991, very few teaching positions have been eliminated, so average class size is relatively small—about 17 students for English and social studies classes, and 20 per class in math and science. By contrast, 25 or more students was the average class size for all subjects at Hull. One veteran English teacher at Rindge and Latin confided that her total student load has gone from 110 a decade ago to 80 or so now—or what Hull teachers had once enjoyed in their school's heyday. Now the Hull teacher load, as we saw, is 120—about the national average.

What difference does class size make? There is considerable disagreement about its importance among researchers, and the large body of research on the effects of smaller classes on student learning is not conclusive. In fact, when the dominant mode of instruction in high schools is "chalk and teacher talk," class size may be irrelevant: you can lecture to 25 people as easily as you can 12. However, Theodore Sizer and many other educators argue that personalizing education—rather than merely lecturing—is what makes the most difference in improving students' incentives for learning. Knowing each student well is a precondition for personalization; a high school teacher simply cannot deal with 100 or more students in a day and expect to know them well. Sizer advocates a total teaching load of no more than 80 students, in order to allow for personalization.[2]

Continuing public pressure for school improvement has led the eight-member Cambridge school committee to adopt a variety of innovations over the past two decades. In 1979, Cambridge became one of the first cities in the country to voluntarily provide a remedy for de facto segregation in its elementary schools, through a system of "controlled choice." Previously, children had been assigned to their neighborhood public schools; today, parents list three preferences out of the city's thirteen elementary schools, and final assignments are made with both the parents' preferences and racial balance in mind. This choice plan has become a model for other cities around the United States.

Cambridge's public education system has seen a number of changes since 1968, when it was one of the first in the country to develop a small, less structured, alternative high school program, now called the Pilot, as an option for students. Several years later, another small but highly structured alternative program, called Fundamental, was instituted. In 1977, the city's two separate high schools, Rindge Technical and Cambridge High and Latin, as well as its two alternative programs, were merged into one comprehensive high school and housed in a brand-new building. The Pilot, Fundamental, and Rindge Technical and Vocational programs—all programs "of choice"—each retained a small core group of students and faculty, as well as their distinctive identities, while the remainder of the high school was randomly divided into four administrative "houses"—known as A, B, C, and D—of about 500 students each.

Since the merge, the number of courses offered at the high school has steadily proliferated. Until 1990, students in the alternative programs and the four houses could select from more than 450 different offerings listed in the CRLS course catalogue. Ranging from advanced placement courses in all academic areas to "Autobody Design," from "Model Engineering Technology" to "Theater Design," the list of choices is staggering and more than what many small colleges are able to offer.

In recent years, the high school has also initiated a number of model programs to retain potential dropouts: in-school day care for adolescent mothers, a work/study internship called the Enterprise Co-op, and an intensive bilingual basic studies program for immigrant adolescents who lack the language skills to be in a conventional bilingual classroom. In 1990, the dropout rate was 21 percent, which was average for the state. Of those who remained at the high school for four years and graduated, 44 percent went on to four-year colleges, and an additional 19 percent attended two-year colleges. The combined average SAT score for the 1990 senior class was 859 out of a possible 1600.

The patchwork of programs described above survived with only minor changes through most of the 1980s. In 1987, however, a number of different concerns and proposals combined to create a strong force for change.

Evolving Change: A Mandate and a Counterproposal

Since the early 1980s, both the Pilot and Fundamental alternative programs had been heavily oversubscribed. Even though these two programs were philosophically very far apart, the parents of more than half of the incoming ninth-graders requested one or both of them as their first choice. Admission was therefore by lottery. The students who were refused were confronted with a bewildering array of houses, programs, and course offerings from which to choose. Rumors began to circulate that one house was for the "preppy" kids, many of whom were white, while another was for the predominantly black "jocks." Yet a third house had been designated for all of the school's intensive bilingual education students, a large percentage of whom were Haitian. Increasing numbers of white middle-class parents requested that their children be placed in the "prep" house. There was a growing number of complaints about not being able to get into the smaller programs and about the difficulty in making sense of the other offerings.

Responding to parental concerns in 1987, then-superintendent Robert Peterkin and the Cambridge school committee decided to create two new programs with distinctive identities within the existing high school: a math/science "exam school" and a school for the performing arts. They had not counted on what happened next—a storm of protest from those who worked at the school.

The reaction from faculty and administrators to this school committee decision was overwhelmingly negative for two reasons. First, most of this group had served many years in the Cambridge system and had worked together for some time to make the newly merged Cambridge Rindge and Latin High School a safe and high-quality school. As a matter of principle, they resented changes being imposed upon them from above when they had not been consulted.

The second reason for resistance to the newly proposed programs resulted from concerns raised by a group known as Concerned Black Staff. This group issued several reports and a series of recommendations in 1986–87 that addressed the problem of the underrepresentation of minority students in the upper-track and advanced placement courses at the high school. A number of the faculty, both black and white, felt that the two newly proposed programs would siphon off additional resources for those very able, white middle-class students who were already well served by the school.

In 1987 the Key Results Committee, consisting of elected

members of the high school faculty and administrators, had been formed to monitor a strategic planning process that had been undertaken at the high school. As a result of the storm of protest against the newly proposed programs, the Key Results Committee was asked by the school committee to study the proposals for the new programs and to make recommendations.

A comprehensive self-evaluation of Cambridge Rindge and Latin, written by a team of faculty and administrators in the fall of 1991 for the New England Association of Schools and Colleges, summarized the work of the Key Results Committee:

> This group, working with the principal, undertook a yearlong major research effort, visiting exemplary schools of similar urban size and population, and familiarizing themselves with the several major commission reports and benchmark critiques examining American high schools at that time. The result was a serious reappraisal of everything from the school's sense of mission to the organization of its classrooms.
>
> Agreeing with the critique presented by Sizer, Powell, et al. in *Horace's Compromise* and *The Shopping Mall High School*, the Key Results Committee felt that, like many American high schools, we were "doing pretty well with the upper level and lower level kids," but that there was a substantial population of "kids in the middle" who could be served better. A math/science exam school and performing arts house would provide more options for students who already exercised many options in the school. The committee instead proposed concrete measures to boost house identity, improve school climate and the quality of teaching and learning for all students, and enhance the professional lives of teachers and other staff. These measures were compatible with and built on the recommendation of the Concerned Black Staff.
>
> "Parents want their children to be known by their teachers, to receive personal attention, and to be involved in a

> place which professes some distinct purpose," the Key Results Report said. In other words what was wanted for the whole school was the sense of community and identity, long term staff/student contact, close guidance and mentoring associated with the more self-contained alternative programs.
>
> From experience in our own school we know that school-within-a-school settings have to be developed and owned, conceptually and emotionally, by the faculty—whose efforts to make them succeed, in turn, need to be supported, politically and financially, by the administration and the broader community. Achieving such settings is an enormous undertaking—requiring equally enormous commitment!

Nancy Burns, currently a math teacher in what was then known as House D, served on the Key Results Committee. She described some of the highlights of the experience: "We went around observing at a number of excellent schools. Some were doing some very different things and having a lot of success with at-risk minority kids. John F. Kennedy High in New York City made a big impression on me. They'd broken a big high school down into much smaller units. It made me question the whole "shopping mall high school" idea. I began to think that kids don't succeed at math for reasons other than academics. Kids need identity and structure in school. They need the feeling that there are teachers and a place that belongs to them. Small groupings also gave teachers more of a chance to work together, to learn from each other, and to be more accountable to each other and to students." (The phrase "shopping mall high school" comes from a 1985 book by Arthur Powell, Eleanor Farrar, and David Cohen which compared the typical comprehensive American high school to a large shopping mall that offers students a degree of anonymity and course choices, but too little quality or coherence in the curricula.)[3]

The 1988 Key Results Committee report made a number of recommendations for creating a revised mission statement for the high school, and for curricular and administrative restructuring. Members of the committee drafted a new mission statement which was adopted by the whole faculty in 1989. It reads:

1. The primary commitment of the Cambridge Rindge and Latin School is the preparation of students to be literate, competent, educated, skilled, informed citizens—appreciative of the arts, capable of critical thinking and problem solving, and able to function effectively within a complex, interdependent and pluralistic world.
2. We propose to create a learning community for staff and students
   a. that is safe, caring, consistent, fair, flexible, open and democratic;
   b. that meets the needs of students, parents, staff and society through educational programs small enough to promote individual fulfillment, yet broad enough to encompass the complex interdependency of the world community;
   c. that attempts, in its philosophy, structures, and interpersonal relationships, to mirror an ideal world: peaceful, equitable, just and free; and
   d. that achieves educational excellence in an environment which promotes mutual respect, fosters human dignity, and, in particular, recognizes, respects, and celebrates racial and cultural differences.
3. The development of such a learning community entails
   a. a continual striving for innovative responses to changing situations;
   b. an analysis of our current administrative and curricular structures to inform a rethinking of our school, particularly as these structures relate to the culture of the classroom, the function of the teacher and the form of the teaching, and to interrelationship of all educational programming; and
   c. a curriculum that engages students through its social

and ethical relevance and nurtures intelligence of every kind (e.g.: verbal, logical, mathematical, aesthetic, kinesthetic, introspective, social).

4. The school recognizes and affirms its intimate, integral relationship with its community. Close collaboration between the school and the community is vital to the school's survival and success as an institution.

The focus of the committee's recommendations for curricular restructuring was on creating core programs—wherein students would all take the same English and social studies courses, and have only limited choices for math and science—for all ninth- and tenth-graders within the existing houses. It was proposed that groups of teachers in English, social studies, math, and science act both as teachers and as advisors to the same 100 or so students for a portion of each day. Houses would be encouraged to evolve their own distinctive pedagogical approaches and program themes for these grades, while eleventh- and twelfth-grade students would still take courses throughout the school.

Following the widely praised innovation of "controlled choice" for the thirteen K–8 schools in the city, all programs within Cambridge Rindge and Latin High School (the three existing programs—Pilot, Fundamental, and Rindge Technical and Vocational—plus the three houses A, C, and D) were to be reenvisioned as programs of choice. (House B was eliminated and its staff disbursed throughout the school in 1988 due to reduced student enrollment.) All incoming ninth-graders would fill out a common application on which they would list their three choices. A schoolwide controlled-choice lottery, much like the one that existed for elementary schools within the system, would be developed to ensure proportional representation of categories of race/ethnicity, gender, and residential district.

The administrative recommendations of the Key Results Committee's report strongly affirmed the importance of involving faculty, parents, and students in implementing and monitoring restructuring efforts. It called for the creation of a schoolwide policy council, which would consist of elected representatives of the faculty, parents, and students. The twenty-two-member Transitional Advisory Committee—which consisted of the principal, one parent, two students, teachers, and program and curriculum leaders—was voted into being by the full high school faculty in December 1989 and began to meet regularly in March 1990. Their charge was described in the ballot distributed prior to the 1989 vote:

> The Committee will strive to ensure that various house programs and curriculum initiatives are broadly understood, coordinated and compatible. It will coordinate the efforts of Key Results, Parent Advisory, School Improvement, Staff Development, and other major committees which influence school priorities and direction.
>
> The Committee's goal will be to help achieve consensus about the school's overall structure and direction, and to facilitate orderly change.
>
> By the end of the fall semester of 1992, the school will recommend a representative advisory/policy-making body that best serves its needs for the future.

The Key Results Committee report had a galvanizing effect. Soon after the report's release, a group of faculty from House D began to meet weekly with their house administrator, Ruben Cabral, to talk about what kind of program they wished to create. This working group developed a master plan for House D—henceforth to be known as the Academy. The Cambridge school committee approved the creation of the Academy as the fourth program of choice for the high school in December 1989. House C administrators and faculty also developed a proposal for a new program name and focus, called Leadership, which was approved by the school committee in June of 1990. Meanwhile House A, which was already the most requested house because the community perceived it to be the most academic, retained its name and developed a fairly conventional academic high school program.

Thus, by the spring of 1990, all three houses had written descriptions of their programs. These were circulated, along with already existing descriptions of Pilot, Fundamental, and the renamed Rindge School of Technical Arts programs, to the parents of all incoming ninth-graders. The proposal to create an arts house and math/science exam school had been replaced by the evolution of six "programs of choice"—three existing programs and now three new offerings—and a new form of organization for a comprehensive high school.

Leadership for Faculty Empowerment

In September 1990, all the new programs were in place. Two months later, the school put on its first-ever orientation night to present the new choices and describe the application process to next year's incoming ninth-graders.

On a cool autumn Wednesday evening, the large modern auditorium of Cambridge Rindge and Latin High School is nearly full of parents, many of whom have brought their eighth-grade children along to find out about the programs offered to incoming ninth-graders.

"Close to three hundred and fifty families," boasts the acting assistant principal as he continues to greet latecomers with information packets. "That's two thirds of the incoming ninth-grade class. By far the best turnout for a parent night we've ever had!"

The high school, with 2,100 students, has more than a 50-percent minority population, but as I look out at the audience, white parents and students predominate.

Nine school administrators—one black, two female—sit with Ruben Cabral at a long, white cloth-covered table on the stage, which has been decorated with a few large houseplants for the occasion. Ed Sarasin, the principal, moves to the podium to speak. His tone is cordial but matter-of-fact as he welcomes parents, introduces the people on stage (polite applause for each), and then briefly explains the purpose of the evening. It is to acquaint parents with the six different programs at the high school to which they can now apply for their children. He describes each in a sentence and states that "the purpose of the decentralization is to be more responsive to the needs of students and parents."

One of the handouts in the information packet goes on to explain that while "programs of choice may differ in theme, emphasis, and management, they provide equal opportunities for all students. . . . The School-Within-a-School model creates the advantages of a home base, the opportunity for close monitoring of student progress, and a stronger, more personal relationship between families and the school. At the same time, it provides student access to the widespread resources of a large, comprehensive high school," meaning that kids can still choose from more than 450 different course offerings.

Now a guidance counselor explains the selection process. Families put down their first three choices on a form which must be sent in by January 16; programs are balanced for equal representation of minorities, range of abilities, girls and boys, and so on; parents are then informed of placements by mid-March; 80 percent will get either their first or second choice.

Now each of the six program administrators, or housemasters as they are called, gets up in turn to talk about his or her program for five minutes or so. The presentations are, for the most part, informal, chatty, factual—Pilot is located on the fifth floor and has 225 students who call their teachers by first names; there are twelve different technical training areas in the vocational program; the Leadership School stresses community service and cooperative learning; Fundamental offers a highly structured learning environment with two hours of homework a night, and so on.

After the first four presentations, the program descriptions begin to fade, blur, and sound the same.

Short and round, with thick graying hair and square, metal-framed glasses, Ruben Cabral, housemaster of the Academy, appears a little more formally dressed than his colleagues in his dark suit. When his turn finally comes, Ruben opens with a warm comment about how rewarding it is to have such a large showing of parents. It is the first gracious note of the evening. He then goes on to talk in an organized, clear, and succinct manner about the Academy, which came about, he says, "from a process of analysis and self-discovery and subsequent decisions about the program by teachers." Ruben summarizes what he says were the teachers' decisions in a style that is both succinct and intellectual:

- *that the program would be a community of learners, not a place of just teaching. Ruben quotes Theodore Sizer's metaphor of "student as worker, teacher as coach";*
- *that cooperative learning is best fostered by learning how to learn;*
- *to try team teaching to break the isolation of the classroom and allow teachers to talk together about students' needs and interests;*
- *to do cross-cultural education to reflect the variety and richness of many cultures (all Academy ninth-graders are strongly encouraged to take a foreign language; they are not allowed to have free periods in their schedules);*
- *to be attentive to the individual needs and concerns of students;*
- *to create a more democratic process, not just for teachers, but also for parents and students;*
- *to emphasize the arts (all Academy ninth-graders must take an arts offering);*

- *to move toward evaluating students on the basis of research projects in different courses;*
- *to require seniors to do community service;*
- *to emphasize understanding of knowledge as a whole entity; (the curriculum is integrated, as much as possible).*

After all the presentations, Ed Sarasin fields a few questions from the audience in the theater. There are several about procedures. One woman asks what percentage of the women and minorities in each program go on to college. Ed assures her that no one program is "the *college prep program," and that all the houses send just about the same percentage of kids on to college. Checking his watch now, he indicates that the time for the large group presentation is over. Next on the schedule are opportunities to meet informally with the program administrators over coffee and dessert in the cafeteria and to tour the building with student guides who each carry two helium balloons—one black, one white.*

The crowd files out quickly and migrates down a brightly lit labyrinth of halls, heading toward the cafeteria. Student lockers, painted in bright primary colors, stand flush against the walls on either side most of the way. The murmuring of voices and the scuffling of feet on the terra-cotta floors echo loudly back from the white cinder-block walls. Here and there, a few display cases shine with the usual athletic team trophies and photos, but there's also one with student art and another near the large, modern library room that contains books about diverse cultures. No dim, outdated flickering fluorescent lights; no graffiti. Built thirteen years ago and hailed then as a breakthrough in "humanized" high school architecture, the building still shines as though new.

Ruben stands in a corner of the cafeteria, surrounded, as

are all the other program administrators, by a tight knot of a half dozen or so concerned parents. Several parents complain to Ruben that all the programs sounded alike. One asks, "What's really different about the Academy?" He replies, "The curriculum. We're not a school, but a place of learning. We're concerned that students are challenged individually but also that they learn how to work in a group. Students learn more from teaching each other than from sitting and listening to a teacher. We're also concerned that learning be more whole, more integrated. This year, for example, change is a theme in all the ninth-grade classes." To another parent, he explains, "We have built change into the process; the moment we feel comfortable is the moment we're starting to fail." As the group of parents move on to be replaced by another, Ruben says with a smile and an expressive wave of the hand, "Come and visit anytime. Come talk to the teachers."

Ruben's reference to "self-discovery" and his invitation to "come talk to the teachers" were not just program hype, I came to discover. He believes that what makes the Academy program truly different begins with the thinking that faculty in his house have done together over the last few years.

Recalling how "professional" the Academy faculty's original proposal presentation to the school committee had been in the spring of 1989, Cambridge superintendent Mary Lou McGrath observed that Ruben had "really encouraged teamwork all along the way. He's never defensive, always willing to take risks, very committed—empowering."

"Empowerment" turned out to be a key word in a number of interviews at Cambridge Rindge and Latin. Principal Ed Sarasin described "empowering teachers" as both a means and an end of school improvement. Unlike Hull superintendent Claire Sheff, whose reasons for restructuring were primarily to find better ways to serve students, both Ed's and Ruben's responses to the question of why we need school reform began with their concern for teachers.

Ed Sarasin argued, "What has hurt education is that we've allowed teachers to stay in their individual classrooms with the doors closed and have only worked with the few who want to change. The real challenge is not to just work with those people, but to work with all teachers out of the classroom. . . . You need school reform, but reform is more a form of faculty empowerment, rather than defining on a national level the three R's. School reform will be successful when teachers assume responsibility not only for teaching, but also for what and how things are taught, when they see themselves as part of the whole. Teachers need to define the problems, make a plan, assess progress, and make changes. Until you can make teachers become researchers in the classroom, there won't be change."

Ruben and Ed have worked closely together for thirteen years, since both were first hired as administrators for the newly combined high school. While they disagree on some issues related to curriculum (Ed is a strong advocate of maintaining a broad selection of course offerings for students), Ruben has nevertheless felt supported by Ed in his efforts to work with faculty to create the Academy. And Ruben, like Ed, believes that school improvement begins with giving teachers more responsibility and a stimulus to change.

"Teachers need personal and professional growth. They're a captive labor force," observed Ruben. "New programs help them rethink everything they do—especially team teaching. . . . One of the most cruel things that affects teachers is the loneliness of the classroom. . . . And it is very hard for administrators' evaluations to have any effect whatsoever on the improvement of teaching. Only peer observations and team teaching can. It creates intellectual stimulus for both teachers and students. Supervision also then becomes less threatening. It becomes program development for a team, rather than a criticism of what an individual teacher is doing."

In the same interview, Ruben went on to describe how he became housemaster, some of his ideas on leadership, and the evolution of the Academy:

"Education was initially the last thing I wanted to go into. . . . But I couldn't return to Portugal for political reasons, I was tired of waving banners [as a community activist], and I decided that education was the first priority. At that time [1974], 75 percent of the Portuguese kids were dropping out of the high school. It was another area where one could intervene. I thought I'd do it for a few years.

"I taught Portuguese and social studies for three years. It was very frustrating. I enjoyed the top-track kids, and they did well, and the lower track kids did fine, too, but I had very little patience, and I didn't feel challenged. I felt constrained; nothing could be changed.

"I had a position equivalent to dean of student affairs for a year. Then the housemaster position opened up, and everyone at the high school sort of decided I should apply. I had a chance to study with Lawrence Kohlberg at Harvard at that time, but I decided I could get a Ph.D. anytime. [Ruben later completed his doctorate, studying part-time.] Here was a challenge, a chance to start from scratch—a new superintendent had come in, merged the two high schools, and so had been able to fire the principal and thirty-three others, including all the department heads. I would be the first immigrant to have an administrative position in Cambridge. It was important for the Portuguese community, and for the kids to have a role model. And I knew I would succeed—even when people were telling me I wouldn't because of my accent, or because I would not be big or strong enough to break up a fight.

"The first meeting with teachers, I only spoke for a few minutes. I said to the teachers that before they were profes-

sionals they were people, that I would have an open door, and that I wanted to rebuild the school. I also told a joke—that I was hired because I was the only person they could find who was shorter than the principal, who is also short. Then we had some nice desserts and refreshments.

"Right away, I knew I had to neutralize some teachers and demolish others. I neutralized first by creating an advisory council that met weekly and that represented all factions of the faculty, not just my friends. Then we had regular faculty meetings to decide a number of policies. For me what policy they came up with was not the issue, it was the process. We would meet in small groups, and I always put someone in each group who would create tension but not disruption. The small groups would report back to the whole group at the end of each meeting, and the written notes would be the basis for the next meeting. I still use the same process."

"What about the ones you had to demolish?" I wondered aloud.

"I confronted them at every opportunity, but always on the issues, on principles. After a while they became isolated, lost their voice.

"I've had the same plan for thirteen years: the goal is the betterment of everybody. I see myself as never doing things, but as getting things done by creating the right interaction between people. Getting the right resources focused on the right problem. The whole thing is to set up the right interaction with people. . . . You have to continually remove obstacles, to express the common vision—that's one of the most important things we can do [as leaders]—and then you have to create the right conditions for people to act on that vision. . . .

"Sometimes you have to create a problem to keep people moving—put a wrench in the well-oiled mechanism to bring it to a stop—like asking uncomfortable questions.

Education should be uncomfortable, unsettling. But the problem is people can feel betrayed or paralyzed when you do that. They may even see it as a breach of faith. Five years ago, I started the discussions on 'desegregating' the bilingual program [having bilingual students attend classes throughout the high school]. The whole house faculty rose up against me, and I didn't talk about it again for two years. I told them I respected them. But it was from that confrontation that I brought them into a deeper discussion of what they're doing, which led to the Academy proposal."

Ruben's leadership style is complex. He believes in teachers and knows that they cannot be "made" to change or grow, nor can meaningful programs be developed without teachers' active involvement. But as the interview above suggests, Ruben doesn't sit and wait for teachers to come along with good ideas. He prods, he cajoles, he argues, he inspires, he sometimes even manipulates—all means to the end of encouraging teachers to rethink and reassess their work. This description, from the notes I took at the first Academy faculty meeting of the year in 1990, reveals Ruben's unusual blend of assertiveness and deference with the teachers:

Ruben is the first to arrive at the library for the after-school faculty meeting. He goes around politely but crisply informing students that a meeting is about to take place and they have to leave. Now he waits at the doorway, a handful of agendas in one hand, rattling change in his pocket with the other.

Faculty are slow to gather for the meeting. They spread themselves around the large room, five or six to each of half a dozen tables. Ruben opens the meeting with a brisk, upbeat description of parents' positive responses to the pre-

vious week's parents' night. "Eight have expressed interest in participating in a parents' council," he informs the faculty. "And all systems are go for the ninth-grade program. All students' scheduling problems seem to be solved—" A teacher interrupts with a student's unresolved schedule problem. Ruben is focused and responsive, and the problem is quickly straightened out. Several others are mentioned by other teachers and dealt with similarly.

Next come several long announcements from faculty. The first is about the upcoming blood drive, and there is a good deal of humorous banter concerning unlimited cookies and how quickly the body replaces the blood. The next announcement has to do with the formation of a gay and lesbian support group for students, which produces neither looks of surprise nor disparaging remarks from any faculty.

After twenty minutes, the meeting breaks up into four smaller working groups which each have a specific task. I go with Ruben to observe the ninth-grade teachers' meeting. Ruben opens it with just a simple, "Any problems?" There is a brief discussion of several special education kids' needs. Teachers do most of the talking, and the conversation has a practical, problem-solving tone and takes no more than three minutes.

Ruben then introduces the next topic: "I believe we should encourage students to read books in addition to what is assigned, out of class. Each department could develop a reading list with the expectation that students read a book a month from the list, which we could check in advisor groups. What do others think?"

There is a five-minute discussion, with several teachers offering suggestions, such as starting more modestly with articles and also encouraging students to read school publications with student writing. Ruben seems responsive to these ideas and ends the discussion with a question: "Could I expect copies of articles or book lists in, say, a week?" There is no disagreement.

For the last half-hour, teachers present. The first presentation is of a "banner project" idea, by a math teacher. Something to do with each student making a square incorporating the idea of the "golden rectangle." Faculty ask what that is, and there is a lot of easy laughter as the teacher answers in ways that no one except another math teacher could understand.

Finally, another teacher gets up and says she will present a cooperative learning lesson plan, as requested by Ruben. She talks about how to use existing worksheets in small groups—something that she says a number of teachers have wondered about. After explaining how to do it, she says, "But that wasn't what Ruben wanted me to do." And then she presents ideas for a non–subject specific brainstorming activity as a way to ease into cooperative learning.

Ruben sits beside faculty as a part of the audience and says nothing through this part of the meeting. The tone of both presentations and of the questions from faculty is informal, collegial, professional.

In individual interviews, Academy faculty spoke repeatedly about feeling empowered, respected, and trusted by Ruben.

Nancy Burns described the process of developing the Academy's founding proposal: "After the Key Results Committee released its report, Arnie Clayton [a teacher] came along and began to talk about the successes a team of faculty were having working intensively with bilingual kids in the Basics Program [a very individualized and supportive remedial academic program, developed by Arnie Clayton for students who can neither speak English nor read and write in their native language]. It was along the lines of what we had seen when the Key Results Committee had visited the John F. Kennedy High School in New York. I got excited, but I thought we didn't have the staff to pull it off. Ruben said, 'Yes, yes, we can do it!' He's a real yes man!

So a group of about twenty of us began to meet in our planning period—in the spring of 1988—to talk about ideas and develop a proposal. Ruben sort of facilitated. He'd pose key questions, and we'd try to answer them, but it was definitely created by the faculty. It was fun! Limits were not a part of our discussion. It was also very empowering—sharing ideas and concerns and the sense that because you're there in the trenches, you know best what's needed."

Another teacher who was also involved in the creation of the original Academy proposal had a similar perception of Ruben's role. "There was no question from the beginning that Ruben wanted the active participation of teachers. I felt that every step of the way he was listening, weighing our views, willing to try things our way even if he thought it might not succeed."

The results of a two-page, twenty-one-item House D faculty referendum on the Academy proposal, taken prior to the school committee presentation in June 1989, reflected broad support even from faculty who were not involved in its creation. The least supported aspect of the program—extending the team teaching concept to tenth grade—still had a more than 90-percent favorable rating. The final question on the ballot asked whether or not faculty would like to teach in the new program. Seventy-three percent, or forty-nine faculty out of sixty-seven, said yes; 22 percent said they were uncertain "at this point," and only 5 percent (three faculty) said they had no interest in participating.

I talked to one of the teachers who had voted against the proposal. He felt he'd had little say in the move toward team teaching ninth-grade students. "It was the administration's decision," he said, implying that bureaucrats had imposed this idea on teachers, as they had been doing for years. "We've seen it all come and go. So we'll do cooperative learning for a while."

However, unlike the teacher quoted above, a teacher who had recently moved to the Academy from another house felt that Ruben was far from the usual, run-of-the-mill administrator.

"He's different from the others—like with the two planning periods we have. Most administrators would be up here checking on us, to see if we really were using the extra time to plan together. But Ruben doesn't do that. He doesn't take attendance at house faculty meetings, either. The result is his attendance is better, and people come tell him when they can't be there. . . . Ruben has given us lots of support. He tells us we're the professionals, that there's no such thing as problems, that we can figure it out for ourselves."

What, more specifically, has the Academy faculty figured out? What has "empowering faculty" meant for students? For answers to these questions, we need to consider more concretely what teachers hoped to achieve and then to observe classes.

The Academy in Action

The following quotes are taken from the 1990 Academy brochure, which Ruben and the teachers wrote to explain their program to students and parents:

> The Academy is a new and exciting response to the needs of students, the aspirations of parents, and the professional goals of the faculty. During the past few years this staff has been engaged in the examination of our educational program. This process entailed the thorough questioning of the nature and purposes of all our daily activities, the assessment of the socio-cultural context of students' lives, and the creation of a healthy and effective educational environment. The result was the development of a master plan for the organization of a new school that reflected the collective thinking and resolution of our faculty.
>
> Central to our program are five basic principles: cooperative learning/team teaching, diversity and cross-cultural education, attention to individual needs in the context of community, shared decision making, and emphasis on the arts in the curriculum. We discuss each below:

1. Cooperative Learning, Team Teaching, and Learning to Learn

The Academy instructional program is based on the premise that students can and should learn from each other. Teachers, working together in teams, model the learning behaviors we seek to foster in our students. Ultimately, by focusing on learning how to learn, our aim is to prepare students for a lifetime of learning and personal development.

2. Diversity and Cross-Cultural Education

The Academy student body is drawn from applicants in such a way as to reflect as closely as possible the racial and ethnic diversity and the various neighborhoods of Cambridge. This principle of selection extends to The Academy curriculum and program activities, which draw from a variety of cultural traditions.

3. Individual Needs and Concerns

The program focuses on the needs and concerns of each individual in the context of the Academy community. The central programmatic focus in this regard is the Advising Program, which includes all Academy students, grades 9–12.

4. Decision Making

The governance of The Academy is based on a democratic model for decision making. The Academy observes the principle of direct learner participation in the educational process.

5. The Arts

Recognizing the importance of the arts in the education and development of every individual, we regard the arts as the sixth major subject area and as an integral part of our curriculum. They will be taught both as independent disciplines and as integral parts of the course of study throughout the curriculum.

Much of the wording for this brochure was taken from the original thirty-page master plan for the Academy, its founding proposal. It is, therefore, a very public set of goals. And, in my school experience, it is a very radical and ambitious set of goals, as well. How do these goals actually translate into practice for ninth-grade students in their classes and for their teachers in team meetings?

I observed dozens of classes during my year and a half at Cambridge Rindge and Latin. What follows is based on field notes I took while shadowing an Academy student for a morning in February of 1990, six months after the program had begun operating. Dwayne (not his real name) is a young black man whom I had picked at random and who allowed me to follow him while he attended his four major academic classes (his other two class periods were taken up with a computer literacy course and an extra-help tutoring session each day). It was in most respects a typical day in the Academy.

At the beginning of homeroom, the PA announcements throughout the school are blaring out birthday and Valentine's Day greetings to individual students through the halls and classrooms. Students reading cordial messages to other students—a nice touch.

At the Academy office, where the copy machine, phones, and teachers' boxes are located, the lone secretary is handing out candy mints. The phones ring incessantly as adults rush in and out, briefcases and bundles of books and papers in hand. The atmosphere is frenetic.

In homerooms, pairs of teachers have five minutes to take attendance and to talk to the twenty or so kids in each room. These are their "advisor groups." Today students are taking a trivia quiz on famous blacks. They are asked to identify the following: Stokely Carmichael, Thurgood Marshall, Julian Bond, Michael Jordan, Colin Powell, Arthur

Ashe. All appear to know Jordan, a few know Powell, but most of the rest are unknown to students.

While this is going on, a black student whom I shall call Anton comes in late and immediately goes over to one of the teachers to ask for help on a math problem. Tad is a science teacher and is also Anton's advisor. With long, curly, blond hair and a ready smile, he appears to be in his late twenties and at least fifteen years younger than most of the teachers in the school. Were it not for his tie, he might even be taken for a student—except for the fact that he, like almost all of his colleagues in the building, is white, while the majority of students are black, Asian, or Hispanic.

"Where you been? Good to see you," Tad greets Anton before they huddle over the student's paper. The two talk quietly until homeroom is over a few minutes later.

In first-period English, eleven students sit in a horseshoe configuration facing the teacher (six students are out on a field trip). The teacher begins with a review of answers to a quick fact quiz on the novel Les Miserables. *Then she asks students to do a one-paragraph "free write" in their notebooks, which she says she'll collect, on whether they think Jean Valjean did the right thing by going back and turning himself in.*

"Now don't forget about all the good things Jean Valjean has been able to do as mayor," she reminds them. Students write for about ten minutes. While they write, the teacher circulates from desk to desk, occasionally encouraging or quietly nagging students with comments like, "That's good, Anita," or, "Josh, you can write more than that—you always have so much to say in class."

Afterward, she engages them in a "discussion" of questions: Was the bishop a good person? Even though he lied to the police? When is it okay to lie?

Students' answers tend to be monosyllables. It's as if the teacher has to pull words out of kids' mouths. But the teacher insists on total attentiveness. When a student's attention appears to wander, she immediately notices and calls on that student. Nine out of the eleven students are called on or participate in some way before the music comes on, signaling the end of the period.

For second period History, the same group of kids moves next door. Here too, the teacher, a man in his mid-forties, is working on Les Miserables. *Students are asked to pair up to discuss and write answers to four questions on a ditto the teacher hands out. The teacher's directions include the following: students have to cite specific references from the book for their answers, they have one and a half periods to complete the sheet, and then there'll be a general discussion of the following questions:*

1. *Would you have wanted to live at the time the novel takes place? Give one reason yes, and one no.*
2. *Which character do you most and least admire—excluding Jean Valjean?*
3. *Which episode is the most significant to you?*
4. *Describe the economic and social dichotomies in the book.*

The students are very slow to start. In only one or two of the five pairs is there much interaction between students. Other groups try to listen in on their answers. The teacher circulates around the room, talking quietly to students throughout the period—trying to explain, coach, cajole.

One girl seems on the verge of tears as she stares off into space, totally uninvolved for most of the period. A boy with bright, hand-drawn and highly stylized cartoons covering his jeans has a large black-and-blue mark beneath his eye. From whom or what, I wonder?

In third period Algebra 1, there are twenty-four students. [Only four are Caucasian, an issue I will consider later in this chapter.] The teacher explains to me that students worked in the computer lab the previous Friday on math games. For homework, they were supposed to have written up one solution to one of the games, explaining which solution they'd chosen and why. She begins the class:

"Those of you who were in the show last Friday did a terrific job! But since you missed class, you didn't do the lab. So I need you to come to the front of the room now so I can assign you to groups. The rest of you pair up with your lab partners. You are going to listen to each other's papers and critique them. Quickly now, you only have till quarter-past. Do all the rest of you have your papers?"

Several students admit they don't.

"You were supposed to have them done. You'll have to come in after school one day this week before the final drafts are due on Thursday to finish them up. Okay, stand at the back of the class, and I'll assign you to a group."

She manages to get all the students who have not done the work into groups where at least one student had, and they look at the completed papers while she goes from group to group, observing, making notes, and occasionally asking and answering questions. But before she answers a question she always throws it back to the group first, to make sure they've tried to give an answer.

In one group of four that I observe, the only white student—a girl—is the only one with homework. But when she wonders why a negative number has to be stacked last in a game, it is a black boy who offers a ready explanation: it's because they're the lightest.

The teacher stops them after fifteen minutes and asks, "Okay, what made groups successful today?"

"Listening to each other," one girl replies.

"Yes, what else?"

"Not talking and making noise?" another answers tentatively.

"Okay, now how many groups were there where both lab partners had their papers? Only one group—that was the group that was the most successful."

I go now with Dwayne to his locker and then on the long walk to his science class, in the older part of the high school. The walk takes four minutes or so of going up and down stairs and snaking through crowded corridors. At one point along the way, the only black male faculty member that I encounter all day is standing outside his room in the hall. He asks Dwayne and other students who pass by to remove their hats while in the building—a widely disregarded school rule. Dwayne and the two or three others in my view all oblige him by holding their hats an inch off their heads with one hand until they are twenty feet or so down the hall; then they drop them back onto their heads.

In fourth-period General Science there are sixteen students. [Three are Caucasian; again, we'll return later to this issue of racial disparity in math and science classes.] Unlike other classrooms, which are painted in the standard institutional colors and decorated with only an occasional poster, this room is painted bright green and filled with live plants, as well as numerous bright posters of plants, flowers, and animals. The entire back wall is covered with a photomural of a forest. A poster about famous black scientists is prominently displayed on another wall.

The teacher congratulates the girls involved in the Haitian assembly last Friday, then tells them that they and others who aren't caught up on sheets on time zones for their folders will have to meet with her after class. She also reminds them that sheets on longitude and latitude and seasons have to be there as well. They'll have a unit quiz on all this work later in the week.

She then uses the board to give a lesson on season and time changes due to the earth's rotation around the sun.

"When is there less play time after school?"

Several students mutter unintelligible answers. So the teacher tells them, "Winter."

"Why do you come in at five in winter, and at eight in the spring?"

A student mumbles something about Daylight Savings Time.

The teacher goes on to try to show, through a drawing on the board, different positions of the earth at different times of the year, relative to the sun. Her illustration is somewhat confusing, even to me.

"Why is the equator hotter than the poles, when they're closer?"

Now the teacher uses two pine cones, to try to show the bulge where the equator is. Several times she says half-apologetically that she'll bring in a model tomorrow which explains it better.

For the rest of the period, students work in groups of three on a five-page fill-in-the-blanks worksheet entitled "What Causes Seasons?" I notice that the three white students work together. Within groups, some of the students—mostly the guys—work separately and do not discuss the questions. Occasionally, one will just give another student the answer—"It's C for that one." Only rarely do groups talk together about what the right answer might be. I watch two boys help a third try to figure out which way is clockwise.

Students stay more or less "on task" until the music comes on, announcing the end of the period. The teacher hands out a review sheet for homework that is very similar to what the students have just filled out.

Goals and Outcomes

The original Academy master plan called for teams of four teachers—of English, social studies, math, and science—to work with the same group of students, much as was proposed in Hull. Also similar to the original Hull High School design was the idea that Academy teachers share common planning periods and teach thematic units together, trying to integrate knowledge as much as possible. As in Hull, in the Academy's first year some aspects of the original scheme were implemented successfully, while others were not.

In 1990–91, all of the Academy's ninth-grade English and social studies teachers were paired up, and these teams of two did share the same groups of students and at least one common planning period each day. While I observed no actual team teaching—that is, pairs of teachers working together in the same classroom—the English and social studies teachers whose meetings I observed frequently used their shared planning periods to talk about problems that students whom they had in common were having. Occasionally but less frequently, I also observed teaching pairs plan units to overlap or integrate aspects of what they taught—much as we saw in the description of the two classes that dealt with *Les Miserables*.

However, I was told by Ruben and several teachers that numerous scheduling conflicts did not permit teachers from all subject areas to have either common planning times every day or even to share the same group of students. Tad, the young science teacher who was helping the student in homeroom, was very committed to the ideas of the Academy, but his schedule—a more or less typical one for math and science teachers—did not permit him to be as involved with Academy students and teachers as he would have liked. Out of the five classes he taught in 1990–91, only two had some Academy students. He told me that his applied science class, for example, had 50 percent Academy kids, but they went to four different math teachers. The teacher with whom Tad was supposed to work most closely didn't share the same planning period.

There were other scheduling problems as well. The complexities of the schedule and room assignments were such that not all Academy classes were held near one another. The high school building—actually two multilevel structures—is large, and classrooms can be quite some distance apart. The one time Tad and his colleague in the math department tried doing an integrated lesson, they could find no room where the class might stay for two periods in a row and they lost so much time getting kids from one classroom to the next between periods that it wasn't worth the effort. Most of the math and science teachers did not have back-to-back class periods, so that even if they had wanted to team teach, the schedule just wouldn't allow it.

The lack of adequate common meeting times affected other aspects of the design as well. Initially, Academy teachers had planned to meet all together once a month to develop common curriculum themes across all their courses. They were able to use some of their released time in the spring of 1990 to outline a thematic unit for the first quarter (on revolutionary change), but after school started in the fall, it was hard to find time for such planning. Monthly faculty meetings were usually taken up with all-faculty concerns like how to "do" cooperative learning, and the union contract (a more or less typical one) prohibited teachers from being required to stay late more than once a month. Academy teachers had to give up the goal of developing common themes for all ninth-graders.

What do teachers talk about when they get together for team meetings? Most often, an entire period will be spent talking about one student's problems. A teacher will describe an incident or a set of behaviors of concern and compare notes with other teachers who have the same student. Together they try to decide what's going on with the student and what intervention—like a talk with a guidance counselor, a call home, or an after-school conversation—might be appropriate. What follows is a description drawn from my field notes of the team meeting I attended after shadowing Dwayne for the morning. The meeting was fairly representative, in both tone and content, of many that I observed.

Four teachers of math, science, and research technologies crowd around a small table in a corner of the library. It is the third such meeting they've had this year.

Tad begins the meeting by describing his encounter with Anton, who came in late to homeroom this morning. Tad thinks Anton is "on the edge." His mother is a drug addict, he tells the group, and he was removed from her home five years ago. Since then, Anton has lived in a different home every year; he now lives with his mother's former husband, who is not the boy's biological father. Tad says the man is very authoritarian but also very concerned, and that he calls the school constantly to check up on Anton.

Tad goes on. "Last Wednesday, I saw Anton on the fringe of a group that was talking about going up to Malden for a gang fight. So I just tapped him on the shoulder to say hi as I passed by. So the next day, Anton came by my classroom after school for some extra help. He waited for an hour while I finished up with another student. We had a long talk about a lot of different things. Anton told me that if I hadn't noticed him, he probably would have gone with 'that bad crowd' to the fight. He also told me about how he can't talk with his stepfather. I tried to reassure him that was normal. Then he told me that there was a lot of 'bad stuff' going around about his mom—some of the kids in school evidently know about his mother's drug use 'and other stuff.' Anton also talked about the work he's doing for his homeroom on a 'Brady Bunch' trivia quiz. He told me he'd lived with his grandmother for a year, and the only thing to do was watch TV. 'Brady' was his favorite show, so he became an expert. He knows more than anybody in the whole school about that show, but he once asked me, 'Why can't I have a life like they do?'"

The other teachers all appear to listen attentively to this rather detailed story. Then Anton's math teacher reports that Anton's failing because he missed seven days in a row in the last two weeks. But he has *shown up for the last three days. They wonder if perhaps he may be coming around.*

The conversation about Anton now over, and with only five minutes left until the end of the period, I ask the group how they use their common planning periods. They tell me that they spend at least 50 percent of their time talking about specific students who are having problems—much as they did today, and as their peers at Hull did, also. They like being able to talk about specific kids. One teacher elaborated: "It helps when you find out the problem you're having with one kid isn't just yours, that other teachers are seeing the same thing. Also, you can get on top of problems much faster—talk to the advisor of a kid who's having problems. We can make switches quickly when a kid's in the wrong math or science class. We just do it informally between us, try it out for a few days to make sure it's right, and then inform the guidance counselor. Under the old system, getting the paperwork through the counselors for a switch could take two weeks."

"There are still problems, though," another teacher explains. "There isn't enough overlap between the applied science course and the other ninth-grade science offering, 'Intensive Biology,' for example, so that the switch doesn't always work."

The group reported that they also value the time to talk about their classes. According to one, "It's really great to have a chance to bounce ideas off one another, get feedback about what's working and not working, and how another teacher handles similar material. So much of what teachers do is done in isolation." Another popular topic has been how to make their classes more interdisciplinary, but that's not happening as much as they'd like. Not enough time to plan together, they say.

Based on these observations, what have Ruben and the Academy teachers achieved in their first year of operation? What progress did they make in implementing the three essential components of the change process: setting clear academic goals or outcomes, creating core values, and nurturing greater collaboration?

Unlike the Hull ninth-grade teachers, who had so many different priorities that they did not know where to begin, Academy teachers concentrated on trying to make a few clear changes in their classes. Cooperative learning was the choice of many as a goal for change and is also the first academic goal mentioned in the Academy brochure. (Cooperative learning is a comparatively new strategy for high school teaching; students work in small groups and help one another master the assigned material, while teachers circulate from group to group to give assistance. It is an innovation about which many Academy faculty feel strongly.)

Veteran teachers like Nancy Burns and Arnie Clayton, both of whom assumed administrative roles in the Academy for the 1991–92 school year, believe that cooperative learning is the heart and soul of what they are trying to do differently. Through cooperative learning, these teachers argue, students learn to be more intellectually active and more socially responsible.

"Kids learn better with it, they feel more empowered and more confident," Nancy said. "Their confidence level going into tests is better because they've had a chance to try out their ideas in front of two or three others before the test. . . . Cooperative learning also helps kids see different ways of thinking about a problem, makes them more active in their own learning, and gives them lifelong skills."

Arnie agreed, saying, "Cooperative learning is essential as a learning tool because it gives students control over their own learning, rather than having someone talk at them the whole period. It fosters mutual responsibility, teamwork, and shared leadership."

Cooperative learning was, in fact, being practiced in one form or another in many of the Academy classes. In math and science classes that I observed through the year, students worked in pairs or larger groups of fours and fives close to 50 percent of the time. While there were comparatively fewer lessons formally structured as cooperative learning activities in English and social studies—perhaps because these classes were smaller to begin with—these teachers also stressed the importance of students learning from one another and "becoming more active in their own learning."

The problem, however, is that one can use cooperative learning formats within the traditional framework of a very teacher-dominated and "coverage-centered" classroom and have changed nothing substantive. We saw that in one of the faculty meetings a teacher was, in fact, showing others how to "do" cooperative learning with the same worksheets and lesson plans teachers had always used. Cooperative learning, while important as a means for motivating students, is a teaching strategy, not a goal. It is a means to an end—an end that still remained undefined for many teachers in the Academy during its first year.

Having clear academic goals means having a clear set of answers to the question, What should all students know and be able to do? While the *academic* goals remained undefined in the Academy's first year, two years of discussion among a core group of teachers had produced some clear benefits. By all observable criteria, more work was being demanded of—and done by—Academy students than of students with comparable test scores and dropout rates in Hull and other schools. In interviews with students, I discovered that they spend an average of one and a half to two hours a night on homework. Academy students wrote more frequently and were required to develop their ideas and opinions more fully. As we also saw, teachers went to great lengths to get students to participate in class.

Compared to the fill-in-the-blanks final exams that ninth-graders in Hull took, Academy students had to do much more analytic writing on their final tests. The last part of the English final exam for the team that I observed required students to write a three-paragraph essay comparing and contrasting the theme of love in three of the six novels and plays that students had read during the year, and the final exam for the social studies class consisted entirely of short essay questions.

The same team of ninth-grade teachers also required each student to do a final project—an oral presentation and a seven-page typewritten research paper, complete with a six-item (minimum) bibliography, on a civil rights or women's issue of their choice. The teachers insisted that the papers had to be without spelling errors and "letter-perfect" or they would not be accepted. When a girl tried to turn in a paper that had a footprint on page five of an otherwise perfect paper, the social studies teacher turned it back to her. When the student said she did not have the money to buy a new ribbon for her mother's printer, the teacher simply told her that she would have to wait until she could afford the cartridge before she'd be allowed to turn the paper in. He took nothing off for the tardiness, but he would not consider compromising his standards.

Unquestionably, Academy students were asked to do more work and were being held to higher standards than students in many other urban high schools, however, the *academic competencies* they were expected to master remained vague at best. Too often, the work required of students was more memorization than thinking. Assigning more homework and making sure it gets done does not automatically prepare adolescents for "a lifetime of learning and personal development" or teach them to "learn how to learn," the stated Academy goals. It only means students are more busy.

Having to "cover" a curriculum often gets in the way of developing real competencies. Teachers were covering a curriculum—in this case, the book *Les Miserables* and the history of the period as a part of a larger curriculum about change—without having defined what it was they expected students *to know and be able to do* by the end of the year. Having clear academic goals should not be confused with curriculum coverage. Even when individual teachers have high standards, students can serve "seat time," get passing grades, and still not be able to demonstrate mastery of specific skills by the end of the year. The push by teachers to cover a curriculum unconnected to real competencies or to students' interests and needs is part of the educational problem.

To understand how even a creative and challenging course of study such as the one these teachers developed can contribute to the problem of students' passivity and lack of competencies, we need to return to the classroom and try to see the world within and beyond school through students' eyes.

The Curriculum versus Competency: A Student's Perspective

Academy teachers worked very hard to engage students—nagging, coaxing, and cajoling nearly all students into responding—in most of the classes that I observed. In fact, they were working too hard. In many cases teachers were doing too much of the "thinking work" in order to jump-start students. At the same time, preoccupied with trying to get students through specific curriculum hoops, they missed some opportunities to take advantage of students' spontaneous interest and energy and engage in more active, authentic thinking and learning. Too often caught up in their traditional roles as information givers, many teachers did not see or did not know how to respond to genuine sparks of feeling, energy, and interest that came from students. An English class that I saw one spring day provided subtle but powerful examples of such missed opportunities:

Students sit in a horseshoe around the teacher's desk at the head of the room. She stands in front of her desk now as students open their notebooks. The homework was to pick a passage from the play they're reading, Even Colored Girls Get the Blues, *that was especially moving or upsetting. The teacher hands out notebook paper and asks students to write down the page number and first few words of their chosen quote. Then she asks them to write a paragraph about what the play is about and the "themes or messages in the play."*

After they've written for ten minutes or so, the teacher begins the class discussion. "So, Sue, what is this play about?" [The names here are pseudonyms.]

"I didn't read it," Sue says very quietly.

"Sue, I'm crushed. Raymond, didn't she miss a great experience?"

Raymond looks down at his desk. "I didn't read it."

"Did anyone else not read it?"

No one says anything.

The teacher continues, "So what happens in the play?"

What follows is a fifteen-minute teacher-prompted recital of plot highlights—the rape, prom night, marital problems, and so on.

Having reviewed the plot, the teacher asks the first "opinion" question. "How would you describe the tone of the play—sad, angry, despairing?"

The only white male in the class replies, "It sort of reminds me of women's support groups."

"Is that a criticism? Are you talking from experience? Are the issues in the play only women's issues?"

Now Dwayne [the student whom I had earlier shadowed] replies, "I can picture a group of women sitting around on stage, talking, with spots shining down on 'em—"

"Did you read the stage directions? Are they sitting? No, they're dancing. What does the dance part mean? It's a way for them to express their feelings—especially anger. There's lots of anger in this play."

"No, really?" Dwayne mutters quietly, with obvious sarcasm.

"Who's the anger directed at?"

"Us!" Dwayne says.

"At the men," the teacher agrees. "But is it all anger? There's some affection, too."

"Some of these women seem invincible," Dwayne observes.

"Some of you have said we should have read this book sooner—"

Again Dwayne comments under his breath, but loud enough for most to hear. "Yeah, if we'd read the book sooner, we would have liked the course."

"Why should we have waited?"

"'Cause you were trying to bore us," Dwayne taunts with a smile.

"We've been reading books and plays about change— Metamorphosis, 1984, Julius Caesar, Tale of Two Cities, Les Miserables, Hard Times, Enemy of the People, Doll's House*—were all about changes. So we've been leading up to this book."*

"Are we going to read better books after this?" a girl asks.

"Well, the next book we'll read is Cry, The Beloved Country. *It's about South Africa—"*

"I want to read Roots,*" one girl declares.*

Another agrees, "My sister's reading that in college, and she says it's really—"

"Back to the play, where are these women from? They're from cities, aren't they? What's important about cities?"

"It's real life. The country isn't real," offers one girl.

"I think you're being 'city-ist.' What's more real about the city? Have you ever lived there?" another challenges.

Students talk back and forth between themselves. It is one of the few examples of a student-sustained discussion in all the classes that I have observed. They take different points of view about which is more real, city or country.

The teacher lets several exchanges go by before finally contributing a point of view. "Well, the suburbs are more sheltered—"

"I wasn't talking about the suburbs. I was talking about country—farms and like that," a girl rebuts.

"Maybe it's not a matter of one being better than the other. They're just different." Now the teacher tries to steer the conversation back to the play. "But what is important about these women's experience in cities? There's more danger for women in cities, isn't there? If you were in Boston alone at midnight, would you feel scared?"

Most girls raise their hands, so does one boy.

Another boy replies, "Depends. If it was First Night [the popular Boston New Year's Eve citywide celebration] I wouldn't be."

Kids start to talk about their First Night experiences as the music comes on over PA, announcing the end of the period.

A careful analysis of this class discussion reveals several missed opportunities to engage students in a much more active manner, as well as to require more serious intellectual work of them. Both students' specific reactions to the play and their more general criticism of the course were ignored or deflected, and thus critical thinking was thwarted, while the teacher pursued "the curriculum."

Perhaps the first missed opportunity was when two students out of thirteen confessed to not having read the play. The teacher might have asked why. She might also have asked other students to tell these two what they were missing, instead of making it a matter of having personally disappointed the teacher. (Later, in the chapter about Brimmer and May, we will see examples of classes where ninth-grade students are successfully given more responsibility for running classroom discussions.)

The more serious missed opportunities occurred in the discussion of the play and the other literature students had read through the year. The teacher started with an intellectually engaging, "student-centered" homework and writing assignment—asking students to identify passages which moved them. But instead of asking students what they'd chosen as important passages and why, as a beginning point for discussion, the teacher asked about "the tone of the play." In the way she posed the question, she partially answered it as well, and in doing so limited the possible number of "correct" replies to three—"sad, angry, and despairing."

Instead of answering the question, two students—Dwayne and a white male—began to talk about how the play made them feel: the first, with a comment about women's support groups, and the second with how he visualized the play on stage. The teacher's replies to both students' comments did not encourage discussion; one student was reminded that he's never been to a women's group, while the other was told to reread the stage directions.

Next, the teacher directed students to consider the underlying anger in the play. But as soon as two boys attempted, once more, to talk about how the anger toward men in the play made them feel, the teacher abruptly changed the topic, reminding them that there's a lot of affection in the play, too. Rather than deal with students' feelings, the teacher quickly went on to try to draw a very abstract and tenuous connection between everything they've read through the year. "It's all been about change," she informed them.

Dwayne's angry remark about how boring the books have been inadvertently opened up another opportunity to engage students. Suddenly, several students wanted to talk about the choice of books for the course. Two girls expressed a clear interest in reading *Roots*, a book that certainly has academic merit and is apparently of much greater interest to students than the next book scheduled, *Cry, The Beloved Country*.

It's quite possible that the teacher ignored the students' interest because *Roots* was not available in the school book room, so it seemed to her that assigning it was not an option. But she never explored the nature of their interest. Why did they want to read this book? What did they want to learn? To know? Students' replies to these questions might have revealed new ways the teacher could engage them. And if a teacher really wants to respond to students' interest in reading, he or she need not be bound by what may be available in the book room. (In this case, if they had decided as a group to read *Roots*, some students might have been willing to buy their own paperback copies; others could have shared or gotten copies from the library. Or some students might have elected to read it out of class and then give a report to the rest of the group for extra credit.)

Sadly, the teacher returned to the "curriculum" for the day—a continuing discussion of the points she wanted to make about the book. The class eventually degenerated into a safe but aimless and intellectually empty discussion of "city versus country." While the teacher may think this is a chance for students to engage more actively, unless such discussions are structured around thought-provoking questions or moral issues, students are merely trading uninformed opinions on comparatively unimportant subjects.

After class, I talked to Dwayne, who confirmed my observation that while students enjoy their Academy classes to a degree, and feel cared for by teachers, they are not often as intellectually challenged as they might be.

Dwayne received a grade of seventy-nine (a C+) in English first semester. English and the social studies class that followed it back-to-back were his favorites, he said, "because you get to express yourself and learn from other people around you, not just the teachers. You get to see things from different angles." He also felt that "Academy teachers care about students. They know who you are—you're not just some dude sitting in row three." He confessed to me, though, that he had never read all of any book that had been assigned. "I can usually get most of what I need to know from discussions." And when I asked Dwayne how much of the time he "had to use his mind in school," his reply was, "There's nothing for me to really think about in class. They don't give me anything I can use my mind on. The only thing I had to think about this year was my paper for social studies on why Spike Lee is so controversial."

To motivate students to be more active in the learning process, teachers must take more seriously students' personal, emotional responses to what they're learning. Teachers also must listen for students' real questions and nurture their curiosity. In the class described above, some students showed real interest in talking about the male-female tensions in the play, for example, but the teacher shut the discussion off. Who knows what other interests related to the play might have been revealed in students' homework. And who knows how many more students might actually *read* a book—like *Roots*—that they had chosen together. Unless teachers are able to tap students' experiences, interests, and responses to the subject material and the world around them, teachers invariably end up having to do too much—too much coercing and cajoling, too much of what should be the students' thinking.

The alternative is not a simplistic return to the faddish 1960s "free school" notion of just letting students do what they want—the greatest fear of many school reform critics. Rather, it is to develop curricula through a dialectical process which brings together the world of adult competencies with that of students' needs and interests. It means working with students in ways that enable them to be true partners in the learning process, rather than adversaries. With the above description in mind, we are in a better position to understand three essential steps related to setting clear academic goals:

1. *Teachers—in collaboration with parents and community members—must define what students are expected to master—to know and be able to do—in each class, at the end of each academic year or at other critical points in a student's education, and, finally, in order to earn a high school diploma.* Mastery should not be defined in terms of "seat time served" and subjects "covered," as has been the case. For most students, what is covered in school—whether it's a Shakespeare play, the Battle of Gettysburg, or how to calculate the circumference of a circle—is just a bunch of stuff to be memorized for a test and quickly forgotten. The task of high school education must be redefined. It is not to fill students up with information, but to teach them to use intellectual tools and make sense of the world. The traditional, information-saturated curriculum is badly out of date. Acquiring information must now be seen primarily as the means for teaching competencies and gaining mastery, not as an end in itself.

In the sciences and math, students must be required to demonstrate "know-how"—to show that they know how to use powerful tools for understanding the world and transforming it. Students must show that they can use science as a method of inquiry, not just memorize a list of phyla or elements. Students must show they know how to use mathematics as a problem-solving tool, not just recite a times table. In the humanities, students need to demonstrate that they can reason and communicate clearly—both orally and in a variety of written forms. Students also must show that they know how to develop and apply a knowledge of history and literature as a means for understanding the world around them.

2. *Teachers must discuss with students what skills or competencies they will be expected to exhibit in clear terms well ahead of a projected completion date.* We will see how Brimmer and May ninth-graders were told at the beginning of the year what

they were expected to master in English by the end of the year. In fact, they were actually given the final exam question in the first weeks of the school year, so that they could more clearly know what was expected.

High school students' most common unanswered question is, Why do I need to know this; when will I ever use it in my life? Having a clear road map of where they are going, students can then discuss with the teacher whether these competencies are truly important and why. With a clear understanding of both *what is expected* and *why* they are learning certain things—beyond doing it because the teacher tells them to—students are far more motivated to work harder.

3. *Teachers must involve students in the learning process along the way—in choosing books, projects, and topics, as well as in assessing progress.* There are many ways in which academic competencies can be mastered and demonstrated. Students will be far more motivated if they are permitted choices within the curriculum and engaged in a collaborative process of making decisions and periodically assessing results.

Academy teachers sometimes tried to involve students in a discussion of how to improve their classes, but teachers—perhaps too caught up in their traditional role as "answer givers"—often cut off discussion by providing the solution to problems before students had time to really consider them. The beginning of a social studies class that included the same group of students in the English class described above reveals another fine effort by a teacher, but one that resulted in one more missed opportunity:

As the students straggle in from English next door, the teacher has them pull their chairs into a circle. All this week, students have been doing oral presentations of the final project papers they have written. Now the teacher sits down at a student desk in the circle and begins the class.

"Before we start, I want to mention something—I feel you're not responding to one another's presentations. You're waiting for me to say my two cents' worth. So I'd like you to fill out a sheet for each speaker: you put down the topic, what article you read, the major points covered by the presenter, some of the questions you have, points you'd like to follow up on, ideas or topics covered that you hadn't anticipated, how your original opinion has altered, et cetera."

"What if you don't have any questions?" Dwayne challenges.

"I'm sure you'll have some—the whole idea is to keep yourself intellectually alive, and not veg out when you listen, just 'cause you know your history teacher likes to talk. Okay, let's get on with our presentation for today . . ."

The teacher's instincts—to "play back" to students behaviors of theirs which concern him—are good. But after having posed the problem as the lack of response to one another's presentations, the teacher goes on to solve it immediately, all by himself.

A better tactic would be to ask students *why* they seem unresponsive to one another's work. The topics—date rape, feminism, prejudice, and so on—are of obvious interest to the students, but perhaps by trying too hard to channel their responses in a narrowly academic fashion the teacher inadvertently cuts off discussion—and thinking, as well. Students doing the presentations could select the short readings *they* think are most relevant for others to read prior to their presentations and then end with *their* questions for discussion. They could also ask their peers for the feedback they want on their presentations.

Teaching students to ask for and give help to one another is a part of the "process approach" to teaching writing,[4] but it is rarely used in other classes. Here schools could borrow a new "best practice" from business—the idea of creating a "learning organization." Business consultant Peter Senge describes using a process for organizational improvement in which discussion of goals and better ways of achieving them is a continuous, collaborative endeavor.[5] In an informal talk at Harvard in 1991, Foxfire founder Eliot Wigginton described an approach he uses to involve high school students in a regular monitoring of progress toward goals which the class establishes for itself at the beginning of the year. (In his book, *Sometimes a Shining Moment*, he also advocates involving high school students in overall course and teacher evaluation.)[6] We will see numerous examples of this more active engagement of students in their own learning with descriptions of Brimmer and May classes in the next chapter. It is central to Theodore Sizer's idea of "student as worker" and is, I believe, one of the most crucial strategies for overcoming student passivity.

When I described the missed opportunities I'd seen to Ruben, he was neither surprised nor defensive. In private, Ruben talked comfortably about the gap between rhetoric and reality in the Academy. "You have to take one thing at a time," he said. "Creating teams was the first step—a way to generate more thinking about teaching and curriculum. That by itself won't necessarily change things. But administrators can't mandate change from the top, either. What I'd like to do is create a new position like Dean of Studies—someone who would spend most of his or her time in classrooms observing, giving suggestions to teachers, and raising curriculum issues."

The two teachers in the descriptions above did not have the benefit of such assistance and had been working together for less than a year when the descriptions were written. By the end of their first year of working together they had come to understand the need to relate the curriculum more consistently to issues of interest to students, as we saw from the final project assignment they gave. They were also beginning to listen to students' suggestions about other books to read and speakers to invite into classes. After months spent observing them, I was deeply impressed by their competence and dedication. It was clear to me that they would have welcomed more feedback on their teaching.

As Ruben implied, teaching strategies such as those discussed above do not come by themselves. Teachers need training—both coaching in their classrooms and opportunities to observe others. They also need time to solve problems together and to get to know students well. Such time to reflect, address problems, and get to know individual students is a rare commodity in schools, as we have seen. Finally, teachers need a clear mandate to emphasize competencies over curriculum, and they need help in setting overall curriculum priorities. Too many communities continue to tell teachers what more they must teach, without suggesting what might be deleted.

Creating clear academic goals based on competencies rather than curriculum coverage requires a larger conversation—and is not something that educators can do alone or in a vacuum. Teachers cannot decide on their own what is most important for students to know and be able to do. Nor can they stray very far from the high school curriculum path so familiar to most adults without community "permission." Developing a school- and communitywide consensus on what's worth knowing is essential. This is a problem underlying all school reform efforts and one to which we will return in the last chapter.

In large schools like Cambridge Rindge and Latin, a number of institutional roadblocks stand in the way of the more intensive community and teacher collaboration that is required to develop new curriculum goals and teaching strategies. Institutional factors also affect the development of and commitment to core values.

Dealing with Race and Class: Core Values

As suggested earlier, the idea of core values raises difficult questions. Core values must affirm, paradoxically, both individual self-development and the importance of community. Should certain values be promoted over others? Who should decide?

Leaving aside the question of universal values (to be discussed further in the Brimmer and May chapter), the choice, emphasis, and wording of specific core values must vary from school to school, as they do from one community to another. Individual schools need to create their own codes of ethics to nurture in more specific ways both personal growth and community. When considering which core values to choose for their school, educators and community members must discuss the particular circumstances and needs of their students. Schools obviously cannot undo all the economic and social effects of poverty and racism, but the development and expression of appropriate values is how schools best deal with issues of race and class. A discussion of core values at Cambridge Rindge and Latin will help answer the question, What more can schools and communities do for the students most at risk?

To better understand these issues, we need to go back and listen to Dwayne once more.

As I came to know him—and he to trust me—Dwayne revealed himself as someone very different from the apparently detached, many might say lazy, posturing rebel we saw in the classroom. When he was given an opportunity to discuss issues of real interest to him, a much more deeply thoughtful and engaged side of Dwayne emerged. The difference between how Dwayne "plays the school game" and what he really thinks provides a powerful lesson about the gap between the often comparatively trivial classroom rhetoric and the deeper reality of students' concerns, interests, and thinking.

I asked Dwayne, who was only fourteen, why he admired black filmmaker Spike Lee, the subject of his research paper (the one assignment all year that he said really required him to use his mind). His unedited response:

"Spike Lee is the only activist we have right now. . . . Blacks need a political revolution, a way to get minorities in power, and a revolt against negative aspects—like drugs and weapons. Nobody should be able to buy an AK-47 or a kilo. . . .

"Yesterday I went to this guy's house—a friend of my older brother's. The kid had a MAC 10 [a type of machine gun] just sitting on the table. Usually I'll hold a gun, if it's just a semi-automatic or something. But I was afraid of that thing. I didn't even want to touch it.

"If I was President, there'd be no such thing as a MAC 10. War'd be something you play on Nintendo. War in other countries, war in the streets—it's crazy! We fought Hussein for oil, but when I'm dead my kids won't be able to sit out on a nice day like this. They'll have to live in some gas chamber."

Dwayne went on to tell me that he's observed four shootings in the last year and a half, and every few weeks or so he's asked if he wants to "spot" or deal by sixteen-year-olds who drive BMWs and give him hundred-dollar bills "to go buy some lunch." It's tempting, he said—especially when his father has to wait a month before he can even give him fifty dollars for a new pair of sneakers.

Dwayne is luckier than many poor black students. He has obvious intellectual gifts, and he has a lot of support from his parents. When I went to interview them, I counted eighteen pictures of their three children on the walls and shelves of their tiny, cramped living room. It was a kind of shrine to family. But Dwayne's father knows little of his son's struggles and temptations. His wife was laid off from her job a year ago, and now he's worried about what to do when the facility where he works closes later this year. He told me proudly of his son waiting patiently for fifty dollars for new sneakers and then finally turning the money down, saying he could wait a few more months (perhaps Dwayne hid them at home, or perhaps his father chose not to notice Dwayne's brand-new hundred-dollar Nikes).

Dwayne also feels some support from his teachers and from the college students who act as tutors for him three afternoons a week in an Upward Bound program. He wants to be a psychiatrist some day, he says, so he can help other people the way some adults have helped him. Yet in spite of this support and his own gifts, he remains very much at risk and on the edge—failing three classes, often alienated in the two he does well in, and deeply afraid of being drawn into either drug dealing or the gang wars that he thinks are likely to erupt in Cambridge over the summer. "It's scary," he told me. " 'Cause I look around in my classes now and figure some of the kids won't be coming back in September."

What more can schools do to help Dwayne?

Celebrating Diversity

The commitment some urban schools like CRLS now make to "celebrate diversity" as a core value is a very important first step toward keeping minority students in school. In my observations of day-to-day life at the Academy, I saw a number of examples: clear and frequent attempts to acknowledge the achievements of diverse cultures in all-school assemblies (and the faculty's appreciation of their students' performances in them); the "famous African-Americans" quiz in homeroom; numerous posters and displays throughout the school which highlighted the achievements of minorities; and the opportunity to learn more about minority leaders and issues in parts of the curriculum. Through such efforts, students learn that the worlds of culture and of achievement are not all-white. Dwayne needs to know that his dream of becoming a psychiatrist is not just a fantasy—that other black men and women have gone before him.

Nurturing a sense of pride and respect for the different contributions of minorities may be a precondition for establishing a climate of general respect at all levels—for black, brown, and white, for students as well as adults. At Cambridge Rindge and Latin, I was impressed by the ease with which students seemed to relate to one another, and to teachers, and with the lack of any apparent racial tension in either classrooms or halls. My interviews with Dwayne and others confirmed my sense that there was a basic climate of respect and tolerance in the school. The result was that the school felt safe and comfortable for all students, and there was comparatively little testing or "acting out" of disrespectful behavior in classrooms.

Respect and safety are necessary but insufficient as values for success in school. Students must believe that they have a fair shot at succeeding, that what goes on in classes relates in some way to their lives, and that there are adults in their lives who care whether they succeed or not. All three are frequently missing in most high schools and were continuing problems at CRLS, despite the commitment and effort of many there.

Individualized Learning

The detrimental effects of ability grouping—or "tracking"—on many students' motivation to succeed in school is now widely documented.[7] Students relegated to the "standard" or "basic" tracks believe themselves to be "losers." Unfortunately, so do many of their teachers. The results—low-quality work, high dropout rates—point to a self-fulfilling prophecy, one that disproportionally affects children from poor and minority families. Nevertheless, most American high schools still have three to five academic tracks in all subject areas. This practice, and the stereotypes that underpin it, belie schools' rhetoric—and the American belief—that everyone can learn and has an equal chance to succeed.

In my account of the history of Cambridge Rindge and Latin, I referred to the concerns of a group of faculty about the tracking of minority students in the high school. Their report documented the low percentage of minority students who were in college-level and advanced placement courses. Faculty feared that minority students were being discouraged from taking such courses—and thus from being more academically successful.

Aware of the considerable literature about the detrimental effects of tracking, Academy teachers were committed to trying to eliminate the practice. As we saw, Academy English and social studies classes were not tracked in ninth grade. Upper-grade courses in these subjects remained tracked throughout the school, however, and science and math courses in the Academy continued to be somewhat tracked, though less so than before. Entering ninth-graders can take either first-level algebra or geometry for math, and either biology or a course on the principles of science.

Still, the correlation between even this reduced tracking and race persisted. There was a very low percentage of minority students in the more advanced ninth-grade math and science sections that I observed. For example, in Dwayne's algebra class there were about twenty minority students out of a total of twenty-five, while the more advanced ninth-grade geometry class that came in the next period had a total of only twelve students—three of whom were Asians, and none of whom were black or Haitian.

It is comparatively easy to describe the destructive effects of tracking on all students, especially minorities. Finding solutions, however, is far more difficult. We saw that in Hull the ninth-grade teachers struggled to find ways to work with students of very different needs and abilities in the same class. This was also true in the Academy.

I talked at length to the teacher of the "Algebra 1" class described earlier in this chapter and mentioned above. I observed her to be an outstanding teacher and deeply committed to the idea that every student can learn. (This class was large because she had volunteered to take a group of "low ability" students out of another class where the teacher was having problems.) This teacher told me that in a test of basic computational skills she had administered at the beginning of the school year, her students ranged all the way down to fourth-grade level in math; only two out of twenty-five were at grade level. Sadly, such disparities are the norm in most subjects in American high schools.

Proponents of "de-tracking" like to talk about how teachers can use cooperative learning to teach students of different abilities in the same class, but this teacher had been using cooperative learning in her classes for several years; in fact, she was now teaching the technique to other teachers in the school. Cooperative learning, no matter how successfully employed, cannot by itself bridge the gap between students who may be the same age but as many as five or eight grade levels apart in a given subject area.

The solution, then, is not simply to eliminate tracking. As a society, we must move beyond polarized black-white, liberal-conservative debates and find new ways to resolve the often-conflicting values of true equality of opportunity and real intellectual challenge to all students. Every student must believe he or she can succeed—can learn what is necessary for both personal growth and useful work. And every student must be involved in work that demands real intellectual rigor.

Anne Wheelock and others have described some examples of successful untracked middle schools where "low ability" students' academic achievement was improved and the "top-track" students continued to do well while also learning how to get along with students different from themselves.[8] However, differences in students' abilities and aspirations become more extreme at the high school level, and so we do not yet have many replicable models for untracked ninth- through twelfth-grade schools. Theodore Sizer and others are suggesting that high schools might offer two diplomas—a "basic" one that all students would earn by the age of sixteen or so, and an advanced diploma for the more academically inclined students.[9] While I believe that this is a strategy worth pursuing, in the meantime we must individualize learning to a much greater extent than is being done—or even discussed—in most secondary schools.

When I taught high school English and social studies, I had a great deal of success with students of wide-ranging abilities through a combination of mixed-ability seminars and independent-study tutorials. My students met in seminars twice a week, when they presented projects and discussed both individual and group readings around common questions and themes of interest to all. The rest of the week, all students worked on individual projects and assignments. I used that class time for biweekly conferences with every student, during which I gave supervision and extra help.[10]

It took me four or so years of research and development, both teaching and reading, to learn to do this work well with students of all abilities. Likewise, new possible diploma tracks will require systematic investigation over time—and some risk—but such new approaches are essential if we are to achieve both equity and excellence in our schools. As a society we cannot afford to give up either one.

Authentic Conversations: Letting the "Real World" In

While Dwayne worries about gang wars and struggles to make sense of the "craziness" he sees all around him, he remains silent during the English-class discussion about city versus country. And while he wrestles with the choices he confronts in his life and wonders what kind of world his children will have, in the social studies class he asks the teacher what to do if he doesn't have any questions.

In Dwayne's eyes, the world of school asks comparatively little of him and often seems silly, while the real world is deeply confusing and even overwhelming. It is not merely the bureaucratic "cracks" through which students fall; it is in this enormous intellectual and emotional gap between two worlds—the "play" world of school and the real world of violence and conflict—that we lose many young people.

Teachers can make significant progress in closing this gap by allowing students' "real world" experiences, interests, and deep questions to become part of the curriculum in ways that I have already outlined. For classes to have life and vitality, and to engage students more fully, we need to risk more authentic conversations. Making students' real moral dilemmas and concerns legitimate topics for class discussions and further study must be a core value.

Caring

Redefining the curriculum as a set of competencies really worth mastering, creating an environment that truly respects differences, equalizing educational opportunities, and encouraging students to pursue their individual interests, questions, and real concerns in the classroom—all these help students to become more engaged and active in their own learning. But there is yet another factor that is required to motivate students to learn. For students to care more about their schoolwork, they need to know that what they do in school matters to parents or other adults close to them. Students need to know that there are adults in their life who *care* about what they learn, and who care for them as individuals.

In the previous chapter, I referred to the work of James Comer, who described the loss since World War II of the structures that supported minorities' motivation to do well in school—family, community, and church.[11] When they worked well, all three communicated to young blacks that there were people who knew about and cared what they did. Comer argues that a crucial ingredient for minority students' success in schools is having parents or other adults who are informed, involved, and interested in their schoolwork, and Nell Noddings has written persuasively about the importance of caring for the intellectual and moral development of *all* children.[12]

Encouraging caring adult-student relationships may be the single most important effort we can make to increase *all* students' motivation to succeed in school. Such relationships must be founded on much more than mere respect. Respect isn't enough for the students in our three schools and elsewhere who are emotionally cut off from the world of adults. They need relationships with adults rooted in trust, intimacy, and care.

Advisory Roles for Teachers

Teachers can contribute to creating a more caring environment for students by learning roles that will be new to many: working together in teams and being advisors to students.

Individual teachers, seeing perhaps a hundred students a day and working in isolation, cannot possibly come to know and care about the needs of all their students. Nor can guidance counselors, who typically have a load of between three and six hundred students and whose main job is to do class schedules and get students into colleges.

We saw that both at Hull and in the Academy, where teams of teachers worked with the same group of students and were given time to discuss student progress, teachers spent considerable time talking about individual students. Many fewer "fell through the cracks," in one teacher's words. In so-called Comer schools, this idea is taken a step further. Teachers serve on "mental health teams"—along with guidance counselors, school psychologists, and perhaps an area social worker—to monitor the progress of the most "at-risk" students. When they discover a problem, the group creates an action plan, and one individual is assigned as a "case manager" to follow up and report back periodically.[13]

But what about students who are not "at risk"? Do they, too, need more caring and community? Significantly, the top priority of *students* for improvements in all three of our schools—as well as in the four California schools included in the Claremont study cited in the previous chapter[14]—was closer teacher-student relationships.

We learned that in Hull teacher-student relationships were uppermost on the minds of the student council representatives when the principal, Bob McIntyre, had a candid conversation with them about what was wrong with the school. They told him they felt that many teachers at the school just didn't care about students. The results of a poll the Academy's student government sponsored in the winter of 1991–92 showed that what students wanted most was to get to know faculty better outside of class. (Faculty, too, observed that they needed to do much more to build community in the Academy, as we will see.) Finally, when Brimmer and May students discussed ways in which their school climate might be improved, they came up with a proposal that more time be provided for student-faculty fun events which would build community.

The solution to which some schools have turned—and one

that Cambridge Rindge and Latin had made efforts to implement—is to create teacher-student advisory groups. Groups of about fifteen students are assigned to one teacher, and the group meets weekly.

At Central Park East Secondary School, a leading member of the Coalition of Essential Schools founded by Deborah Meier, advisory groups meet for about four hours a week to talk about what's happening in individual students' lives, in the school, and in the world. Advisory groups frequently go on trips together and deal with more sensitive topics such as sex and health education and substance abuse. Most college counseling is also done in advisory groups. Most important, teacher-advisors have the primary responsibility for knowing how students are doing in all their classes and for communicating with parents through periodic phone calls, conferences, and even home visits.[15]

In time, successful advisory groups become a kind of extended, or in some cases even substitute, family. Students can say important things and feel heard by an adult and their peers. Young people can laugh and cry and feel they are cared for. Advisory groups can significantly enrich students' school lives and so help reduce dropout rates dramatically. While less than 40 percent of New York City high school students graduate within four years, at Central Park East—where teachers work with comparable groups of students but in many of the new ways I've described—the graduation rate is 71 percent. And of those graduates, more than 90 percent are attending college.[16]

Teacher-as-advisor is a new and often difficult role for many. Teachers need a great deal of training and support to be successful. They also need an adequate amount of time to do this additional work. In our earlier description, we saw that the science teacher, Tad, was trying to advise Anton—as well as his other students—while taking attendance and listening to school announcements during the ten-minute homeroom period at the beginning of the school day. It wasn't enough time, and so Tad, a young teacher without a family, frequently met with his advisees after school, something that not all teachers can or are willing to do.

It wasn't always that way. Cambridge Rindge and Latin once had a teacher-advisor program (called TAP) in which teachers were given a regular advisory period during the school day to work with students. But the school committee eliminated the program as a money-saving measure, while keeping the auto repair classes, the advanced placement courses, and more than 400 other academic offerings. It didn't matter that preserving advisory groups was the first priority for the majority of Academy teachers. It was not their decision to make. The problem of dealing with a politicized bureaucracy is one to which we will return.

Parental and Community Involvement

A striking finding in my study was the minimal degree to which parents of students in these three schools were involved with, or even aware of, discussions about how to improve their children's schools. Despite two years of professed intentions to involve parents in decision making at both Hull and the Academy, in neither school is there yet any involvement of parents in any decision-making group. In all three schools, administrators have made efforts to inform parents about change, but parent meetings have remained rather poorly attended. As a result, parents of students in these schools were not very well informed, as I discovered.

I interviewed the parents of two ninth-grade students from each school. At the end of the 1990–91 school year, I selected students whom I'd observed to be more or less representative. With respect to the levels of academic achievement, at each school I selected one student who was getting good grades and one who was not.

I asked each parent what contact they'd had with their child's school that year and what they knew about ongoing changes. One Hull parent, a recently divorced woman, had had one conversation about the death of her son's grandfather with a school guidance counselor, but could not remember the man's name.

She had not attended any meetings at the school, was not aware of any new programs, and thought that school had been "fine" for her son that year, despite the fact that her son's grades were C's, D's, and an F.

At the Academy, Dwayne's parents were unaware of any innovations or change in the school and hadn't been to any meetings, but his father had spoken twice to Dwayne's counselor on the phone about his son's grades and was deeply concerned about his school performance. "If I could, I would send him to Catholic school. You have more discipline," this father told me.

The other Academy parent I interviewed, a divorced woman who had immigrated from Taiwan nine years before, spoke very little English. She'd had no contact with the school all year and was unaware of any new programs. My questions about the school seemed to make her feel uncomfortable. Because of the language barrier and the fact that she worked most evenings, this woman said, she couldn't even help her daughter with homework, let alone get involved in larger school issues: "I don't spend much time with [her]. All she shows me is her report card. She asks me some questions on homework, and I don't know how to teach her."

Only one parent selected for interviewing, a self-employed computer consultant who was the father of a Hull student, was both well informed about and involved with school-change efforts at his child's school. He had a strong interest in education, a large number of children in the school system, and had been asked to serve on a systemwide advisory committee. He was well aware of the curriculum innovations in the ninth grade and had attended several open-house meetings. His answer to my question about how the school year had been for his daughter was informed and articulate: "She had a pretty good year, although I don't feel she was as challenged academically as she should be. She should be exposed to more primary sources and less predigested learning."

All three of the "uninvolved" parents were in some sense financially at risk and could not take time off from work to find out more about what their children were doing in school. Interestingly, while many business leaders decry the state of our schools, and some even donate goods or services, rarely do employers grant parents paid time off to go to parent-teacher conferences or to do volunteer work in schools.

Other adults—not just parents—are needed in schools. Businesspeople are needed to work with school-based management teams, as company managers did in the seven Massachusetts schools described briefly in the Hull chapter. They are also needed as mentors. Serious mentor programs, which are sustained over a period of years and have strong company support, can provide many "at-risk" students with a badly needed interested adult presence in their lives. Mentors are also a potential bridge for adolescents to the adult world of work—a way of connecting what they learn with the skills they will need. Instead of donating an occasional computer, businesses might best contribute to educational improvement by creating incentives and programs for parental and community involvement in schools. Polaroid Corporation has created several model programs.[17]

Simply inviting parents to become more involved is not enough. James Comer describes how many poor and minority parents feel unwelcome in schools.[18] They often feel confused or demeaned when they talk to people whom they see as authorities. A symptom of this problem at Rindge and Latin was the comparatively small turnout of minority parents for the meeting that introduced the new high school programs to parents. Despite the considerable efforts of administrators to reach out to minority parents—translating program descriptions into four languages, for example—the composition of the audience did not come close to representing the 54-percent minority school population.

Over the past fifteen years, Dr. Comer has worked with educators in New Haven and elsewhere to develop a successful methodology for involving parents in the life of schools. The first step is to create a governing council of teachers, administrators, and parents, so that everyone feels they have a voice in decisions and an equal partnership in educating young people. (I argue that students must also be a part of the school improvement process as well.) The second step is to involve all parents more fully in the life of the school—beginning with social events which are less threatening than meetings with the (often white) authorities. In time, the school comes to be seen as a true community center, and parents more readily move into a variety of volunteer classroom roles. The results, in terms of students' improved attendance and increased interest in their schoolwork, are often dramatic.[19]

The problem in middle- and upper-class schools is often quite different. Preoccupied with their children's performance and future success, many parents in these schools are frequently overinvolved in their children's schooling and often assume they know better than the teachers what their children ought to be learning. Their goal, however, is not to change the school, but to make sure their own children have all that they need to get into a "good" college. The parents of one ninth-grade girl at Brimmer and May told me proudly that she planned to attend medical school, and that their chief concern about the school was that she was not getting all the math and science she should have. They'd been in to the school several times to talk with school administrators about the problem and had had the girl moved to a more advanced section in math. (The following year she was sent to another school—her third in four years.) Brimmer and May teachers observed that the girl's real difficulties were not academic, but social; believing herself to be smarter than her peers, she rarely participated in class and tried to take over in small-group work.

The other Brimmer and May parent I interviewed, a woman who had been divorced for some time, was in close touch with her daughter's advisor because the mother was very concerned that she wasn't doing well enough in school. This mother told me that she was on the phone almost weekly to the school and tried all kinds of threats and bribes to get her daughter to do her homework, to little avail. When I interviewed her daughter, it became clear why the focus on improving the girl's level of achievement wasn't working. She told me that there was no one home when she came back from school every day, and her mother was often traveling for weeks at a time for work. "It's boring and lonely at home, so I turn on the TV instead of doing my homework," she said. "I feel sad sometimes because there's not much parental influence in my life."

These two examples typify, in my experience, the kind of parental involvement one finds in most wealthy suburban public and independent (that is, private) schools, where parents are all too often less interested in what students are learning and feeling—in whether they feel happy or challenged or creative in school—than in how well they are doing. Parents must understand that, What grade did you get on the test? is a question that conveys a very different meaning than, What did you learn that was interesting today? Worrying about a student's school achievements in terms of how they may look on a transcript for college or how they affect a child's future is not the same as caring. Young people need to know that parents, teachers, and other adults care about them as human beings and are interested in their real thoughts and feelings, not merely in how well they perform. (In the next chapter I will describe some strategies for adult-adolescent conversations that can lead to real understanding and caring; and in the final chapter we will consider the larger question of how parents judge quality in high school classrooms.)

Many parents become less involved in their children's education as their kids grow older because they don't know how to help. The subject material is too difficult. The problem becomes even trickier with a very different high school curriculum based on competencies rather than curriculum coverage. If kids don't have any lists of facts to memorize for tests to show their parents, then what can parents do to assist, and how can they know their children are learning? Just as teachers need training to learn new ways of teaching, so parents must learn how they can support their children's schoolwork in new ways. The fall back-to-school night that most high schools host should focus on programs that help parents learn how to be better informed and more supportive of their children's learning.[20]

Collaboration: Limitations and Successes

The two major goals that I have described so far—creating consensus about competency-based academic goals and developing core values in the context of a more equitable and caring community—require greater teacher, student, and parent collaboration. But collaboration, to be meaningful, must lead to action. "Collaborative" advisory committees meet endlessly in too many bureaucracies—schools, colleges, nonprofit organizations, even corporations—but rarely do lists of recommendations result in real decisions, in change. *Teachers, parents, and students must have the authority, as well as the responsibility, to implement their collaborative decisions.*

We saw that Academy teachers were empowered by administrators to collaborate in the creation of a new program, and that the school board allowed them to bring it into being "from the bottom up." But Ruben and the teachers struggled under serious constraints as they tried to set their own program's goals and priorities while remaining a part of a larger school. Their struggle reveals both the limits to collaboration in the large bureaucratic structures that characterize most American schools and how an exceptional group of educators can and do collaborate under adverse circumstances.

We have already seen how the need to accommodate a school-wide schedule with more than 400 course offerings severely constrained the development of significant parts of the Academy's master plan. Lack of coordinated meeting times for classes and groups of students was ongoing and obvious to all—and a deep source of disappointment to many of the teachers who had worked on the original proposal and been told by Ruben that they could "do it all."

I observed a number of other political and bureaucratic struggles that undermined greater collaboration among Academy teachers and threatened the further development of the Academy program. In fact, Ruben's job began to appear to me as much more political than educational in nature. Within the school, he seemed to be constantly dealing with different factions—trying to keep some at bay, satisfying others, pursuing what the Academy needed with still a different group. The struggle and pressures of having to work within the constraints of a large and complex school bureaucracy seemed unrelenting. Ruben frequently used language and metaphors from his military experience in Portugal to describe aspects of his work.

For example, Ruben struggled all through the 1988–89 school year with several members of the in-school middle management, the subject area coordinators, over the Academy's proposal to have some subjects meet only four days per week, instead of five, so that teachers would have additional time to plan collaboratively. "They accused me of wanting to water down the curriculum, of 'creating morons,'" Ruben explained. "I don't like confrontation. I prefer to work with people, and to go in having counted my votes. But I fought the battle and I won. I had to wave the school committee's decision [authorizing the creation of the Academy] in front of them, even to question the integrity of some of them. I was almost physically sick. Part of the reason I'm so tired now is a result of that."

Ruben also was pushing constantly for a greater share of the school's overall budget for textbooks and supplies. The two longstanding high school "choice" programs—Pilot and Fundamental—each had their own budgets, as well as the authority to hire their own faculty, but the Academy did not. Ruben had frequent conversations with principal Ed Sarasin, who acknowledged the inequities and was supportive of the Academy's efforts. But his hands were tied, Ed finally told Ruben, by the superintendent; reallocating resources and granting the Academy greater autonomy for hiring and scheduling were not his decisions to make.

The struggles with the superintendent, the central office bureaucracy, the local union, and the school committee were ultimately the most difficult and disheartening for Ruben and some of the most active teachers within the Academy. The sequence of events described below illustrates the difficulties many committed teachers and administrators face as they try to change their schools.

Early in January 1991, Cambridge superintendent Mary Lou McGrath called a meeting of all the housemasters and the principal from the high school. She was apparently concerned about the growing competition between the housemasters for scarce resources. She had also heard some complaints from students and parents that students had fewer choices of courses because of the efforts of the houses to "block schedule" their students and teachers, putting English and social studies or science and math classes back-to-back with the same group of students so that teachers could plan interdisciplinary units and work more collaboratively.

However, several people who attended the meeting told me that the way in which the superintendent raised these issues was felt to be both personal and insulting. She apparently accused some housemasters—without specifying whom—of being "on ego trips" and of trying to "fatten resumes." After having appeared to be supportive of efforts to create different houses with distinct programs in the past, at this meeting she said that the house programs were cutting too much into students' choice of courses and that she'd hired an evaluator who would set to work immediately to do a full-scale assessment of the high school's restructuring efforts.

I talked to Ruben several days after the meeting, and he was extremely demoralized. He felt that the personal attacks were deeply unfair. He also thought that initiating an evaluation after a program had been in operation only a few months was totally unreasonable.

Earlier in the fall, Ruben had been offered a position as head of a new educational foundation in Portugal. He'd turned it down, feeling that he had both deep personal ties and work still to do in Cambridge. But this latest attack, on top of all the other struggles within the school, was too much for him. A few days after the meeting with the superintendent, Ruben submitted a six-page single-spaced letter of rebuttal—and his resignation. He decided he would take the job in Portugal.

"I can't work in a bureaucracy any longer," Ruben told me. "You go so far and then something happens that has nothing to do with the program—it's very debilitating. In a perverse way, I almost wish Reagan's idea of vouchers [parents being able to choose their children's school, private or public] had gone through. At least it would have shaken up the bureaucracy."

For Ed Sarasin, the central administration was also his biggest concern. When I asked him what he saw as the most difficult challenge for the next school year, he replied without hesitation, "The degree to which central administration will allow us to do what we want to do. In its truest form, the real success of school-based management is sharing decisions and having confidence in people who make decisions—even though they're not perfect and may stumble. The issue is to what degree central administration will give us true school-based management." When I asked him what he liked least about his work, Sarasin continued, "It's the politics—the pettiness—that drives me nuts! They ask your opinion on things they know you agree with. And they ignore you on the things they know you disagree with. The central office deals with issues solely on the basis of political expediency."

Ruben and Ed have long shared a commitment to teacher empowerment and shared decision making. Ruben's decision to resign now provided them both with an opportunity to push teacher empowerment and collaborative decision making one step further—as well as to try to ensure the survival of the program they had created. The struggle over who would succeed Ruben as housemaster of the Academy provided me with an opportunity to observe, firsthand, problems related to the "political expediency" to which Ed alluded.

Ruben believed that if there were to be "open hiring" for his position, the program would be imperiled; the position might remain unfilled for a long period of time, and the program would be allowed to drift and gradually disintegrate without a strong "advocate and defender" in the bureaucracy. Another administrator would eventually get the job, but whether this person would have the same commitment to the teachers and the program was uncertain at best. Ruben told me he'd seen too many people hired to fill a minority quota or because they were friends with someone in the central office, rather than because of their competence and commitment to an educational philosophy.

So Ruben and Ed proposed that Ruben's position be filled by two teachers who would be elected by the faculty and who would both administrate and continue to teach part-time. The proposal describes the two positions in the following way:

> One of these teachers will hold the position of Dean of Administration and will be responsible for the overall daily management of the program (including supervision of discipline, attendance, payroll, coordination with programs and departments, etc.).
>
> The other teacher will hold the position of Dean of Studies and will be responsible for the overall management of the academic program (including supervision of curriculum delivery, staff and program development, support for the cross-curriculum teams, etc.).

Also stipulated in the proposal was the principle that anyone from the Academy faculty could run for the positions, but only as part of a two-person team. Elected teams would hold office for three years and receive a stipend for working additional days. The Academy faculty discussed and approved the proposal, with 74 percent voting yes, at a meeting in late March 1991.

While Ruben's resignation was sudden, his idea of having faculty assume administrative roles was one he'd talked about to faculty for some time, and he'd already singled out two individuals whom he felt would be outstanding for the job—Arnie Clayton and Nancy Burns. They had consistently provided real educational leadership to the house and were widely respected by the faculty. But the question remained, Would the bureaucracy accept a new model for the administration of the house?

Ruben had always tried to involve faculty in decision making, as we've seen, and an elected "executive committee" of the Academy faculty, called the Faculty Council, had been in place since the beginning of the year. Consisting of five teachers, two guidance counselors, and Ruben, this group was intended to help run the Academy, but they had rarely met through the year. There were too many other meetings and priorities. Now, however, the group recognized that they would have to work hard to get their radical proposal adopted by the end of the school year, and so they began to meet weekly at 7:30 A.M. for forty-five minutes before the start of the school day. They drafted letters seeking consideration of their proposal to the president of the Cambridge Teachers' Association (the union) and to the superintendent, and began to prepare for face-to-face meetings with these individuals, as well as for the school committee presentation they knew they'd have to make.

Meanwhile, Ruben formally announced his departure at the April 23 Academy faculty meeting. He would be going to Portugal immediately to help get a school like the Academy started, he explained, and so two faculty who did not want to run for the newly proposed positions would fill in on an interim basis. His final comments to the faculty were brief and emotional:

"I don't believe in charismatic leaders. And, as you know, I view administrative positions as a kind of trap. It doesn't allow for faculty leadership and for faculty to grow and try new things. That's why we've proposed abolishing the posi-

tion of housemaster and having two faculty administrate. Members of the Faculty Council and I went to talk with the superintendent and the president of the CTA yesterday, and while they have many questions, and details need to be worked out, they are in general support of the idea of trying this as a three-year experiment. This is an important experiment, and like many things we've done, it's unique. We need to learn as we go along.

"But we always have to remember that it's the pedagogy that's most important, not the administrative structures. It's the creativity, professionalism, and trust of teachers working together. As you know, I don't believe in problems. Tragedy and disaster are the outcomes of isolation and loneliness."

While faculty support—both for the new model of administration and for Arnie and Nancy—remained strong, the support of the teachers' union and the superintendent was far less certain. For reasons that were never made clear to Academy faculty, the Cambridge Teachers' Association wanted only one teacher to have the position, not two. And the CTA lawyer argued that a teacher-administrator could not be involved in teacher evaluation—in fact should not even be allowed to observe other teachers in classrooms—because it would be contrary to the union bargaining agreement. Some Academy faculty, including several CTA representatives, began to wonder why the CTA appeared to be so unsupportive of a plan that empowered teachers. Similarly, while the superintendent had been encouraging in an initial meeting with a group of Academy teachers, she had prepared nothing in writing for the school committee, and many wondered whether she was, in fact, waiting to see whether a majority of the school committee favored the proposal before she endorsed it publicly.

The school committee discussion of the proposal finally took place on May 14, 1991.

The meeting starts half an hour late in the high school cafeteria. School committee members straggle in and talk informally with one another and with central office staff while all wait for the meeting to begin. Finally, Alice Wolf, mayor and ex-officio chair of the committee, calls the meeting to order. Old business and reports consume the first forty-five minutes of the meeting.

Finally, at about 8:30 in the evening, "new business" agenda items come round. The Academy Faculty Council representatives, plus principal Ed Sarasin, are asked to come forward, and they assume seats at a cafeteria table facing the horseshoe configuration of three tables at which the committee sits. The group's presentation to the school committee takes no more than fifteen minutes, and now Alice Wolf asks the first questions. She wonders about the role of students in the development of the proposal. She also asks about guidelines for the job with reference to gender, ethnic diversity, subject area, and so on. One of the teachers says no plans exist to develop guidelines, and she urges them to consider it. This idea is seconded by another committee member, who reminds the group of the system's mandate on affirmative action.

Another committee member, James Rafferty, is concerned about the precedent of teachers from only one house—the Academy—being able to apply. He's also worried about the election of a teacher for a supervisory position who will have to be responsible for evaluation. "Will this person feel the need to go easy on colleagues because he was elected?"

Ed Sarasin replies that these questions need to be addressed but stresses that "the beauty of this is as an experiment; nothing is engraved in stone. We don't have all the answers. We are looking at a better way to run a school system, and we'll learn along the way. We'll evaluate on a yearly basis." He also speaks strongly about the integrity of this group of teachers.

James Rafferty persists: "People I talk to are concerned that things are always changing. What's the correlation between this effort and student achievement? And what about the report the superintendent was supposed to give us months ago on long-range goals for the management of the high school? . . . Look at the number of acting and unfilled positions. . . . Where does this fit in?"

An older school committee member, former mayor and longtime Cambridge politico Alfred Vellucci, now speaks. He rambles on for more than ten minutes in a kind of disjointed stream-of-consciousness: "There's gonna be a revolution—school committees are gonna be done away with. Parents know something. They're a lot smarter than most people think. There's too much psycho-babble in education today. . . . Someday, there will be a board of governors here. What would they do? What would you do if you were in House A? They laughed at Galileo five hundred years ago. They excommunicated him. He said the earth moved around the sun. I'm saying the same thing. The bucks are getting tighter and tighter. The bureaucrats are making mistakes and mistakes. They're building up debts. You have no say. They let you come here and talk, but you have no say. You think about what I'm saying. Someday teachers will have a big say about what's going on in education. But the bottom line is the dropout problem. If you have a good system, you don't have dropouts. Nobody seems to have the answer. Good-bye and good luck."

No one seems to know quite how to pick up the thread of the meeting after this meandering monologue. Finally, Alice Wolf asks about what in the Academy plans addresses the issue of dropouts.

Several Faculty Council members respond. Tad talks about the team meetings every Friday as being a way to be in communication with teachers about how students are doing in all classes, socially as well as academically, so that Tad can be more helpful when he meets with kids after school. "I feel I can reach these kids a lot easier when I can talk to Nancy and other teachers about what's going on in kids' lives." Arnie mentions that the Hispanic dropout rate in the Academy is lower than that for Caucasians.

"How many in the ninth-grade Academy class have dropped out this year?" Wolf asks. No one has the answer.

Alfred Vellucci goes on the offensive. He attacks the "lily-white" makeup of the group of faculty in front of him. "Why are there no minorities among you?" He shouts. "It's a disgrace. I'm going to tell the voters. I'm going to talk about this on TV. The voters should know. I'm going to expose you."

As Alfred Vellucci speaks now, one of the Academy Faculty Council members gets up and leaves. Alice Wolf quietly but firmly asks her to come back.

"We were the ones who were elected," is Arnie's quiet reply when Alfred Vellucci is finally finished.

James Rafferty now jumps in and says, "Shouldn't that set off an alarm for you?"

Frances Cooper, the one black school committee member, reminds the group that minorities comprise 54 percent of the total enrollment in the Academy. "I support the idea of experiments, and I applaud your efforts, but it is simply unacceptable that everyone presenting—the leadership here—is all white."

Arnie mentions to the committee that the third house administrative position—that of assistant housemaster—will remain the same and is currently filled by a minority woman.

Another school committee member, Henrietta Davis, now has her opportunity to ask questions, and she wants to know how the Academy is working overall and also how teachers will be evaluated. She's also concerned about how the existing assistant housemaster, who's full-time, would work with the teachers who were only part-time administrators. Finally, she asks about whether they know of any precedents for this kind of position elsewhere.

Finally, the superintendent speaks for the first time. She says that while real issues remain to be worked out—title, salary, and especially evaluation, which is a major concern of the Cambridge Teachers' Association lawyer—she is very supportive and excited about the proposal. "I feel very strongly that the Academy is the kind of program that deals best with preventing dropouts by knowing and caring for kids."

The one school committee member who has not spoken now takes a turn. He says that he thinks "the Academy will produce graduates that can be competitive and can fill out applications for jobs and so on. I liked the idea in the original Academy proposal of pre- and post-testing and of school-based management. But you all have to develop efficiency standards—especially with declining resources and the competitiveness that's gonna happen in the future. You gotta get the most money out of the dollar you're gonna spend. I have to answer to the taxpayers for that. Let's all move together and try to make the best of it, and I want to come and visit and help in any way I can."

After more than two hours of discussion, the committee votes to table the proposal and to continue the discussion in a week.

This school committee meeting began better than many I have observed in other school districts. Several people initially asked thoughtful, policy-related questions: Had students' reactions been solicited? Were there precedents elsewhere for this kind of position? Would a teacher elected by peers still be able to act as a supervisor? Other questions—What was the dropout rate at the Academy this year?—were less well considered. Eight months into the first year of a new program is much too soon to do any kind of evaluation, and any number that might be given would have to be looked at as part of a much more thorough comparative evaluation of all programs. This, along with comments related to program evaluations and unfilled positions at the high school, seemed to be a misdirected effort to prod the superintendent into action on an altogether different set of problems.

However, this meeting—like so many in other districts—went seriously awry when some committee members began to talk about race and to give political-sounding speeches. Whether it's educating "gifted" students, sex education, test scores, or dropout rates, too many controversial topics are discussed by school committees in ways that may placate constituencies, but contribute nothing to possibilities for change. Race-related issues *are* central to broader issues of school reform, as I have discussed; in this meeting, however, it appeared to me that most of the comments made by the school committee members on the subject were meant more for the cable-TV camera in the room than for the teachers presenting their proposal. The dearth of minority teachers in the school came as no surprise to school committee members since they had regularly discussed the problem for many years. In fact, the school system had begun a vigorous affirmative action program in the late 1980s and had made real progress in recruiting qualified minorities into teaching and administrative positions. The school committee members knew this—they'd helped engineer it.

Although not members of minority groups themselves, the teachers present at the meeting were all deeply committed to being educational advocates for minority students. They were widely acknowledged to be some of the very best teachers in the school. As mentioned above, one of them, Arnie Clayton, had created a basic studies curriculum for bilingual students that was a model program and had dramatically reduced the dropout rates for Hispanic and Haitian students. If school committee members did not know that, they should have. Yet the comments of several committee members suggested that it was wrong, solely because of the color of their skin, that these faculty members had been elected by their colleagues to represent the Academy. And when the committee members did nothing to stem the insulting, blatantly political tirade of Alfred Velluci, the teachers felt further humiliated.

Ultimately, the meeting—and the roles played by the teachers' union, school administration, and school committee—is a powerful lesson in the politicization and bureaucratization of education, and in the consequent waste of resources and demoralization of dedicated teachers and administrators. Rather than having to face the school committee without help or support, Academy teachers should have first worked with the superintendent and a representative of the CTA to refine a proposal which would have better anticipated the school committee's concerns. Once in the meeting, the role of the school committee should have been confined to asking only long-term, policy-related questions about the proposal. The chair should have ruled out of order overt and covert speechifying, as well as more detailed operational questions. School committees in too many American communities consider themselves experts on all facets of education and have become political entities which attempt to micromanage schools.

As a result of this lack of collaboration in the preparation of a presentation and the lack of clarity about the appropriate role of the school committee, a decision which should have taken half an hour or an hour was discussed for more than two hours, only to be tabled. The meeting was an enormous waste of time for the thirty or so people who participated—time that was needed to discuss pressing educational issues.

My conversations with Academy teachers after the meeting shows how this way of managing schools also erodes teacher morale. One teacher said, "They say they're all for teacher empowerment, but listening to that man Vellucci tell us how wrong we were was humiliating and degrading. I'd *never* talk to my students that way. If I did, they'd walk out. . . . The minority issues are complex. It isn't as if we're unaware of it or haven't talked about it. All of our minority teachers are in the bilingual program. They all have young kids and don't want to come in at seven-thirty in the morning for meetings or stay after school. And two of us had asked Filimena [the assistant house administrator, who is a black woman] to come and sit with us when we made our presentation, but she didn't want to. . . . Besides, look at the school committee. Only one black. Who are they to talk?"

Many comments made at the next Academy Faculty Council meeting several days later suggested that these teachers had also been upset by the lack of respect shown them at the school committee hearing. What was extraordinary about this council meeting, though, was the way in which the group rallied and worked together to deal with the school committee's complaints. It was by far one of the most focused and productive meetings I have ever observed among teachers in any school, an example of effective and efficient collaboration that shows what educators can do when they have been allowed to work together over time to create—and defend—an educational program they believe in deeply.

It's 7:35 A.M., and all but one member of the council, plus Rob, who is the interim house administrator, are crammed around a table in a tiny, bare-walled, windowless room. The last member rushes in now, appearing disheveled and disorganized, saying she's lost the first paycheck of her life since she started working at fourteen. Everyone talks for a few minutes about how rattled they all were by the school committee meeting.

But then they all quickly focus on a draft questionnaire

for faculty that one member has prepared in response to school committee concerns. It asks Academy faculty to vote on three items: first, to affirm their initial support for a three-person administrative team (the two faculty leaders plus the existing assistant housemaster); second, to vote on whether to open the faculty leader position to anyone in the entire high school who is in agreement with the Academy's principles; and, third, to amend the Academy charter to add the same paragraph that talks about minority representation to the Student Council to the description of the makeup of the Faculty Council ("Appointments will be made by the House Administrator, as necessary, to insure a balanced representation of all groups").

One teacher now wonders why they've heard nothing from the superintendent since the school committee meeting and also why she seemed so nonsupportive in the meeting. The group agrees to drop off a copy of their questionnaire at her office and also to call—"We won't get through, but at least it will be recorded by the secretary that we tried."

Next they talk briefly about handing faculty the questionnaire versus just putting it in boxes. They agree to do both, to get a quick and full response.

Now the question arises about whether they should send a letter to the school committee or to Alice Wolf about the humiliation they all felt at the hands of Alfred Vellucci and some of the other committee members. One teacher suggests some possible language for a letter. Another teacher makes a joke about a "witness protection plan" for all who sign such a letter.

The focus of the conversation now shifts to talking about how they let themselves be victims, that when one of them walked out, none of the remaining group said anything or stood up for themselves at the meeting. Nor were they supported by the CTA representative. They talk about what they'll say if it happens next time. One actually practices the words she'll say to Alfred Vellucci and to Alice Wolf, the chair, if it happens again.

Someone suggests they get back to issues of concern to the committee. One that remains is the concern about how faculty can do evaluations of fellow teachers. Rob talks about the difference between summative evaluation, which may be for a job or contract or tenure, and formative evaluation, which is more like peer coaching. The group quickly agrees that they will have to figure out a plan for the former, even though "it's not happening at all in the rest of the school and it's really the peer coaching that is what we want and need—it's part of why we developed this proposal in the first place."

They return to the issue of how to deal with Alfred Vellucci, and one of the group agrees to work on a draft letter for their next meeting. The meeting ends abruptly now after forty minutes, as teachers jump up and rush off to cover their homerooms.

Despite the fact that a very high percentage of Academy faculty had returned their questionnaire and approved the three referendum topics by from 72 to 84 percent, all of the teachers at the next Faculty Council meeting one week later were clearly very nervous about the showdown with the school committee. They felt they shouldn't have to say anything more, but they were concerned that they'd not heard a word from the superintendent.

Excerpts from their brief conversation suggest the depth of their sense of vulnerability and anxiety:

"I feel like resigning from the Key Results Committee because of the way the superintendent has treated us."

"Ruben really abandoned us. Maybe we can fax him something—"

"Yeah, a bomb!" They all laugh.

"I'm feeling more and more powerless."

"The Academy had a lot of problems this year because of the schedule. The reason why the faculty leader position is so important is because we need someone who really understands the problem."

"I've heard that five of our brightest ninth-graders are leaving at the end of the year because we haven't done all we promised in the Academy—"

"We haven't done any community building. No trips or meals together."

"What Vellucci did last week was a classic case of abuse and enablement—in the way that Wolf and the other committee members let him get away with that."

"More and more it feels like a tug-of-war between the teachers and everyone else in the system, instead of us all working on common goals together. We never talk about anything educational. It's all just politics."

The meeting of the school committee the next night was anticlimactic. After an hour and a half of other business, the Academy proposal finally came up as the last item of the evening. One member of the committee who came late to the meeting started to speak, and the superintendent took him into the next room to explain a confidential report. The motion to approve the positions for one year and to let the superintendent pursue negotiations with the Cambridge Teachers' Association was approved with no "nays" and without discussion.

Immediately after the meeting was adjourned, the superintendent came up to the table and shook Arnie Clayton's hand, saying, "See! I told you it would work out. We just don't want to tip our hand to the Teachers' Association."

Later, one of the Faculty Council members talked about how degrading it had been to go around and ask all the Academy minority faculty to "show their faces at this stupid meeting—and for nothing! In the twenty years that I've been here, I've only attended one or two school committee meetings. I'm no good at figuring out the politics of all this. If this is what it's like, if this is the politics you have to go through, then that's not how I want to spend my time!"

At the last Academy faculty meeting of the 1991 school year, Arnie Clayton and Nancy Burns were unanimously elected to the two newly created positions. Ed Sarasin attended the meeting and was last to speak: "It took the courage of people in this room to endorse and support this proposal. It won't be easy, but it's an outstanding opportunity. . . . I hope that in three years, five or six teams will be up here running for these positions. The beauty of this is that it gives you a chance to try administration and then go back to teaching if you want. I believe in making creativity part of the process. You lose sharpness once you've been an administrator for a while. You have to fight the tendency to be lethargic or indifferent. Nancy and Arnie will press us—I hope that everyone in the room will have a chance to try it. . . .

"I don't think this process would have been as successful in another house. It's your commitment to the Academy—your willingness to say, It's our problem together. We're not there yet, but we're a lot closer to where I want us to be—closer than I ever thought we'd get."

I agree, and I do credit the superintendent and the school committee for giving much more than lip service to the idea of teacher empowerment by supporting the development of the Academy and the creation of the new positions. This is certainly a great deal more than many school districts have accomplished. However, what even progressive bureaucracies have the power to give with one hand, they have the power to take away with the other. The Academy teachers succeeded in their collaborative effort to defend their program in spite of the politicized struggles described above, and at some real emotional cost to them.

This see-saw struggle continues to the present, as we will see.

Inmates Running the Asylum

Several times since Arnie and Nancy were elected, I've returned to the Academy for periodic updates. One of the first changes I noticed was the large computer-printout banner above the office that reads: "THE ACADEMY: WHERE THE INMATES RUN THE ASYLUM."

The last time we talked, in July 1993, Arnie and I were interrupted seven times in one hour by people coming in and out of his open door—mostly kids. But Arnie never lost track—nor momentum, nor enthusiasm—as he discussed how the Academy has continued to evolve and become a stronger program.

The ninth grade still has the same core group of teachers working together to refine the program. The curriculum is now based on a set of themes that are much closer to student interests. "The Impossible Dream," for example, looks at how different societies have dealt with issues of justice, power, "haves" versus "have-nots," and students' own roles in creating a more just society.

Extending the Academy's interdisciplinary studies and team teaching to tenth grade had been proposed in the spring of 1991, and it would have been a logical next step for the ninth-graders who'd already been in the program for a year, but it was vetoed at the last minute by the superintendent. During the 1991–92 school year, the school received a grant for curriculum innovations related to drug abuse prevention. Arnie used the additional planning time and the opportunities to work closely with several of the high school administrators that the grant afforded to create a much stronger plan to extend the Academy to tenth grade. Called Project America, this interdisciplinary humanities curriculum was team-taught for the first time in the 1992–93 school year and looks at the American experience in literature, history, geography, art, and students' personal experiences.

In response to my questions about how the model of "faculty leader" was working, Arnie said, "There's never enough time in the day, and there are so many things to do all at once—I feel my two classes aren't as good as they have been. I sometimes go in and teach on automatic pilot, and I'm not sure doing this job and teaching *two* classes is viable. But it's very exciting. It's a different feeling having no bosses. Teachers who've been marginal for years are really pulling their weight now. They see Nancy and I out in the halls all the time talking to kids and taking classes for people, and I think they feel more of a sense of shared responsibility. Ruben was a good leader and very respected, but it's different now. We're all in this together. If we don't do it together, it won't get done."

The Academy's student government has been increasingly active over the last two years. There are regular all–student and teacher "community meetings," and more frequent field trips and social events. Tenth-grade students also now act as mentors to incoming ninth-graders. According to Arnie, these student-initiated activities help create a stronger sense of community and are an important part of what makes the program work.

We see, then, that the Academy continues to evolve as an important educational model. The teachers are talented, committed, and very hard working. But the program exists, nevertheless, as a part of a complex and very political bureaucracy. So it is fragile—limited in a number of areas and highly vulnerable.

The original Academy plan called for eleventh- and twelfth-graders to remain in the program and work on a competency-based diploma. That idea is now gone—too hard to schedule in a school where the parents of college-bound students insist that there be a wide selection of courses. Arnie also suggested that the limits imposed by the seven-period schedule have kept teachers from working toward defining and assessing what all Academy students should know and be able to do by the end of tenth grade—a step which he believes would strengthen the program further.

After tenth grade, Academy students now become a part of the regular tracked high school—with the opportunity to choose from among 400 course offerings, but with no sense of belonging to a smaller, more intimate community. Arnie says the Academy's student government is planning reunions, and he thinks students will do fine. I remain unconvinced. A growing body of research, as well as the practical experience of increasing numbers of educators, suggests that smaller high schools—with 400 or fewer students—have lower dropout rates and are less violence-prone than large high schools.[21]

The local union has continued to impose another limit on the Academy's realization of its original plans. One of the primary reasons for creating Arnie's and Nancy's positions was to have teachers who could act as coaches for other teachers—to do what is sometimes referred to as peer supervision. Arnie has no interest in formally evaluating teachers in order to decide whether or not their contracts should be renewed. He was asked to become certified so that he could perform this administrative function and refused. But he does feel teachers want and need more help and feedback on their teaching. The union, however, has remained adamant that he and Nancy not be allowed in the classroom when other teachers are working—so that teachers are not put into the position of having to "supervise" peers. Arnie is hopeful that the newly elected union president will not oppose the necessary change in the bargaining agreement, as the previous one had done.

Arnie's major concern, though, is both keeping students in the Academy and attracting new ones. Many ninth-graders transferred out of the Academy at the end of the 1992 school year, when spots became available in what had been their first-choice program. More incoming ninth-grade students have selected the Academy as their first choice in the last two years, but Arnie feels that they have to do a lot more recruiting. The problem, according to Arnie, is stereotypes. "People still think of the Academy as the bilingual house [the major program focus prior to the high school's reorganization into separate programs]. Ours is also the only house where all of the classes are heterogeneously grouped instead of tracked. It's not a place they want to be, even though our students' test scores are the second-highest and very close to Pilot's [the most popular program choice], and our top kids say they find their classes with cooperative learning and different kinds of kids a lot more interesting. It's going to take a lot of time to break down old stereotypes." Parents of college-bound kids worry about SATs, so Academy teachers must begin marshaling all the research that shows kids learn better in mixed groups.

"If we don't have more kids choosing the Academy, then we won't have a program" was the way Arnie summed up the recruiting problem. The experience of the Academy, as well as Brimmer and May's experience in the educational marketplace, points to several fundamental problems with the school reform strategy of "choice," which we shall consider in the final chapter.

It would help if they evened the playing field, Arnie said. The two long-established programs, Pilot and Fundamental, have their own budgets and the ability to make their own hiring decisions, and the Academy still does not. According to Arnie, the superintendent pops her head in every now and then to say what good things she hears, that the Academy is her favorite program—but the continuing inequity of resources has not changed.

Still, Arnie refuses to play politics in the system. "Ruben thought he could accomplish things that way, but I don't believe in it. . . . I only go to school committee meetings when I have to." When I asked him what were the chances the school committee would renew his and Nancy's joint position in 1994, he said, "If they do away with the job, then I'll be happy to go back to the classroom full-time. If you don't have anything to lose, then you can't get caught up in their games."

While it remains to be seen whether Arnie or Ruben's strategy for dealing with the central office bureaucracy and school committee politics is the more successful, the experience of the Academy raises basic questions about the viability of a small high school program within the context of a large comprehensive institution—with all of its diverse constituencies, pressure groups, and bureaucracy.

Shortly before he went to Portugal, Ruben allowed himself to be even more critical of the bureaucracy than before: "The truth of the matter is I'm glad to be getting out. I'm tired of fighting the bureaucracy. There's more and more of it. Why do we need a business office when we do all the purchasing and payroll here? Why do we need a personnel office when we are the ones who should be doing the hiring anyway? What do the assistant superintendent and the superintendent's cabinet [a group of central office middle managers] contribute to improving schools? Most of our energy goes to fighting the system instead of changing it. We need schools that are completely outside the system. How do you dismantle a bureaucracy?"

Indeed, what would school reform be like without a central office bureaucracy, in a smaller school with a master schedule that enabled teachers to meet and plan together? What would school reform be like without a politicized school committee? Without a union? How does school reform work in a school where classes are small enough to allow teachers really to know students, and where adults have spent years together developing and refining ways to engage students more actively "as workers" in the classroom?

Our final school—Brimmer and May—is such a place.

THREE

The Brimmer and May School

Schools aren't preparing kids for the kinds of tasks that we need them to be able to do now and in the future. The country is quickly losing ground in the international marketplace because students aren't trained to be good thinkers and good workers. The majority of kids are shuffled through the system. They aren't challenged. They know what they need to do just to get by and it's not much.

—Anne Reenstierna
Headmistress of the Brimmer and May School

The Evolution of a "Coalition School"

Unless you know it's there, you have to look carefully to find the school nestled in this lovely tree-lined street in the affluent suburban Boston neighborhood of Chestnut Hill. Most of Brimmer and May's small, irregular-sized classrooms are located in three stately Victorian houses that look no different from neighboring residences. Even the trim playing field looks more like a park than a school. Only the two newer buildings, with their tall, sweeping roofs, suggest something slightly out of place. A modest campus, by either public or private school standards, yet it is home to a very ambitious and exciting educational endeavor.

The 1990 Brimmer and May admissions brochure opens with a "Message from the Headmistress." Anne Reenstierna writes:

> Brimmer and May is a member of the Coalition of Essential Schools, a national organization of schools committed to excellence and educational reform in partnership with Dr. Theodore Sizer and the Brown University Education Department. As a Coalition School, Brimmer and May works hard to teach students to use their minds well. We challenge our students to question, search for solutions, formulate and test hypotheses, and make reasonable judgments. In classrooms at Brimmer and May, students lead discussions, critique one another's work, ask critical questions, and ac-

tively engage in their own learning process. We develop questers and life-long learners.

Theodore Sizer's critique of American high schools and the principles for high school reform that he and his colleagues have evolved have become an explicit part of the core identity of the Brimmer and May School. Yet for much of its history, Brimmer and May would hardly have qualified as an innovative school. Rather the opposite.

The school traces its beginnings to the founding of two Boston schools—Miss Folsom's in 1880 and Miss Brown's Classical in 1887. The two schools merged in 1939 to form a private all-girls college preparatory day school for grades seven through twelve, with a coeducational program from nursery through sixth grade. In 1954, the school moved to its present location in Chestnut Hill.

Brimmer and May has always prided itself on offering a fine traditional education for young women—the word "traditional" having been prominently featured in the school's catalogues for years. Though somewhat overshadowed by the larger and more well known Winsor School for girls, also located in the Boston suburbs, Brimmer and May nevertheless enjoyed a good reputation and modest but steady growth in enrollment through the 1950s and 1960s.

With the economic recession of the 1970s, however, enrollment began to decline. Qualified students who could afford private day school tuitions became harder to find, and as the school struggled to cope, several male headmasters came and went. By 1975, enrollment had dropped to an all-time low of 126 girls. A female head who was appointed in the early 1980s managed to put the school on a sounder economic footing by enrolling an increasing number of students with learning disabilities.

In an interview in the spring of 1989, Judy Guild, then assistant headmistress and head of the Upper School, described the situation she encountered when she first came to the school in 1984 as a math and English teacher: "We had a total school enrollment of about a hundred and eighty students then, with sixty-five or so students in the seventh through twelfth grade—what we call our Upper School. While we had a very traditional curriculum, we tried hard to give kids a lot of extra help one-on-one. Our reputation was increasingly that we were a school for learning-disabled kids. . . . But the problem was that some faculty lacked the necessary training, and the faculty as a whole was not working well together. Teachers were very autonomous. We had no clear educational philosophy, and we didn't even know that was the problem. When Anne Reenstierna was appointed head in 1985, the main thing people said they wanted in a new head was someone who could open up communication."

A soft-spoken woman with a somewhat shy demeanor, Anne Reenstierna was the product of a good traditional education—first in an all-girls Catholic high school and then at Wheaton College. Like both Claire Sheff and Ruben Cabral, nothing about Anne suggests anything "revolutionary." But as more and more books and business leaders echoed the call for changes in education in the early 1980s, she began to think seriously about the school's need for a different kind of educational as well as administrative leadership.

"I began reading a number of books on school reform," Anne explained, "and one of them was Sizer's book *Horace's Compromise*. In the spring of 1986, I bought copies for the trustees and all the faculty and asked them to read it over the summer. When they returned in the fall, I met with Upper School faculty every other week to talk about ideas. Then, in January 1987, I stopped meeting with the group in order to let Judy Guild, whom I'd appointed head of the Upper School, try to gauge the degree of support for our becoming a member of the Coalition of Essential Schools. The faculty seemed open to trying some new things, and so we decided to work with a core group of the interested ninth-grade faculty. I asked the trustees for their support, and they voted in favor of our becoming a Coalition school. We wrote our application to the Coalition in the summer of 1987 and were accepted in the fall. During that summer, teachers came in voluntarily and worked very hard with Judy to plan a new ninth-grade curriculum. Their main focus was on creating an interdisciplinary aspect to the ninth-grade program and also trying to figure out how to make students more responsible for their learning—student as worker."

Parents were officially informed of the school's alliance with the Coalition and of the new emphasis in the ninth-grade program at the school's regular back-to-school night in the fall of 1987. Judy and another teacher described the program, taught a sample lesson which emphasized the principle of "student as worker," and then invited parents to attend classes, if they wished, at a subsequent open house. Judy recalls the ninth-grade parents as having been generally very interested and supportive. "We were very lucky to have a great deal of support from the families of girls in that class," she observed.

So, by early fall of 1987, the school had clearly set a course toward exploring new educational ground—with trustees, parents, and teachers all having given their blessing, at least formally, to the journey. By the 1989–90 school year, when I first visited Brimmer and May, the school's new academic focus was already beginning to attract more parent interest. Although the average SAT scores of seniors that year was 938—somewhat lower than at many private schools—Brimmer and May was no longer known as a school for learning-disabled students. Total K–12 school enrollment had climbed to about 260 students, with 55 girls in grades 9–12. (Part of the improvement in the school's enrollment was due to the fact that grades K–6 became fully coeducational in 1989.)

The school worked hard to attract a more diverse group of students than is usually found in private, or "independent," schools. Minority enrollment was 14 percent, only slightly above the private school average of 12 percent. (At Brimmer and May almost all the minority students were African-American, while in most independent schools the largest percentage of minority enrollments is Asian-American. That year, black students accounted for only about 5 percent of the total national independent school enrollment.) The tuition Brimmer and May charged was comparable to that at other private day schools—$11,600—but 35 percent of the school's students received tuition aid, compared to the private school average of only 23 percent.[1]

The approximate cost per student of running the Upper School was $10,000, with 95 percent of the budget covered by tuition. Most independent schools are only able to cover 80 to 85 percent of their costs with tuition. Annual giving and income from endowment make up the difference. Since Brimmer and May had only a tiny endowment, it kept costs down by paying teachers somewhat less than other private schools in the area and considerably less than public school teachers. In 1990, the median salary at Brimmer and May was about $22,000—approximately two thirds of the average teacher's salary in Massachusetts public schools at the time.

What that tuition bought, when compared with the $1,500 less per student spent at Cambridge Rindge and Latin, was smaller classes. The student-teacher ratio at Brimmer and May is seven to one, with class size ranging from five to fifteen. The smaller classes and reduced numbers of students each teacher had to work with each day greatly facilitated Brimmer and May's implementation of Coalition principles, as we will see.

Student as Worker, Teacher as Coach

More than 150 schools nationwide were members of the Coalition of Essential Schools in August 1993—18 of them independent schools. (An additional 435 schools are either in the active planning stages or are exploring Coalition membership.) Putting the new principles into practice, however, is another matter, and very few have gone as far as Brimmer and May.

Anne Reenstierna and Judy Guild, and the teachers with whom Judy worked over the summer of 1987, made several key strategic decisions as they considered how to begin implementing

Coalition principles in classrooms. First, they decided to focus their change efforts initially on just one class—the ninth grade. They also decided not to try to implement all of the nine Coalition principles at once.[2] If initial efforts were successful, they planned to revise teaching methods and curriculum materials in the higher grades and to incorporate other principles, one year at a time.

The conversations between Judy and the teachers of ninth grade that summer were initially broad-ranging, but after considerable discussion, they eventually focused on several key Coalition principles. The most important of these, according to Judy, were "student as worker, teacher as coach," and interdisciplinary learning.

Two years later—in 1989, when I made many of my class observations—these were still seen as central themes for the school. In an introduction to Brimmer and May for visiting faculty from the Walnut Hill School in April, Anne summarized her school's goals as a Coalition school. Her key points, as I noted them in my field notes, included the following:

1. Adolescents should learn to use their minds well;
2. Learning should become personalized;
3. There should be greater emphasis on cross-disciplinary teaching;
4. The governing metaphor for school should be, in Theodore Sizer's words, "student as worker," rather than "teacher as deliverer of instructional services."

Anne also stressed the theme of student as worker in her opening remarks at the first all-school parents' night that I observed in May of 1989. She said, "Student as worker means that we view the student as the principal worker in the classroom, not the teacher."

For the four years that Judy Guild served as the head of the Upper School and lead Coalition teacher, a hand-lettered poster hung on one wall of the small room that served as both her office and teaching space. It read:

Explorer:	Let's give this a try.
Matchmaker:	What you're saying is a lot like what Sue is saying.
Skeptic:	I'm not sure I see good reason for saying that.
Carpenter:	Let's make what we're saying more solid.
Will Rogers:	Let's find a way to make the incorrect statement correct.
Sherlock Holmes:	I think we've overlooked something important.
Librarian:	Here's a passage that supports your point.
Journalist:	Takes notes and summarizes points made.
Map-maker:	Makes a visual chart of where the discussion didn't go, who did, who didn't speak.

I asked Judy about the poster at our first meeting early in the spring of 1989. She explained that it's a list of student roles for class discussions from a workbook, published in draft form by the Coalition, called *Student as Worker* (no longer available). In my classroom observations and interviews with students, parents, administrators, and teachers over the next several years, I came to understand that the metaphor of student as worker was not mere rhetoric, but rather reflected a clear and conscious commitment of many in the school community to have students become more active and more responsible for their learning in the classroom. It was a kind of shorthand many in the school used for their academic goals, as we will see.

In the Classroom

One of the first ninth-grade English classes I observed, taught by Judy Guild, was a discussion of Romantic poets:

Eleven ninth-grade students are crowded around the small rectangular table in Judy's office reading a photocopied passage from Wordsworth on the characteristics of the poet.

"Okay, what are some of the characteristics of the poet?" Judy, their teacher, asks.

"Able to feel more deeply," comes an immediate reply from a student. Four other students offer answers as well. Another student says, "Capable of having an out-of-body experience."

"Where does he say that? Or is that your opinion? Your opinion is important, but right now we want to understand what Wordsworth is saying," Judy replies.

From this point on, students refer to specific page and line numbers and specific quotes as they discuss the question. Discussion continues until the teacher asks, "So what does all this mean—where do we go with these abstract, heavy ideas?"

Judy addresses her question to the student sitting at the center of the table, who then leads the rest of the discussion. The student moderator focuses the class by saying, "I think we know that the poet believes the connection between man and nature is very important. Now maybe we should read a poem and analyze it."

Students then discuss "Ode" for the next half an hour, with every single student making at least one comment. All but one student sitting at the corner of the table seem attentive—sitting up more or less straight, eyes following the discussion, periodically checking points in the poem, making notes, and so on. The discussion is led by the student to whom the teacher had turned at the beginning of class. The teacher comments only occasionally to clear up a point of general misunderstanding, to ask for evidence from the text, and so on.

At one point, a student says, "I looked up 'ode' and it means [she quotes a dictionary definition from her notes]."

"Why does he use that word in the title?" another student asks.

Four students engage in a lively discussion of the question while the teacher continues to observe.

Finally, the student moderator asks, "Do you think we've discussed everything? Are we ready to move on?" Students express general agreement.

After about an hour of class, the teacher says, "Okay, I think we're ready for a summary now."

A student [whom I later learned had been designated as the "recorder"] reads aloud from her notebook about two pages of concisely summarized notes, and then asks, "Anyone have anything to add?"

Several students suggest additional points. The student recorder then says, "I'll copy these over tonight. I can probably xerox copies for everybody before lunch tomorrow."

Judy turns to another student, who had been asked to keep a tally sheet of all student participation in the discussion. She reads from her sheet: "We need to hear from [four names are mentioned], and Alice talked kind of a lot."

A student comments, "I think some people like poetry more than others, that's why some people didn't talk as much. They don't relate as much to poems."

"Who doesn't like poetry?" Judy asks.

Three hands go up without hesitation.

"Okay, we have ten minutes and one poem left. Why don't the three of you who don't like poetry choose the last one for us to look at?"

The group quickly decides to look at the last poem. It is briefly discussed in the same way the others have been. At the end, a student says, "I found some neat metaphors." Three other students read aloud metaphors they liked, as well.

Discussion continues, but now there's a good deal of noise in the hall—primarily girls' loud conversation as another class has let out. Several students yawn. (The class has been going for an hour and twenty minutes! This is the first time I've seen students' attention collectively lagging during the entire period.)

"Anything more?" the teacher asks. She turns to the student secretary again, who reads several more sentences from her notes. The secretary ends her report by saying, "I didn't get all your metaphors, though. Can you give them to me later so I can include them in the notes?"

"Which poems are you liking the most? Which ones do you want to write about?" the teacher now asks.

Students refocus their attention as the teacher goes around the table and hears each student's answer. She then briefly reminds them about the form they should follow to "explicate" the poem in their written assignment. Judy ends the class with an enthusiastic, "Nice job today!"

As students file out the door, I hear several say, "Thank you, Mrs. Guild."

After students leave, I overhear a brief conversation in the hall between the teacher and one girl who had been participating the least of any student.

"Were you prepared today?" Judy asks. The girl shakes her head and looks down. Judy says she knows it's a difficult time for the girl because her parents are being hard on her for not making honor roll, but still, she can do better. The girl nods her head in agreement, not looking up.

The teacher then consults briefly with the student secretary who has been waiting just outside her door about how many pages of notes she had—twenty-some. "That's a lot. Try to condense them," Judy suggests.

Ninth-grade History. Students file in and immediately take seats in a semicircle. Neal, their teacher, asks them to settle down and then says, "Do you remember what was on the board yesterday? We were considering the question, Was France ripe for revolution in 1789?"

"Yes, 'cause there was lots of fighting and struggling going on between the three estates," one student immediately replies.

"Economically, no, 'cause there was so much debt," another student rebuts.

Neal asks, "Could that be argued the other way?"

He now divides the class of twelve students into two groups—one of kings and nobles, the other of peasants and bourgeoisie. Each group has to answer a series of questions Neal hands out related to what changes they wanted to see in France at that time and why; they also have to define their positions on various specific issues. Later in the ninety-minute period, Neal explains, they will give their reports to the other group.

The two groups begin by each appointing a leader, and everyone takes out their notebooks and begins to scribble as they talk. They work for a good half an hour before Neal offers them a short break. One group talks all through the break and does not get up from their seats. The other group is back at work within five minutes.

Fifteen minutes later both groups are still hard at work, so Neal tells them they can take the rest of the second period to finish up and present their reports tomorrow.

In all the ninth-grade English class discussions I observed, and in the combined English/history large and small group discussions, students rotated responsibility for leading discussions, keeping track of fellow students' participation, and summarizing important points covered in substantially the same way as in the classes described above. However, in science and math classes there was less general discussion and more individual and small group work.

In a ninth-grade math class, students worked in groups of three for the entire period as they made up questions for one another, using a list of math concepts the teacher had written up on the board. The teacher circulated from group to group answering questions and offering suggestions.

Nancy, the math teacher, described the evolution in her thinking about her classroom work: "I'm less anxious about covering certain quantities of material. I'm more willing to spend time on things that are more interesting, and so I think the classes look different. I'm not the center of attention. Kids have more responsibility for what they're learning. Like homework. I don't correct papers the way I used to. The kids do it in class and have to ask questions when they get something wrong."

Jenny, the Upper School science teacher, also described how her approach had changed: "When I taught ninth-grade science two years ago, it was almost all lecture. It was *exhausting*, making them learn the stuff! And it only reached a certain percentage of the kids. Now I almost never lecture unless all the kids are stuck. They work at their own pace through the text [called *Spice Chemistry*, a book the teacher spent a great deal of time locating]. They work with lab partners to do experiments, and then try to figure out what happened, what the principle was. There are lots of places where they have to stop along the way and answer questions. And they don't go on until they understand the concepts."

In her ninth-grade science class one morning in April 1989, the students were constructing three-dimensional models of different molecules, working in pairs. "Building these models helps them really understand the bonding properties of different molecules—how and where they bond," Jenny explained.

Giving students more autonomy and responsibility in the classroom is very different from the 1960s alternative-school notion of letting students "do their own thing." Judy Guild was concerned that when many people initially read Theodore Sizer's work "they think it's mostly fun and games. They don't understand where the higher standards for academics come in. . . . I give the students a copy of the final exam for the year on the first day of class, so they know exactly what's expected of them—what we're aiming for. I say to them, 'You have a job to do by the end of the year. I have a job to do, too. Let's get to work.' When you really emphasize mastery, it's demanding. When we've spent too much time on something, kids will say, 'We're getting behind. Can we meet at lunch?' "

Excerpts from my notes on Judy's final ninth-grade English class for the 1991 school year—a preparation for their upcoming exam—showed how far she had taken the idea of student as worker and how much responsibility students can assume when the tasks to be accomplished are clear.

It's the first period of the day. Though there is no bell, all but one of the thirteen students enrolled in the class have taken their seats within a minute or so of the announced start time of the class.

"Okay, we've got eighty—no, eighty-two minutes to review the four questions for the exam. Should we spend twenty minutes on each question?" a student begins.

"Mrs. Guild, will you be speaking today?" another asks.

"No, not unless I can't resist." Judy smiles slightly.

"Okay." The student who appears to be the appointed moderator for the day takes a deep breath and continues. "The first question is what are the characteristics of the play as a genre, and the similarities and differences between Richard III *and* Oedipus*." Their other books this year are:* A Separate Peace, Canterbury Tales, Jane Eyre, The Modern Tradition *(a collection of short stories),* I Know Why the Caged Bird Sings, *plus various poems.*

Students take turns reading, from their prepared notes, answers to the two questions. One student, not the moderator, keeps track of who's raised their hand and wants to speak and calls on students in order. She has a chart in front of her with every student's name and marks an X after a student speaks. The staccato nature of student comments suggested both a certain sense of urgency to move the discussion forward, and real mastery of ideas.

"Plays have narrators."

"A common theme in the books we read this year was letting out feelings or breaking out of a problem."

"Short stories have conflicts, morals; poems have to do with religion, the meaning of man and god. The drama form is more free."

"Poems are more abstract."

"Poems can be about anything."

"Poems have rhythmic language and verse."

"That's only true of the ones we've read this year," Judy interjects. (It is twenty minutes into the class, and this is the first time she has spoken!)

A few minutes later, Judy speaks for a second time in reply to a student's assertion that short stories were the earliest form of literature. Judy disagrees, saying that the short story form is a fairly modern invention.

"But that's not what the encyclopedia said," the student persists.

"It depends on what you mean by short stories. I suppose you could think of Canterbury Tales *as a collection of short stories—an extension of oral storytelling tradition."*

After twenty-five minutes, the student moderator interrupts the discussion, reads a list of people who still have to speak on the first question, and says if she doesn't call on some people who've raised their hands, it's because they haven't heard as much from some people.

After a few more minutes on Question One, another student is asked to read her summary notes, and they move on to Question Two: Why does a writer select one genre over another?

Judy interrupts. "I'm concerned that you're not using the

texts to support your answers. They're good ideas, but they're too general."

And a little while later she stops the discussion once more. "A lot of people are talking about morals, but we've spent very little time talking about that. I'm not even sure we can assume that most authors want to teach us something."

"But don't all authors want to teach something?" a student challenges. "They're not just telling about a life."

The discussion continues until a student is asked by the moderator to read her summary of student comments.

The student who has been mapping the discussion reports, "The average number of times people spoke was three." She goes down the entire list of students, mentioning how many times each has spoken, who needs to talk more, who less.

The discussion continues as a student reads Question Three: What are the freedoms and restraints of each genre?

"Novels leap in time and can show a character's dreams and fantasies—their inner thoughts," a student asserts.

"Short stories usually deal with just one character," adds another.

"Wait, can we organize the conversation by type of literature, instead of jumping all around?"

But several girls reply that it's too late, that everyone has done their notes in a different way. The discussion continues:

"Poems have onomatopoeia and alliteration."

"So what does that mean?" Judy wants to know.

"It means that the sounds of words are important."

"The author of autobiography is limited to telling just facts."

Several students challenge this idea, suggesting that authors of some autobiographies can lie or just make things up.

"The main character in an autobiography is the author—you don't get other points of view," another student offers.

Judy intervenes, "You're all saying something important. You're talking about narrative style. The first-person narrative, versus the author jumping in and out of others' minds, which is third person, omniscient."

"The novel we read last year, Pigman, *showed two points of view, in alternating chapters," a girl reminds the group.*

"Canterbury Tales *showed different points of view."*

The timekeeper breaks in. "It's time to go to Question Four."

"Instead of discussing style, form, and content, which you've largely covered in your discussion, why don't you stay with this question about freedoms and constraints for a while," Judy suggests.

"In plays you have to develop character in the beginning. With novels, you have more time."

"There's more freedom in the modern novel, less social constraint. George Eliot couldn't come out and give a political viewpoint. But in Separate Peace, *the author could protest war through his characters. He wasn't afraid of public reaction. But the constraint in modern lit is that it's harder and harder to be original and creative."*

"Very good point!" Judy is clearly impressed.

A student reads the final summary of points made in the discussions, and then Judy speaks. "Let me clarify a few things for the exam. You may bring in your class notes from today's discussion and any prep notes that you have. Text evidence you plan to use should be written out. You can bring in an outline of your essay. You'll have one hour to write it, and one hour to identify terms and passages from all of the books we've read this year."

"Will you go over our thesis statements with us before the exam?" a student wants to know.

"No," Judy replies. "We've been working on this all year. For your first paper, I gave you the thesis. In the second, I gave you part and you developed the rest. The last one you did completely on your own. Part of the point of the exam is to see what you can do on your own. But you can get together and help each other."

The class was eighty minutes long, with no break. Every student was taking notes and seemed alert and attentive for the entire period.

In addition to these classes—math, history, English, and science—all Brimmer and May ninth-grade students take an arts class and a foreign language. The other major part of the ninth-grade academic program is an interdisciplinary class, "Connections," in which students learn study, computer, and research skills. Students take a trip to the main branch of the Boston Public Library and learn how to search for primary source material, for example. Some class time is given over to interdisciplinary humanities projects and discussions. In the last quarter of the year, all students must complete an extensive research paper on a topic of their choice. The research topic must cross several academic disciplines, and students are required to present their work orally to a panel of teachers and to the rest of their class.

Assessing Progress: Clear Academic Goals

In the outset of their change process, teachers and administrators established a very simple but clear academic goal (although at the time it was expressed more as a general ideal): the goal of a Brimmer and May education is for students to learn to use their minds well. That goal would best be accomplished, teachers agreed, by focusing less on subject coverage and more on posing questions, problem solving, and so on. It also meant having students do more of the actual work—making the observations, asking the questions, summarizing the key points, in other words, student as worker. According to the research of John Goodlad, teachers talk between 70 and 80 percent of the time in most high school classrooms—public or independent.[3] By contrast, as we saw, Brimmer and May "teacher talk" was perhaps 20 percent of the class time—and often much less!

There have been two clear results from this focus. First, students have indeed learned to use their minds—often and well. We saw numerous examples of an inquiry-based and analytic approach to learning in the classes described above. Student as worker, or student as active participant in the learning process, is a qualitatively different classroom experience from that of most high school students, one which is much more demanding, more interesting, and more active. Passiveness and docility, the two major symptoms of the failure of high schools that most concern Theodore Sizer and many other education critics, were simply not in evidence in Brimmer and May classrooms. In my observation, these Brimmer and May students raised many more questions and were far more articulate than ninth-graders of comparable—or higher—ability in other schools, and students' writing showed this same high degree of real intellectual competence and skill in self-expression.

The second result of a clear academic focus on students learning to use their minds well is that students are more *motivated* in their own learning process. We saw how active and engaged students were in their classes. Even when dealing with highly academic material, by insisting that students pose the questions and by relating books and other materials to issues of social and personal interest to them, teachers enable students to connect what they're learning with what they think and feel. The motivation to learn becomes more intrinsic and stronger.

When I interviewed students extensively, without teachers present, to ask what being in a Coalition school meant to them, they explained to me that they were becoming more and more motivated to learn. The following are representative comments:

"Students leading discussions is good—much better than teacher lecturing—because you feel you have more of a part in it, you're involved."

"We're a close group and closer to the teacher. You can always go for extra help. Plus there's an energy in class. It's easy to get out your thoughts."

"There's more pressure, a lot more work to do, but also more help—so you don't get frustrated or lost."

"There's more motivation. You want to get work done, 'cause you can learn a lot."

"I would never have thought to use the Boston Public Library for a paper before. Now for sure I'll use it."

"Learning is more fun when you have a role and discussion questions without the restrictions of a teacher."

"I feel challenged to work. I've improved my note-taking skills—it's made me think and given me the confidence that I can solve problems."

"Taking on roles means that the more passive kids are now a lot more active in class, so we all learn more together."

In 1989, after only a year and a half of experimenting with new teaching methods, many teachers began to observe significant changes in the students' classroom behaviors. Judy Guild, who helped coach the other teachers in the development of new Coalition teaching practices, continued to be surprised at the results. Judy's comments help clarify what Brimmer and May educators mean by—and how they assess—students "learning to use their minds well":

"I can really see real differences between what tenth-graders [who were taught by Coalition methods the previous year] and eleventh-graders [who were not] are able to

do—the tenth-graders are so much more able to think and analyze on their own, and they participate more in the classroom. . . . The more I step out of the center of the class, the more students step in. Every year I end up 'teaching' more, and they learn more—but by their taking charge. They're not just clock-watching. . . .

"The single most exciting thing this year was to see kids develop the ability to voice opinions assertively—kids who didn't even know they had opinions or who couldn't say them. When you demand interaction, they begin to see the value and to take risks. I had one little girl who at the beginning of the year couldn't speak loud enough for the girl next to her to hear. She used to leave the class crying because she thought her soft voice was some kind of physical disability. But it wasn't that at all, it was a confidence issue. At the end of the year, she led several seminars for the whole class with no problem. It's incredible to see people start to believe in themselves, to see that much growth."

As Anne and Judy grew more confident of the value of applying Coalition ideas in the classroom, they began to encourage teachers other than those in the ninth grade to experiment. The ninth-grade Coalition teachers started using Coalition-style teaching in their tenth-, eleventh-, and twelfth-grade classes. Finally, Anne and Judy began actively to recruit new teachers interested in Coalition-style teaching.

One of their finds was Neal Brown, who came to the school in the fall of 1989 straight from the Masters of Arts in Teaching program that Theodore Sizer headed at Brown University. Neal had done his practice teaching at Hope Essential High School—a public, inner-city Coalition program in Providence. Initially, he was not interested in teaching in a private all-girls high school, but he was persuaded to take the job because of the school's strong and explicit commitment to the Coalition's principles.

Neal described some of his goals as a teacher: "I want to help kids develop their own opinions and to value their own ideas, and then to express them verbally and in writing. Rather than holding kids accountable for particular dates and facts in history, I want to help students see how they fit into a general scheme of things, to help them gain perspective, to see their lives as a part of a continuum. And I want them to learn respect and tolerance for other ideas and cultures, to be respectful of one another, and to look to classmates for answers, instead of to me."

Veteran science teacher Jenny Prileson also stressed the importance of intellectual skills over subject-area content in reflecting on her goals as a teacher: "I want students to develop a habit of always asking good questions and to question what they may have accepted before—to be skeptics, to look at all sides of an issue. Certainly they have to be competent in the basic skills of a particular discipline, but they have to begin by being trained mentally to ask good questions and to follow up with active investigation."

All four of these teachers agreed on the goals of teaching, and the methods they used as I observed them were consistent with those goals. The results the students themselves reported were also consistent. In my experience, few schools ever discusss their academic focus or educational goals, let alone achieve this kind of consensus; fewer still attain a consistency of practice that reflects the stated goals.

Because of Anne's strong support, and the leadership, persistence, and enthusiasm of Judy Guild, experienced teachers like Nancy and Jenny and new teachers like Neal have made Coalition-style teaching the norm at Brimmer and May in grades nine through twelve. The Lower and Middle schools are also now applying Coalition principles to teaching at their grade levels.

In June of 1991, the school graduated its first group of students who had gone through Coalition courses for four years. Teachers and administrators alike were exceptionally proud of this class. When I asked Anne Reenstierna how well she felt the school had done in implementing the principles of the Coalition, she pointed to several areas where the school needed to improve, but then said, "We've just graduated the first class who've worked under this pioneering approach. They don't test especially high as a group on SATs. The class average was not significantly higher than previous years' classes, and several of the students have real learning disabilities. Yet they did very well in college acceptances. They have a broad knowledge base. And they are interesting, articulate people who are able to make connections and look at things from a global perspective."

Jenny Prileson observed similar traits. "The growth of the twelfth-graders who just graduated was light-years ahead of what I thought they would be able to do when I first had them as ninth-graders. They are confident, coherent adults who can carry on a good discussion with teachers or students. They ask great questions, and they are bold enough to take risks and to say, Hey, let's try something new."

These are all very impressive results, but some might wonder if they are replicable in a public school. Leaving aside for the moment the structural differences—such as size, single-sex classrooms, bureaucracy, and so on (to be considered at the end of the chapter)—are the students who go to Brimmer and May more talented? More motivated? And so perhaps more intrinsically able to learn to use their minds well?

The question is not a simple one to answer. By quantifiable measures such as average SAT scores, Brimmer and May students were much closer to the public than the independent school norms in ability. In 1988, their 938 average was closer to Rindge and Latin's average of 859 than it was to a neighboring private school's, which boasted an 1179 average SAT the same year. There were as many students in that 1991 graduating class who had some learning difficulties as one will encounter in the average public school. In terms of ability, Brimmer and May students do not seem to differ significantly from the populations in many suburban public high schools.

It is true that many independent school students have more motivation to work harder in classes, but doing more of what the teacher tells you because you think you can and must go to college, please your parents, or have a successful career is very different than being motivated to *learn*. In my experience, students in independent schools are more motivated to perform—to succeed—but they tend to learn only what is necessary to get the grade they want. School is often seen simply as a means to the end of getting into a good college and having a successful career. Will it be on the test? and, How much does the test count toward the semester grade? are the two most commonly asked questions in many independent school classrooms. Motivating students to care about competence, learning for its own sake, and using their minds well, not merely to memorize, can be as difficult in independent schools as it is in many public schools.[4]

And some things are even more difficult in independent schools, as we will learn.

Core Values

In the teachers' quotes above we heard frequent references to their interest in students' emotional as well as intellectual growth. It was important to these teachers that students had become more independent, collaborative, and self-confident, as well as more thoughtful and curious. Brimmer and May teachers understood the importance of their role as advisors and met with their student advisees regularly.

Many independent schools profess a commitment to "educating the whole child" and routinely assign students to faculty advisors. Few, however, have taken seriously the problem of the "sense of entitlement" that children from upper-middle-class backgrounds often exhibit, a trait that Robert Coles described so well in his book *Privileged Ones*.[5] Fewer still have gone as far as Brimmer and May has in their all-school effort to develop core values.

Just as core values were essential for many students who

seemed emotionally "needy" and depressed at Hull, and for minority and at-risk students at Rindge and Latin, so, too, are they essential for children from more privileged backgrounds, for similar reasons and for different ones. All students suffer from the effects of profound social and economic changes which have diminished their capacities and incentives for learning, as we discussed in the Hull chapter and will consider again. And, as we saw, many students from poor and/or minority backgrounds also feel like "losers," are deeply demoralized, and lack goals; they need to feel successful and to know there are adults in their lives who believe in them and in their future. Children who are told they are the likely "winners" from an early age, on the other hand, feel a constant pressure to perform—to excel in the classroom and on the athletic field—which tends to make many of them anxious and self-centered, and sometimes less than honest. The attention many high-achieving, success-oriented parents give their children is often conditional or distracted at best, and so these students—who are sometimes indulged more than they are loved—can be extraordinarily egocentric and demanding. Their greatest developmental need is to worry less about their own personal success and learn more about community service and getting along with others from different backgrounds.[6]

The particular emphasis related to core values for individual growth and development in different communities, then, may differ. In Baltimore County, where all schools have been encouraged to develop their own core values, parents in the blue-collar communities hardest hit by unemployment pushed for greater efforts to bolster students' self-esteem; in the affluent Pikesville area, by contrast, the most serious problem among students was thought to be fierce academic competitiveness, and so their parents wanted their school to emphasize more strongly issues having to do with academic honesty.[7]

However, all schools also need core values for social development, for democracy. The two kinds of core values—those that nurture personal growth and those that promote social growth—

are two aspects of the *universal* human struggle for goodness and for community. The list of core values that promote human growth and development is thousands of years old, but it is a short one. Striving to overcome greed and self-centeredness and developing greater compassion, generosity, and moral courage—these universal ethics are at the heart of most world religions, as well as many philosophies of human health and growth.[8]

Dealing with some of the problem behaviors associated with students from middle- and upper-middle-class backgrounds gave Brimmer and May teachers the opportunity to consider some *universal* values and to choose *specific* core values for the school. How they involved students and parents in their discussions, and the universality of the values they ultimately adopted, provide us with an important model which other schools, public as well as private, might follow.

Creating All-School Conversations about Moral Issues

At an end-of-year faculty meeting in June 1989, concerns about student behavior surfaced in teachers' discussions for the first time. Some faculty, hesitantly at first, expressed the view that students sometimes did not treat either one another or faculty with respect. Those who spoke initially feared that perhaps they were the only ones who felt there was a problem, but it soon became clear that many faculty were disturbed by aspects of students' behavior. Some wondered, though, what could be done or even whether a school should deal with moral education. Judy and Anne promised to think about the issue over the summer and to explore ways of addressing it.

Knowing of my previous work in moral education, Judy called me in August to ask if I would be a consultant to the school. Together we developed a plan: first, I would do some interviewing and observing of student behavior and faculty responses in the school; then I'd facilitate a half-day faculty workshop where I'd share my impressions and raise questions for discussion; and, finally, we would then consider ways to involve students and parents in broader discussions.

Focusing for half a day on observing students' nonacademic behaviors and interactions with faculty, it quickly became clear to me what was upsetting some of the teachers. Students routinely interrupted one another as well as adults. They demanded immediate help or attention as they stood beside teachers, they ran and bumped into each other and teachers in the halls, and they shouted to faculty on duty in the dining room to bring them more food at lunch. The faculty was at best inconsistent and at worst indulgent in confronting these behaviors. A few who spotted kids running told them to go back and walk, but many appeared not to notice, while others seemed almost eager to "hop to" when a student demanded seconds at lunch or insisted on more of a teacher's time after class. The environment was hurried and harried; the students clearly felt themselves "entitled," and adults didn't know how or even whether to respond.

These problems were by no means unique to Brimmer and May, as I reassured faculty when I shared some of my observations with them a few weeks later. I described the diminished moral influences of family, religious institutions, and community, and the rise of television as the new teacher of values for many young people. Self-centered behavior has become the norm at many schools, both public and private, and dealing with the problem would require that the entire school community come to agreement on more than just some rules—rather, they needed a set of values, and ways of talking about them, which would help bring out the best in adults and students alike.

But aren't each person's values something personal? some faculty wondered. How could a school come up with values that might apply to everyone—universal values? I suggested a distinction between religious beliefs and practices, which vary greatly, and core values, which are remarkably consistent across all cultures and religions. I encouraged faculty to see if they could come up with their own set of core values by first considering *behav-*

iors. We broke into small groups to talk about three questions: What student and adult behaviors are of greatest concern? What behaviors would we like to see more of at the school? What values do these imply?

The conversations were rich and animated—almost as though waves of pent-up frustration and relief were breaking through the rooms. The faculty were delighted to discover how much in agreement they were. At the end of the day they had no difficulty coming to consensus on four core values that they wanted to promote actively in the school. These were

- honesty
- respect (for oneself as well as for others)
- responsibility
- citizenship

At a follow-up workshop a month later, the faculty developed specific proposals for promulgating a greater awareness of these values throughout the school. They decided to set aside time to involve students in discussions similar to those they'd just undertaken and to create a forum to discuss issues with parents as well; they agreed to revamp the student handbook and to explore ways of structuring lunch so that teachers weren't put in the role of servants; and, most important, they vowed to work more closely with one another to deal consistently with student behaviors.

I was asked to facilitate discussions with twelfth-graders, and to prepare them to lead workshops for students in grades seven through eleven. Some faculty were initially uncertain about the value of student-led discussions of their own behaviors and thought adults ought to be present. I urged them to let the students be the workers here too. Much to the faculty's surprise, concerns about lack of respect for one another and for teachers were at the top of the students' list as well. But students added a concern of their own: teachers sometimes gossiped about students. When I reported this back to faculty, many nodded their heads, and all agreed that faculty-lounge conversations, which can too easily be overheard in the small school, needed to become more professional.

This two-way dialogue is a sharp contrast to the more usual process in schools, in which adults create lists of rules and students test to see if they are for real and in how many ways they may be broken. Being a part of the conversation about behaviors of concern to them—adult as well as student—created a much greater acceptance of the process by students. It helped build a sense of shared responsibility for improving the overall community.

From the beginning of our conversations, however, faculty expressed the concern about whether parents would be supportive of their efforts. They knew they couldn't do it all alone—that there had to be some consistency between what was expected at school and in the home. They were also concerned that some parents would argue that the school had no business teaching values. So I was asked to facilitate a parent/student/teacher evening discussion of moral education.

The process of gaining greater consensus and clarity about the need for core values took a significant step forward in October 1989, when the largest group of parents in the school's history—more than 150 people, representing three quarters of the school's families—showed up for an evening discussion of "Hurried Children, Harried Parents, and Moral Education."[9] After I gave a brief overview of a way of thinking about the universality of ethics and a description of what students and faculty had discussed during the past six weeks, small groups of students, parents, and teachers talked about what the proposed core values meant to them and ways parents might help students be more aware of and responsible for their own behavior.

The evening's discussions ranged well beyond the initial topics in many of the small groups and had several benefits. Students attended different groups than their parents, and so were able to talk more openly about issues adolescents in all schools now face—in particular about the pressures to experiment with drugs, alcohol, and sex at an early age. The next day students commented on how helpful it had been to hear adult perspectives on issues facing them. Many parents left the evening saying that it was the most helpful and informative school-sponsored event they had ever attended, and a number expressed interest in continuing parent support-group discussions.

It is not only the Brimmer and May parents who want this kind of support. Interviews I conducted with the parents of six students, two from each of the three schools studied, revealed their deep concerns about the stresses in their children's lives. When I asked parents, What are some of the issues facing adolescents today? their responses were remarkably consistent and strongly felt, regardless of the school, their child's academic success, or their own marital status:

"Oh God! Drinking and sex—drinking more than anything. My kids are pretty trustworthy, but the pressures on them to get hammered every weekend are pretty intense, and I don't know why. . . . The thing is communication. As long as you're still talking, there's hope."

"Drug addiction, having sex too early. Parents not having enough time to spend with their kids."

"The hardest thing is drugs and alcohol. Parents don't communicate enough with their kids."

"Sex and drugs. Of course, I want them to go to college, but I also want them to get through high school in one piece. I have this image of a lifeline tied around my daughter's waist, and I keep pulling on it when she gets too near the edge. So long as I hold on, she'll get through this."

Now more than ever, many parents need help understanding and communicating with their children. The success of this Brimmer and May evening suggests that school sponsorship of ongoing conversations about issues of parenting and adolescence could be a valuable service, as well as an effective way to improve parent-school ties, in many communities.

As a result of the evening discussion, teachers felt the support of both students and parents to move forward. Core values could now be considered an appropriate—even important—part of the school's goals. By January 1990, the process of revising the student handbook for the next year to make these values and their implications more explicit was well under way. Anne Reenstierna made the four core values of honesty, respect, responsibility, and citizenship—now officially adopted by the school—the subject of her June 1990 commencement address.

After only a few months, adults in the school had already begun to notice a substantial improvement in the school climate. "Faculty are paying more attention to student behavior. They're talking to students about their behavior, and responding to the little things before they get more out of hand," Judy said. "One result is that student detentions are way down, and when a student is referred to me for a discipline problem she shows much more understanding. Everyone seems more aware."

Spending time on the school campus a year later was an altogether more pleasant experience. I witnessed few examples of the kinds of student and adult behavior that had been of concern to many the year before. As the English teacher for the senior class that year, I was deeply impressed by students' overall respect for the school and support for one another. In my more than fifteen years of teaching in both public and private schools, I had never worked with such a thoughtful, motivated, and decent group of adolescents.

However, it did occur to me to wonder from time to time what that class of fifteen young women might have been like if young men had been added into the mix. The decision of the Brimmer and May board of trustees in 1991 to extend coeducation in stages to the upper grades, seven through twelve, brought into question another strong set of core values which Anne and others believed in deeply.

GOING COED: ISSUES OF EQUITY

Anne Reenstierna feels strongly about the benefits of an all-girls school: "I think women still have a long way to go to have equity in the workplace in most professions. There needs to be an emphasis on getting girls to be more assertive—training them to be more outspoken, and to be leaders. To go for the challenges. We need institutions that understand this and give girls and women the special attention they need to take equal roles in our society."

Anne also believes that women tend toward more collaborative ways of learning and working, and that these strategies must be supported in schools. At about the time she read *Horace's Compromise*, she also read *Women's Ways of Knowing*, by Mary Field Blenky, Blythe McVicker Clindry, Mancy Rule Goldberger, and Jill Mattuck Tarule.[10] "One reason the Coalition made sense to me was because they talked about students learning from one another," she explained. "So I thought it was a natural fit with what the research was showing about how women like to learn."

So it was with real reluctance—and some trepidation—that in 1991 Anne brought to the school's board of trustees the recommendation that Brimmer and May go coed in grades seven through twelve, beginning the following year. The problem was economic: while the school had experienced a growing number of applications for the elementary grades and was at capacity for this part of the school, the Upper School remained underenrolled. Boys had to leave at the end of sixth grade, and some of the girls then also transferred to coed schools. Anne had successfully balanced the budget each year, but it required her and others to continue to seek new prospective parents through the summer. With a continuing recession in the Boston area, the task was not getting any easier.

The 1992–93 school year saw boys in grades seven and eight for the first time—as well as a huge jump in enrollments and inquiries for the following year. At the end of the year, I asked Anne how the first year of coeducation in the upper grades had gone:

"When we made the decision to go coed, I thought we might lose something. I worried that boys would take over in the school and that girls would take a back seat. But I've been caught up in the excitement of what's happening in the seventh and eighth grades this year. The place is certainly louder, and feels smaller [necessitating a new addition to one of the buildings], and there's definitely more emphasis on competitive sports. Parents of boys are much more interested and attend games more frequently than the girls' parents, which I find disappointing. But there's so much more school spirit than before—it's palpable—kids enjoy each other's company and don't want to go home. If there's an evening event that starts at seven, they stay. . . .

"As far as I can tell, there's no change in the classroom for the girls. We've had no faculty turnover for the past two years, and I feel this group of teachers is really sensitized and continues to push girls to be leaders and to be outspoken.

"But it may be that boys who come here will get a better and more useful education than in other settings. They'll learn to work more collaboratively. They'll also learn new roles. All the students in seventh and eighth grades do in-school community service, and this year we had boys assisting in lower grades. It was wonderful to see these big eighth-grade guys pouring milk for the four-year-olds. This kind of experience puts them in the helping roles that boys have been traditionally excluded from. It helps prepare them to be better fathers. And when they do outside community service in eleventh grade [a requirement for graduation], that will also change the stereotypes that it is usually

the women who do volunteer work in communities. Now it will be women and men working together."

At Brimmer and May, it is not only the boys who lead, take risks, and must learn to use their minds well. And the girls are no longer the only ones allowed to collaborate, to serve, and to nurture. The school is exploring new ground as it tries to overcome stereotypes that have limited choices for women and men alike, and teaches adolescents to learn together and to respect each other in new ways.

But what about the teachers? To what extent have they learned to work together in new ways—to *collaborate*? In fact, Brimmer and May's transformation had not been either as quick or as smooth as the above account might suggest.

Teacher Collaboration: Recognizing the Need

In the interviews I had completed with ninth-grade teachers in the spring of 1989, a good deal of excitement had been expressed about trying new approaches in the classroom. But when I asked the same teachers what was the "downside to being a Coalition teacher," the replies were equally consistent and deeply felt.

"A lot of pressure," one teacher replied. "Additional work. . . . Sometimes it's overwhelming. We have an extra planning period, but there's a lot of extra work. . . . Sometimes when I leave the meetings, I don't know what I'm doing next week—I don't feel I'm doing anything well." Another teacher answered the question by saying, "It's very time-consuming. With the ninth-grade planning meeting on top of all my other responsibilities (five classes, four preps), I'm required to do more work than other teachers. I also have to be very flexible—giving up class time for our interdisciplinary studies unit. . . . The other thing is a teacher has to be willing to fail along with the students. Lots of teachers aren't willing to do that."

In several conversations, Judy Guild expressed concern about the problem of the extra demands teaching by Coalition methods were placing on herself and her faculty. She explained that most teachers' total loads remained essentially unchanged from before the school joined the Coalition. The school still maintains a seven-to-one student-to-teacher ratio, with full-time teachers responsible for four classes with an average of eleven or twelve students in each, plus supervision of an additional activity such as CityLab, the tenth-grade urban experiential learning program, or Outlook, the eleventh-grade community service program. But additional time had to be found for team planning, for planning workshops to learn more or to introduce others to Coalition ideas, and—most difficult of all—for creating entirely new approaches to teaching many of the courses offered in the school.

A week after returning from spring vacation in 1989, Judy—an energetic woman who was very much the "head coach" for Coalition efforts for the entire school—was plainly exhausted. She said to me, "Preparing for the Walnut Hill faculty seminar was good because it showed how much teachers have internalized, but they've taken risks all year long and they're exhausted from trying to struggle with restructuring their classes while still wrestling with content—it's grueling, trying to figure it all out. I've heard teachers saying they're going to have to come in and work all summer—I'm worried about teacher burnout. We may just have to be dormant with our Coalition activities next year."

Later on, in May, she told me that one of the ninth-grade teachers was leaving after only one year. "I'm concerned. Though she won't admit it, I think the problem is burnout. It's the second teacher in two years. . . . I'm concerned about what we're asking our teachers to do."

The exhaustion of some faculty was not the only source of stress that year. The teachers were also deeply divided in their understanding of—and support for—the philosophy of the Coalition. That not all teachers in the school were enthusiastic about the Coalition's ideas became clear to me in the first all-school faculty meeting I attended, in the spring of 1989. The agenda for the meeting (set by Anne and Judy) was to discuss the Coalition's corollary to student as worker—the idea of teacher as coach.

I sat deliberately in the back of the room at the opening of the meeting, where I knew from experience the skeptics tend to cluster, and took the opportunity to ask several what they thought of the school joining the Coalition.

"Off the record," one woman said, "I was a little uncertain. Sizer's 'less is more' sounds very vague to me. Maybe the ideas have more application in the lower grades or in other subjects, but in [her academic area] we have always done hands-on stuff. The other problem I see with it is that the Coalition doesn't make the content part clear. They seem too process-oriented to me." Another teacher echoed her concern: "I really don't know what it all means. I don't know how I'm supposed to teach differently."

The subtle anxiety and confusion that some faculty felt became more clearly apparent in the small group meeting I attended when the large group broke up to discuss the idea of "teaching versus coaching." My group consisted of ten faculty from all subjects and areas of the school, and no administrator. A partial account of their half-hour discussion follows:

"I really don't want to be doing this," is the first comment made after everyone has pulled their chairs into an oval. The speaker placed herself slightly outside the circle.

The drama teacher suggests they "act it out," and she's promptly made recorder by the group.

"I'm always the recorder," she complains. She takes a large paper doily off the snack table to write on. Banter and confusion continue for several more minutes.

Another teacher introduces a more serious tone with the comment, "When I go over the possessive—I don't know—I'm the teacher."

"It goes back to the question, What is a coach?"

"A coach shows you something, then lets you go off and try it and stays on the sideline."

"How is that different from what we do?"

"Some teachers in public schools just put out stuff all the time—it's all they can do with so many kids in the class."

The teacher who had said, "I don't want to be doing this," now goes into a long description of how kids she gets from public schools have good handwriting, but haven't done much writing. Her kids, by contrast, have done a lot more writing, working on endings, etc., but their handwriting isn't as neat. She uses this as an example of teaching versus coaching. Other teachers follow her comments with some interest.

"It appears that most of us are already doing most of these things."

"When you have to teach history and cover a lot of information, it seems more difficult to coach."

"Judy says over and over, 'No one knows what the Coalition is, we're just trying to find a better way.'"

"I see coaching as having a much more specific goal in mind—teaching isn't so goal-oriented."

"I was under the impression that with the Coalition any kind of discovery is good—it's the opposite of having a specific goal in mind. It's more roundabout than teaching."

"Is there a difference in process?"

"Maybe the difference is in how kids are able to apply knowledge in different situations."

"You teach a subject, you coach a person."

This comment produces a short silence, and then several appreciative murmurs.

"I hope you're taking good notes, Marty."

"I don't know. I'm pretty confused."

An older woman speaks for the first time, "Don't tell anyone, but when we were putting this meeting together, we had to look up the two words in the dictionary. Teaching had no reference to who is being taught. The word coaching sounded more attractive—trying to interest people who might not otherwise be interested. But maybe the differences don't matter so much."

"A classics teacher I heard of who had a nine A.M. *class always began promptly. Once he began when there was no one there."*

"It's a matter of emphasis—"

"They're not necessarily opposite."

The older woman repeats the comment, "The differences don't matter so much."

"Do we need to jump to an example?"

They turn to a language teacher and ask about teaching the verb "to be"—how would she do it by coaching? She doesn't answer.

"So what's an example of coaching?"

The teacher who talked about writing now goes into a lengthy description of how she teaches reading. She talks about how she does not teach rules—about words ending in "ing," for example—until the kids discover the exceptions and ask about them.

"You mean there's more exploring?"

She nods and explains further.

"Let's use that as an example of coaching when we report back."

There's general agreement. Faculty begin drifting in from other groups.

One teacher says quietly, "I hope 'teaching' is not a dirty word."

"No, no!"

"Of course not!"

Opening the Door

That spring, in 1989, it was clear that some faculty seemed to be taking on too much in relation to the school's Coalition programs, while others did not know where or how to begin. Because of the underlying faculty stress and discord, I felt the school was in danger of losing momentum in the change process after only two years. And, as is the case in most public and private schools, there was no forum where faculty might more openly talk about their questions and concerns related to the school's new academic direction.

While ninth-grade teachers had been given some additional meeting time to plan their interdisciplinary class, "Connections," the agenda for all-school faculty meetings was set by the administration, whose first priority was more training. Faculty did not have a say in what training was needed and often did not even know ahead of time what the agendas were for their meetings. On the afternoon described above, I overheard several faculty complaining as they sat down that they didn't even know what the meeting was about. The small groups, by and large, did not discuss in any detail examples of a "teaching lesson" and a "coaching lesson," as they had been asked to by Judy at the beginning of the meeting. They might have, it seemed to me, if they'd understood in advance the purpose of the meeting.

It seemed to me there was both a need and an opportunity to try out ideas related to collaborative decision making at Brimmer and May. While I knew of no precedents in other independent schools, I reasoned that with many fewer bureaucratic constraints and very little middle management, it might be much easier to undertake such an experiment at this school. I thought that if faculty had the opportunity (but were not required) to work together on larger school issues as a team, some renewed energy, a greater sense of teamwork and shared purpose, and new solutions to problems might result.

On a number of occasions, Judy had asked for feedback on what I'd been observing, and so I scheduled a meeting with her one afternoon in late April of 1989 to talk more about issues related to collaborative decision making. From earlier conversations with Judy, I knew that she was concerned about how some "non-Coalition" teachers were feeling in the school, so that was a natural starting point for the conversation.

"I feel like I'm walking on a tightrope a lot," she had confessed. "On the one side, if I don't do training and faculty discussions, I'm afraid we won't go anywhere as a Coalition school. On the other side is teachers who are sick of hearing the word 'Coalition' and don't ever want to hear it again."

I suggested to Judy that some teachers felt threatened by the faculty meeting discussion of teaching versus coaching. They were hearing the idea that coaching is good and teaching is bad, and worried that coaching and teaching content were incompatible.

Judy immediately agreed with me about the problem, and this provoked a long discussion about a range of issues. She knew there were faculty with very different needs—some who didn't really understand "student as worker and teacher as coach" at all, and others who were exhausted from their efforts to transform totally their teaching and curriculum. Why not form a small committee, with representatives from each part of the school, to help her plan faculty meetings and try to get the teachers more involved in problem solving, I suggested.

As the conversation progressed, several times Judy came back to the problem of fatigue and how they'd probably go "dormant" with the Coalition next year, meaning putting any new initiatives on hold. I suggested she consider the word "consolidation," instead—which she liked very much. I also recommended that at the end-of-year faculty meeting she acknowledge the problem of overwork and her feeling that they needed a breather, and that perhaps a good way to do that was to have an evaluation which asked teachers to respond in writing, after small group discussion, to four questions: What are some important things they have learned, professionally, since the school became a member of the Coalition two years ago? What's worked best? What's been most problematic? What modifications or additional changes do they see as necessary?

Judy was concerned that such an evaluation would commit her to making changes. I suggested she introduce the evaluation with the idea that she needed feedback, but could make no promises about change. Then, over the summer, she could look at the responses, perhaps share them with her new faculty committee, then decide where to go and discuss her views with faculty either in the August back-to-school letter or in person in September.

Many of these ideas were ones that Judy and Anne had just begun thinking about themselves, and so she became very excited in our meeting. At one point she suddenly beamed and said, "Yes—just like with students—*teachers should be workers and take on more responsibility, too!* That would sure take some of the load off my shoulders."

Two months later, in June 1989, I heard no talk of going dormant next year. To the contrary, at the end-of-year faculty meetings there had been a positive and energizing review of Coalition efforts by faculty, with the result that Judy Guild, Anne Reenstierna, and a group of faculty had begun to plan some further changes in the Upper School for the 1989–90 school year. To facilitate more focus and interdisciplinary studies, they decided to change the schedule so that all classes would meet three days a week for longer blocks of time, instead of following the five-day-a-week, forty-five-minute-period schedule that is almost universal in American high schools. Also, English and history classes would be scheduled back-to-back, to facilitate teacher collaboration.

Anne and Judy also made the decision to pursue collaborative decision making more formally in the next school year, as well. They did decide to set up a new Faculty-Administrative Committee to advise them and to help plan and facilitate all-school faculty meetings. And Judy decided to revive the dormant Curriculum Committee and begin a comprehensive review of the curriculum as a first step toward defining what all Brimmer and May students should know and be able to do to earn a diploma. She also hoped this committee might help her think about how alternative forms of assessment might be incorporated more fully into the curriculum.

The Committees Go to Work

Halfway through the 1989–90 school year, the new Faculty-Administrative Committee—which consisted of five faculty from all parts of the school, plus Judy, Anne, and the Lower School head—had met several times to plan two all-school faculty meetings for the second semester. Before making any final decisions, however, the committee decided to distribute a questionnaire to generate a list of needs and concerns. Faculty expressed interest in workshops on "writing across the curriculum" (which would explore ways to integrate more writing into all academic classes) and on the problem of standards and consistency in grading, and in a specific goal-setting discussion on moral issues (the results of which were described above). Faculty also wanted to do more fun things like sing together, and so the committee decided to allow time for pleasant, community-building activities in future meetings.

Another immediate faculty concern that surfaced was the need to improve communications between the Lower, Middle, and Upper schools. Faculty members felt that the memos circulated to inform different parts of the school about various activities were not sufficient. As a result, the committee decided to create an all-school calendar. Judy was asked to put all Middle and Upper school events of general interest on the calendar and to distribute it. She agreed to do this, but when she was also asked by the committee to highlight the activities that might be of particular interest to Lower School teachers, she drew a line. Someone in the Lower School had to read the calendar and decide what was worth highlighting—she wasn't going to do their job for them, she told them. The committee understood the point that collaborative decision making meant taking on additional responsibilities and agreed to do their part with the new calendar. They also agreed that teachers should take turns chairing their meeting and co-chair faculty meetings.

One of the teachers on the committee, whom I interviewed in

January 1990, agreed that establishing the committee was an important step and that progress had been made, but she believed it would take more time for faculty committee members to feel free to disagree with administrators and to take responsibility for committee decisions with colleagues.

"It's hard for administrators to hear negative things, but I think Judy and Anne seem glad to have the help. Lately, our meetings have been really upbeat. . . . It was fun facilitating one," she said. "But we as a faculty need to take more responsibility, and not just rely on the administration to fix things. It's really important for faculty to see that it isn't just the administration who makes a decision, it's the faculty on the committee, too."

Reflecting on the committee's work for the future, she said, "It's going to take time for us, as a committee, to develop trust. People are starting to speak out more and seem freer to disagree. Now we need to spend less time on planning faculty meetings, and more time on overview things—like bringing Lower and Upper school faculty together. Everybody wants it, we just need time to work on it."

By January 1990, the Curriculum Committee had begun a systematic review of the syllabi of courses in the Upper School. The review was conceived as a first step toward the goal of clearly identifying what Brimmer and May students should know and be able to do by the time they graduate. Judy described the effect on faculty of a very different kind of professional dialogue: "What I've done is share knowledge [about teachers' courses] that I used to hold to myself. I've said, 'Let's critique this together.' People have been really energized by looking at one another's syllabi. And the course descriptions have become much more thorough because they know their colleagues are going to see their work. . . . When the teachers are no longer anonymous, they're much more professional."

Jenny Prileson, who had served on a previous curriculum committee at the school for several years, saw real differences in the way the group was working compared to the past. "The committee didn't really exist two years ago," Jenny said in an interview. "Now we're much more focused. Compared to where we were as a Coalition school two years ago, more teachers are really more critically examining their course approaches—presenting more essential questions, getting students to do more of the work. As we outline what seniors should know and be able to do, then we can begin to work our way backward and look at what different courses ought to be—whether to do more interdisciplinary courses, as the Coalition recommends. Eventually, we're going to have to make some hard decisions about what courses to offer."

Compared to the spring of 1989, the faculty at Brimmer and May one year later seemed to me and to those whom I interviewed to be more unified and more satisfied. And they were taking more initiatives in their teaching. One faculty member reported to me, "There's more work this year, but there's also a lot of good camaraderie, people appreciating each other a lot. Most faculty are very supportive about Coalition approaches and are trying a lot of different things—more so than last year." Another observed, "There's a lot more interdisciplinary stuff going on this year. Even though the Coalition stuff is a lot of extra work, it's really exciting to work and plan with other teachers."

"Another thing that has changed," Judy said with pride, "is our professional development budget for conferences and workshops. Before, there was always money left over. Now we have to increase the amount available every year, and we still run out. It's been the only added cost for us as a Coalition school."

The increased interest in attending workshops and the extra work teachers had taken on voluntarily in the two key committees seemed to be clear indicators of the heightened sense of professionalism and esprit de corps that teachers reported in 1990. The results are all the more striking when one realizes that these were the same teachers who the previous spring had described themselves as on the verge of burnout. I do not think that such a change in teachers' job satisfaction and willingness to take on additional work can be attributed to the time of year or to the faculty having had additional experience with the Coalition. And, although Anne Reenstierna's decision in the second year to reduce most teachers' loads (from five classes down to four) helped alleviate faculty stress, it seems likely to me that collaborative decision making at the school was an important ingredient in the dramatic improvement in faculty morale and sense of unity.

The experience of shared decision making had been important for the school's two administrators as well. In January 1990, Judy observed that "there is less complaining from faculty because they have a voice. The experiment has worked out well for me, too. I don't feel I have to do it all anymore!"

The 1990–91 school year at Brimmer and May marked still greater faculty involvement in decision making. In her September 1990 opening address to faculty, Anne Reenstierna declared that extending shared decision making throughout the school was one of her major goals for the year, that parents could be made to feel more a part of the school, and that both students and faculty should be more involved in leadership. "I want to increase the size of the Faculty-Administrative Committee this year," she told the faculty. "I also want to involve faculty in developing a new teacher-evaluation procedure, and in the board of trustees' Long-Range Planning and Compensation committees."

In the fall of 1991, the Faculty-Administrative Committee (now affectionately called the Ajax Committee because they "clean up the messes") began to meet approximately every three weeks. While the group continued to discuss issues that arose and to work on planning all-school faculty meetings as they'd begun to do the year before, they also took on the task of completely revising the method of evaluating faculty at the school.

In the past, evaluations based on sporadic classroom visits and yearly meetings with Anne, with input from Judy, had seemed somewhat mysterious and even arbitrary to many faculty. The Faculty-Administrative Committee spent most of the year developing and refining a new system of faculty evaluation, carrying proposals and questions back and forth between the committee and the Upper and Lower school faculty meetings, where ideas were discussed extensively. The result was a highly refined and innovative proposal for a process that would be different for new and experienced faculty. For the first time, the school's expectations for teachers were spelled out and discussed by Anne; the committee also agreed that all future evaluations would begin with an annual self-evaluation and goal-setting session with an administrator. And for experienced faculty, who would now be evaluated only every three years, there would be opportunities to seek input from both in-school and outside peer evaluators and to submit video portfolios of one's teaching.

At Anne's request, I facilitated an evaluation of the work of the "Ajax Committee" in the spring of 1991, while the final work on the new faculty evaluation process was being completed. I administered an anonymous open-ended questionnaire to all members, observed several meetings, and shared the results of my inquiry and recommendations with the full committee. Together, we identified some changes that could improve the functioning of the group for the following year, including: developing and posting agendas, as well as minutes, ahead of each "Ajax" meeting (this was routinely done for full faculty meetings); rotating the chairing of meetings; having formal elected representatives from every part of the school and periodic reports back to faculty; and, finally, involving teachers in helping set priorities for the work of the committee.

These suggestions for change came in the context of an extremely positive overall evaluation by both teachers and administrators. What follows is a representative selection of written comments on the questionnaire that I administered.

"The committee has opened dialogue about evaluations which are a big concern for most teachers. Talking to faculty at our lower and upper school meetings with and

without administrators present gave everyone a chance to speak. Some people even spoke to committee members privately . . . and all teachers have had input."

"Whole school faculty meetings have grown more organized, efficient, and effective—much more helpful and useful!"

"I know things could be much better but they seem enormously improved from when I started working here four years ago. Each year the lines of communication seem to open up more and more."

"Of all the committees I serve on, I feel this one is the most productive. We get a lot of stuff done, and I'm glad that we hear the concerns of faculty. They're going to come out somewhere, and I'd rather they come out here, rather than in gripe sessions in the faculty room."

In June 1991, the new faculty evaluation proposal was presented to the full faculty for their final approval. The vote to approve was unanimous—and was accompanied by both applause and numerous vocal thank-you's to the committee members for all their hard work.

This is not to suggest that collaborative decision making at Brimmer and May doesn't have its naysayers. There are some teachers who feel it has gone too far, and others who believe it hasn't really gone far enough. One teacher complained, "We have to be privy to almost every decision that gets made—almost to a fault. Administrators don't even come in with proposals to choose between, and meetings can get to be very time-consuming." Another teacher observed that the whole process had allowed "sensitive, even threatening, issues to be aired. But I'm not sure they get resolved. And some issues, like the sense of territory some teachers feel about their rooms or special equipment, never get discussed at all."

For administrators, too, the process is often difficult and far from perfect. As a manager, Judy feels—as did Claire Sheff in Hull—that knowing when and how to share decisions remains one of her most difficult tasks. "Usually, if you're an administrator in one place for five years, you get your systems in place and things gradually become a little easier," she told me in June 1991. "But here it has become more rather than less challenging to manage the faculty. I find it harder now because there are so many empowered people, and you have to make sure you don't take power away. The hardest part of my week is running faculty meetings."

Nevertheless, the practice of collaborative decision making has provided new solutions to administrative problems, and it has helped to create a climate that fosters educational change. When I talked to Anne in July 1991 about strategies she had employed for creating change at Brimmer and May, she spontaneously mentioned the creation and functioning of the Faculty-Administrative Committee as having made a real contribution. "If we want teachers to change the way they relate to students, then administrators have to be role models. Bringing faculty into decision making in the Ajax Committee has begun to change the relationship between teachers and administrators." And Judy Guild observed that "if you're going to ask faculty to give up a certain kind of control in the classroom, then maybe you have to give them more power elsewhere to make it work."

Later, Judy reflected further on what this empowerment has come to mean to her and to the school as a whole: "I used to feel threatened if people weren't all going in the same direction. Now I'd rather have devil's advocates than people who just go with the flow. We'll learn more quickly with the critics. What makes a good school is not that everyone is in the same place but that all of us are wrestling with the issues—that the whole school is at least thinking about our mission. Very few people here are satisfied with the status quo. Some may place more emphasis on one thing, some on another, but we're still moving forward as a whole."

In an interview in the summer of 1991, history teacher Neal Brown made a similar observation: "So much of what school reform is really about has to do with just getting teachers to talk together. There's no one way, no recipe for what works. It's getting together to share ideas and really seeing ourselves as professionals."

After four years, Brimmer and May had gone quite far in efforts to redefine teaching and learning and to involve faculty in truly collaborative decision making. Administrators and faculty were working together to implement a common vision of how to involve students more fully in their own learning and faculty in the overall management of the school. And most expressed a great deal of pride at what they have collectively accomplished. At the same time, Judy's observation that there was little interest in maintaining the status quo seems true. I found a high degree of commitment to continuing to both refine the practice of "student as worker" and extend efforts to work collaboratively.

Next Steps: Toward an Interdisciplinary Curriculum

At the end of the 1991 school year, when I asked Anne, Judy, and the ninth-grade teachers about their greatest challenges for the next year, the goal of interdisciplinary teaching was at the top of nearly everyone's list. While a feature of the ninth-grade course "Connections" had given teachers a chance to plan together and work with students on research skills in a common block of time once a week, the Coalition ideal of a more focused, integrated curriculum taught by teams of teachers who are generalists still seemed far away.

"We're close to the vision I have for the school, but we're not there yet," Anne told me. "The part we've achieved is having students actively involved in their own learning, in research, and in sharing what they know with one another. But the part we're not close to is teaching in a true interdisciplinary manner—where English and history are taught together as 'Humanities,' for example. . . . Students need to 'learn for understanding' [a phrase Howard Gardner uses to distinguish real learning from mere schooling][11]—to see the interconnectedness of questions and issues—not just learn something for a specific subject." When I asked why progress toward this goal was slower, Anne responded, "Some teachers are resisting the idea, and I haven't been willing to tell them that they have to do that yet. Last summer, two teachers from different disciplines got grants from the school to work on a combined curriculum, but it didn't really happen."

Interviews with the ninth-grade teachers suggested other reasons why more interdisciplinary teaching was not happening at the school. As a group, they had come to enjoy team planning, but found that it had taken them time to develop trust. Said one, "I've really learned a lot, but it took us two years to feel comfortable with one another, to learn to listen to one another, and to get efficient." Another, who also said that she enjoyed team planning and wanted to do more of it, found that the meetings still weren't as productive as she would like. "It wasn't anyone's fault, but lots of times we didn't have every teacher at every meeting, so things had to be repeated a lot. Also, we tended to get off the track and talk about specific students or groups, instead of the program." Reflecting further, she added, "It's hard to keep the momentum for change going. We instituted a program, then sort of sat on it for a while. It needs new life."

Educational researchers Dan Lortie and Susan Moore Johnson have both written about the obstacles to greater teacher collaboration in schools. In his 1975 landmark study of teachers, *Schoolteacher*, Lortie suggested that many who enter the teaching profession like to retain a measure of control over what they do and so prefer a more individualistic work style, where they can maintain autonomy.[12] Susan Moore Johnson, in her recent book *Teachers at Work*, argues that the way in which work is organized and decisions are made inhibits collaboration in most public schools. Even when teachers want to work together—to teach an interdisciplinary course, for example—there are often too many institutional roadblocks. She observes that there tends to be more collaboration in independent schools, where there is a greater esprit de corps, a stronger sense of common goals, and less bureaucracy with which to contend.[13] (The substantially better working conditions and greater respect shown teachers in private schools keeps many from going to public schools, where they could earn significantly more money—suggesting perhaps that these workplace improvements may be more important for school improvement than higher teacher salaries.)

In my experience, both Lortie and Johnson are right. Most teachers do not have much interest in working collaboratively, and most schools do not value such work. They are closed, self-reinforcing systems. Yet, as we've seen, schools simply cannot change without greater teacher collaboration to develop clear academic goals and core values.

School leaders need to make collaboration an explicit expectation, as Brimmer and May has done. The school's experience suggests that gradually, over a period of four or five years, the workplace culture begins to change, and that with encouragement, many teachers are more willing to collaborate. Those that are not leave. During the first two years of being a Coalition school, Brimmer and May had a significant teacher turnover rate in the Upper School. However, from 1991 until the time this study was completed in August 1993, not one teacher left in grades six through twelve—this despite the fact that the school's salaries are still not competitive with those of other independent or public schools in the area.

Structural changes must accompany changes in expectations about teachers' jobs. Judy Guild observed, "What we need is a more flexible schedule to allow for people to plan more and teach together. Restructuring the school day is the next big step. As long as the eight-period day and five-subject structure remains, teachers won't break out of their individual classroom walls." Teachers I interviewed in June 1991 were interested in doing more collaborative curriculum planning, but they agreed with Judy that the primary problem was time. "The expectation is that we're going to teach in a way that asks more of us," one Brimmer and May teacher complained. "But we have four courses to prepare for each day, committees to serve on, extracurricular activities to oversee, and then the school expects us to show up at school sports events, concerts, and dances in our 'free' time." Another teacher concurred: "There are too many demands on us outside the classroom. To be coaches and advisors, to be here morning, noon, and night—the hours we spend in committee meetings alone is four to five times what public school teachers are asked to do. . . . There is too little time to get the real work of teaching done."

Anne had long felt the need for a change in the school schedule that would allow more time for teachers to plan interdisciplinary curricula and to work on committees. And she had seen what other schools had accomplished—notably Central Park East Secondary School, where teachers plan curricula half a day each week, while students are off campus doing community service and internships. But she was concerned about the reaction of parents. By the end of the 1991–92 school year, however, Anne had decided that for the continuing progress of the school she had to take the risk. She announced that for the 1992 school year, classes would end at 1:30 P.M. on Wednesdays, instead of 3:15, to allow more time for teachers to work together. Students in grades K–6 would go home early that day, while those in grades 7–12 would be involved in a variety of activities—health classes, community service programs, college planning, and so on.

More than forty parents signed a petition to Anne, protesting the change. She wrote back to explain the basis for the decision once more, and to point out that the other four school days had been lengthened to partially compensate; she also set up an after-school day care program. But she kept to her decision.

A year later, in June 1993, Anne was even more sure of the rightness of the decision than before. "The released time for teachers has generated more interdisciplinary curricula and other changes in one year than we'd seen the previous five. At the end of the year, we had students at the fifth- and tenth-grade level do final exhibitions that combined work in three academic areas. Next year there will be a seventh-eighth humanities curriculum that combines yearlong studies in English, social studies, and arts. And I think we'll see more of that at all grade levels in future years."

Creating a "Learning Organization"

We have seen how the change process has progressed over five years at Brimmer and May. At times there have been some significant leaps forward. But there were other times when many were concerned about the loss of momentum to which the ninth-grade teacher referred in the quote above. To avoid stagnation and to make the change process ongoing, Brimmer and May and other schools involved in systemic reorganization must involve teachers, as well as parents and students, in collaborative efforts to continuously critique and improve the school. The change process must become institutionalized through the creation of what corporate consultant Peter Senge, author of *The Fifth Discipline*, calls a "learning organization."[14]

Creating a learning organization requires first that schools develop consensus around explicit goals and core values—as I have already argued. But then there must be regular assessment of progress toward those goals at all levels, and refinements made and new goals set, as necessary. It is a conscious, critical, and dialectical process whereby a broad spectrum of opinions is sought in the analysis of practice, and both goals and methods evolve through self-study as well as the study of best practices in other organizations.

Brimmer and May faculty and administrators have begun this process, but assessment is still sometimes random and haphazard. For example, despite the fact that it was a new, experimental effort, the Faculty-Administrative Committee had no plans to assess their work or discuss ways to improve until I made the suggestion in April of 1991—more than a year after they had begun to meet. Similarly, the ninth-grade teaching team did not, as a group, formally assess their first year or set goals for themselves for the next one.

Of course, formal assessment of goals and practices rarely occurs in most schools, or in other large bureaucratic institutions, unless it is required by an outside agency. Unfortunately, the ten-year assessment that is required of most schools for accreditation by regional agencies is usually pro forma and very rarely results in real change. Unlike in the business world, in which corporations must now restructure or fail, there are no real incentives in government agencies or in the nonprofit world for systematic, rigorous, ongoing assessment. (Even in business, there is often more talk than action.) Critical analysis and evaluation of practice will not happen in most schools or other institutions unless the process becomes a part of the organization's culture.

Discussion and assessment of school goals and practices must be continuous and must involve all teachers and staff, as well as older students and parents. At Brimmer and May, there is general agreement about goals, and teachers are now accustomed to talking about educational and even administrative issues in some faculty and committee meetings. The next step is to make critical analysis of every aspect of the curriculum, as well as specific teaching practices, a legitimate and frequent topic for discussion at each grade level and in every subject area. This would require teachers to observe one another's teaching, to work together, and to coordinate efforts to a much higher degree than has been done thus far.

Another difficult step would be to solicit criticism, suggestions, and greater cooperation from community members and parents. Anne's recent efforts to create a visitors' committee of distinguished business, academic, and community leaders to advise the school is a start—provided she can get them to put in the time necessary to give useful advice. But securing the right kind of constructive parental involvement can be difficult, even in independent schools. Despite five years of back-to-school evenings, numerous talks by Anne, and various Parents' Association events, the parents whom I interviewed knew comparatively little about the Coalition or the specific principles that the school was trying to foster. They were a contented, even supportive, but by and large uninformed group of educational consumers. It will require a more concerted effort—as well as some risk—to involve parents more fully in critical discussions of pedagogy. Anne and I have discussed the idea of establishing a parents' academic advisory committee, similar to the visitors' committee, as a start.

Anne is also interested in involving students more fully in school governance issues by including them on some faculty and trustee committees. While I think this is an important step, my experience is that putting a small number of students on committees dominated by adults does not usually change the substance of discussions. Far more important, I think, is the involvement of students in a critique of their shared work together in classrooms. Again, an occasional written evaluation is not sufficient. As I suggested in the chapter on the Academy, students can make extremely useful suggestions for the improvement of individual teaching and course content, but only when they are given regular opportunities to talk together as a class with the teacher. With practice and encouragement, students are often able to critique their own group performance in ways that contribute greatly to enhanced overall efforts.

In short, establishing a school culture which fosters continuous improvements requires that teachers collaborate in new ways with colleagues, community members, parents, and students. Teachers must lead in the creation of a true learning organization, for adults as well as for students.

The teachers and administrators at Brimmer and May have gone a long way toward achieving that goal. The difference this change of culture has made in the lives of adults and students at the school is very clear. Brimmer and May has become a very creative, stimulating, and caring environment for students and teachers alike. It is a school community that consciously cultivates new habits of the head and heart.

Implications for Public Schools

Brimmer and May represents an important educational experiment on the cutting edge of efforts to develop a new kind of American high school for the twenty-first century. But it is a private, independent school. Can lessons for public schools be drawn from this school's experience? I have already suggested that the school's students were not so very different from the populations of many typical suburban public high schools. So most of what Brimmer and May accomplished in the classroom could also be done in those public high schools where resources can be reallocated to create smaller classes. But the changes we have described are far more likely to happen if we learn the lessons this school has to teach us about organizational structure and scale.

Structure: Local Control

Brimmer and May is not governed by a political entity, but by a small group of parents and volunteers. The school's board of trustees does not make day-to-day operating decisions, only long-term policy decisions such as whether or not to go coed or build a new building. It hires a CEO—the head of the school—who makes all operational decisions. Board members rotate off periodically, and one of the board's committees selects replacements who have a commitment to the school and an area of expertise needed.

When Anne decides to revamp the curriculum, give a teacher more administrative responsibility, or even to develop core values for the school, she frequently informs the board of her plans, but she does not have to waste hours and months waiting for central office approval or preparing a presentation for a school committee. She simply consults with the appropriate people in the school and moves forward.

Some of the better corporations have been practicing for a decade what many public schools are just beginning to understand: *the people who are closest to the problem should be the ones to make decisions and have the responsibility for solving it.* Elected officials cannot be expected to run school systems with any degree of competence. They know too little about educational issues in most cases, are too far removed from the problems, and are too subject to pressures from various constituent groups.

There are now a number of promising experiments to change power relationships and redefine decision making in public schools around the country. The state of Kentucky recently passed legislation which severely limits the power of school boards and gives greater authority to superintendents and individual schools. And in the summer of 1993, Massachusetts passed a similarly sweeping school reform bill, one which also limits the power of school boards and gives greater autonomy to principals but requires them to establish advisory "school councils" with parent and community representation; the new law also allows groups to apply for approval to run autonomous public "charter schools." Chicago schools are now managed by committees of elected parents who then hire the principal of their choice. So-called school-based management is also being tried in various forms in a number of communities, such as Dade County, Florida, and New York City. New York has also led the way in creating thirty entirely new autonomous high schools. The twenty-two public charter schools in Philadelphia are another bold step toward more fully realizing the structural advantages of independent schools.

School-based management does not by itself guarantee a better school, however. In a review of research on school-based management efforts in the May 1989 issue of *Educational Leadership*, Jane David found few examples of site-based management schools whose school councils dealt with any issues "more difficult than creating a new discipline policy or decorating the entranceway."[15] And in a recent Rand Corporation study, *High Schools with Character*, researchers concluded that in efforts to improve inner city schools, "choice and the deregulation that accompanies site-based managed schools create the external conditions for effective schools. But the internal conditions—developing a coherent mission statement and the individual character that appeals to students and teachers—matter equally." The study went on to document the need for, and attributes of, what the authors called focus schools.[16]

It is becoming increasingly clear, though, that the large comprehensive high schools we've been constructing since the 1950s cannot become "focus schools"—schools with clear academic goals which apply to all students, as well as explicit core values. If the metaphor for these large schools was the shopping mall, which offers infinite variety but at the cost of anonymity, then the new metaphor for more effective schools must be a kind of *intentional community* where there is a shared sense of purpose and people feel known and cared for.

Scale: "Face-to-Face" High Schools

Brimmer and May was able to define and implement a demanding set of academic goals not simply because it was an independent school, but also because it was a comparatively *small, autonomous community where people could meet and talk face to face to reach consensus*. The same was true in the Academy, and at Hull—though teachers there did little talking together the first year.

Our three case studies suggest that the size of the "educational unit" undertaking change is an important factor in the change process for schools. Working in teams, developing effective strategies, assessing results, evolving trust, knowing students well—all require frequent face-to-face meetings. While I have not seen research that explores the question of the ideal size for a faculty that is working for change, I am struck by the fact that the size of the faculty "unit" in all three cases was no more than fifty.

A comparatively small size not only enables faculty to work

more closely, it also permits them to know students and parents more deeply and to create a sense of community. Core values best take root in communities where people know one another by name and where communication can be frequent and informal. Recent research and interviews with educators suggest that high schools of no more than 400 students have lower dropout rates and are far less prone to violence and other forms of destructive student behavior.[17]

A greater number of smaller schools need not necessarily mean more school buildings or substantially higher costs. In District 4 in New York City, large school buildings that were once home to single schools now house new and entirely autonomous public schools on different floors—such as the Central Park East Elementary and Secondary schools, which are located in the same building, along with several other programs. Both of these public schools are run at a cost which is no greater than the per pupil expenditures in the supposedly more efficient behemoth schools.

Choices

Creating smaller schools, as well as reducing class size, does mean accepting certain trade-offs. Central Park East Secondary School has an average class size of fifteen, rigorous academic standards, no violence, smoking, or graffiti, and a graduation rate nearly double that of many of its larger counterparts.[18] But it has no varsity football team. No cheerleading squad. No course catalogue with hundreds of offerings. Few of the things, in fact, that most Americans assume to be essential parts of the high school experience.

When it comes to fundamentally improving high schools, we can't have it all—winning football teams, hundreds of specialized course offerings, individualized learning, and high intellectual and behavior standards for all students.

Everyone seems to want school reform, but are most Americans willing to give up certain things in order to have schools with clear academic goals, core values, and collaboration? Is it possible for communities to come to consensus on what's most important in a school—and on what students should know and be able to do?

Or does having more *choices* of where to send one's children eliminate the need for public debate about what a "good" school would look like? If all parents had more *choice*, would they choose well? Is there a "market" for truly better schools? Will the free market mechanism of "school choice" allow the best schools to thrive, while the bad ones "go out of business"?

We will consider these and other questions in the concluding chapter.

FOUR

Some Lessons Learned

What Works

More than a decade has passed since improving education was declared a national priority, yet most schools—especially high schools—remain unchanged. It has proven far more difficult to transform the culture of schools than most critics and policymakers had thought. Through the stories of three schools' efforts, I have explored some of the reasons why.

I conclude that there are three essential, interrelated components to a successful school improvement process: establishing *clear academic goals* based on developing and assessing students' competencies rather than on "covering" subjects; creating a caring community with explicit *core values*; and encouraging many forms of *collaboration* between teachers and with students, parents, and community members. When one or more of these parts is missing, change is thwarted. And when all three are strong, schools can and do transform themselves—though such systemic change is neither quick nor easy.

We saw how too many top-down decisions and a lack of schoolwide collaboration undermined improvement efforts initially in Hull, and how working within a large school and systemwide bureaucracy did the same in the Academy. If schools are given more independence and restructured for more manageable, face-to-face decision making, as at Brimmer and May, new forms of collaboration become more necessary and evolve more easily. With greater professional responsibility and opportunity for shaping individual schools, educators are more likely to take risks, hold one another accountable, and benefit from additional training and outside assistance. With greater respect and confidence, teachers are also more willing to collaborate with parents, students, and community members.

I have also argued that we should attend to the needs of the heart, as well as the head, by creating a school culture that nurtures explicit core values. In the Hull and Academy chapters, I discussed how students' diminished capacities and motivation to learn, as well as new emotional needs, require that teachers establish personal, caring relationships with all students and teach in new ways. But teachers cannot do it all. In both the Academy and Brimmer and May chapters, I suggested some specific ways to encourage parents and other adults to be more fully involved and supportive of students' work in schools.

School communities need to consider the particular needs of their students as they choose which core values should be emphasized to promote *individual growth and development.* Cultural and racial differences must be more than respected, they must be celebrated. Students' sense of hope for the future must be actively nurtured. Rather than creating categories of winners and losers through rigid tracking systems, schools need to individualize learning so that every student discovers his or her unique interests and abilities and believes that personal success is possible. All students—not just those who are poor or at risk—need closer, caring relationships with teachers through the creation of advisor groups. However, excessive individual attention and the unrelenting push for students to achieve rather than to learn can reinforce a sense of entitlement and self-centeredness. Students from middle- and upper-middle-class backgrounds, especially, need to worry less about personal success while learning more about being curious and creative and about getting along with and being of service to others.

And so I have argued that universal values for *social growth and development*—common to the human experience and essential as a framework for community—must also be emphasized in schools. Without greater acknowledgment of our common needs and aspirations as human beings, our social fabric will likely continue to unravel. We need core values that build community to preserve and enhance life in a democracy. Brimmer and May described these values as honesty, respect, responsibility, and citizenship. Individual schools and communities might choose other ways of describing their core values, as well as additional values particular to the individual needs of different groups of students.

Encouraging greater collaboration and developing core values is hard work, but these are less difficult than establishing academic goals. In my experience, there are three essential steps for developing and implementing clear academic goals. First, outcomes must be defined—what students are expected to master, to know and be able to do, to earn a high school diploma, at the end of each academic year, and at other regular points in each course. Second, the goals must be communicated to students—what is expected, why, and, most important, how competencies will be assessed. Third, students must be involved in the selection of books and projects and in assessing group progress toward agreed-upon goals.

I have argued that educators alone cannot and should not decide what students should know and be able to do. Establishing clear, competency-based academic goals requires nothing less than rethinking the purposes of a high school education. We need new kinds of institutional and community collaboration for clarity about the goals of education.

The first challenge is to make clear the need for a serious dialogue about new educational goals—for a redefinition of what it means to be an educated person in the twenty-first century. *The unspoken assumption of most Americans seems to be that the purpose of school reform is simply for high schools to do better what they once did and have done for the past one hundred years*. We don't need anything new, many say; we've already had too many educational fads that failed—like "new math" and open classrooms. Most Americans believe the real goal of educational change should be to go "back to the basics," back to a golden age when schools—teachers as well as students—did what they were supposed to.

But Deborah Meier, founder of Central Park East Secondary School, and other leading educators argue persuasively that there was no "golden age" when the majority of students were more literate.[1] She and others observe that our nation's high schools have continued to graduate an increasing percentage of students who go on to college. The current high school dropout rate is the lowest in the nation's history. This very "success," in fact, may be part of the problem. The academic bar—or standards—may have been lowered somewhat, and test scores have declined, in part because of the increasing numbers of less academically able students who now take the standardized tests and aim for college as the only available path to a good job.

Educators say they should not be blamed for the loss of blue-collar jobs and the consequent pressure to graduate ever higher percentages of students. Nor should educators be blamed for students' diminished capacities and motivation to learn—the result of the increasing influence of "consumer" values, less respect for all forms of authority, and less parental supervision. These are demographic and social changes which preclude a return to the golden age of "Ozzie and Harriet" high schools—if there ever was one.

Impatient with this kind of finger-pointing, as well as with the near universal failure of school reform efforts to date, a growing chorus of education critics and policymakers now argue that all that's needed to change schools are new "market incentives" and national standards. According to some, "de-regulating" the school business and taking away the "monopoly" status public schools now enjoy will automatically make schools better. Free market competition and frequent testing for higher standards will shake up the bureaucracies as nothing has before, they maintain; educators will be forced to figure out ways to accomplish school improvement quickly and will be held accountable to rigorous national standards.

These two entwined ideas—so-called school choice and a system of national standards and tests—were the heart of the education planks of all three presidential candidates in the 1992 election. The only difference between the positions of the candidates was in how far they planned to extend "choice." President Bush wanted such a system to include private schools, and candidate Clinton did not. Shortly after taking office, President Clinton introduced legislation calling for public school choice, as well as new national academic standards and tests. These two policies are being debated currently by lawmakers at both the national and state level around the country. Not wanting to wait for national standards to take effect, a number of states are considering, or have recently passed, legislation which mandates greater school choice and more rigorous testing for achievement of state-set standards. In effect, many state legislators are offering parents more options and educators more control of their individual schools, but at the price of greater regulation through testing.

As a result, the time and energy needed for rethinking our educational goals as a nation is instead being spent on politicized debates about new strategies—strategies that have no clear educational goals and so are unlikely to create change in schools. We will look at each in turn.

The Limits of an Educational "Marketplace"

The idea of creating a kind of educational free market, as outlined (for example) by proponents John Chubb and Terry Moe in *Politics, Markets, and America's Schools*, is to allow parents to choose any school for their child—private or public.[2] All parents would be given "vouchers"—paper credits—for school tuition which could be "spent" anywhere. No longer would individual schools or even local districts have a "monopoly" on the education of children from a particular neighborhood or community. The public money raised through taxation for every child's education would go wherever the parents decided to send the child to school—private or public, out of district, or even out of state.

Proponents of this free market approach believe that schools doing the best job educating children would attract new "customers" and thrive, while those that did a poor job would eventually go out of business. Educational improvements would continue to occur as schools competed for a greater "market share." And, of course, the most successful schools could attract and retain the best teachers, paying them more, as is done with lawyers in leading law firms or managers in corporations. In such a marketplace, a school like Brimmer and May that supplies a high-quality "product" should theoretically prosper, while teachers reap the benefits of higher profits with ever-increasing paychecks.

But the education world is very different from the world of business. Some of the differences are obvious and have been commented on by many critics of school choice. Unlike businesses, for example, schools won't have budgets for TV ads to inform poor and minority parents about their products. These parents are also less likely to have the time and money to travel long distances for better schools. To address issues of equity, schools or government agencies would have to take on the expense of making all schools equally known and accessible to everyone. As we saw in the case of the many programs at Cambridge Rindge and Latin, even with such efforts, the estrangement of many poor and minority families from the entire school bureaucracy makes it difficult for them to exercise their choices as "educated consumers." Recent research has shown that in places where school choice has been available, it is primarily middle-class parents who exercise their choice.[3]

Furthermore, unlike businesses, schools don't all start with the same "raw materials." Schools that selectively admit academically more talented and motivated students will clearly get better results with test scores and college admissions than those that have a high percentage of "problem" students. Some schools would be much sought after, but could not and would not admit all who wanted to go. So long as schools—private or public—have the right to refuse admission to some students, school choice plans will result in a "creaming off" of the most talented students, who would be admitted to "better" schools while other schools were left to contend with increasing percentages of less academically able students in their classrooms. These schools will not just "go out of business," no matter how poor a job they do, for there would be no place to send their students—except to the streets and jails.

Again, unlike companies in the business world, the best schools would not, could not, simply expand to accommodate increased demands for their "product." Many fine schools prefer to stay small, while even those that might seek to improve or expand facilities would have an extremely difficult time raising the money to do so. In the case of public schools, bond issues or tax increases must often be passed; private schools must seek substantial donations from wealthy individuals.

Providing a high-quality education has never been a highly profitable endeavor—not even with motivated, affluent students, and especially not with students who need a great deal of remediation. Even in a well-run private school, tuition usually covers only about 85 percent of the operating costs—the "deficit" being made up with income from endowments and annual fund drives among parents and alumni. And most private schools keep costs down by refusing admission to students who have special needs or learning disabilities. In my view, it is highly unlikely that Christopher Whittle's Edison Project—a plan to create a national chain of for-profit schools that will charge a tuition half that of most existing independent schools—or other similar endeavors will ever turn a profit. If they do, it will be at the expense of students' real learning.

School choice as a public policy may save some motivated, predominately middle-class students from languishing in bad schools, and may further some teachers' and parents' efforts to create more autonomous schools with their own unique identity and cohesive community. These are reasons to support choice. But without a great deal of extra care and expense, choice as a stand-alone strategy will also likely increase the disparities between the haves and have-nots—and the consequent despair and violence—in our society. It is a high-risk policy of educational triage, not a strategy for systemic school reform.

Choice is also a strategy without a goal. Having more choices does not, by itself, define or improve quality. Implementing more choice programs is another way to avoid questions about what *all* schools should aspire to accomplish, questions which might lead to a clearer definition of what is a truly good school.

Choosing for the Right Reasons

For marketplace incentives to work in education, the assumption is that the "consumers"—that is, parents—both know how to judge a quality product and would make rational choices to send their children to the best schools. The example of Brimmer and May suggests otherwise. A closer look at Brimmer and May's experience reveals that the pressures of the educational marketplace—far from providing incentives for continuing innovation, as some education theorists postulate—actually constrains the school's ability to continue to evolve as a model educational experiment. "We're under pressure from parents to provide kids with a million and one course offerings and activities, to compete with the other schools in the area," one teacher told me. "The financial pressures on the school are enormous. We're trying to be all things to all people . . . and we can't."

Despite the qualitative improvement in the school's academic program that students, teachers, and parents have observed since it became a Coalition school, Brimmer and May has had to work very hard to maintain its enrollment and admission standards. From 1979 to 1989, the school had been able to increase enrollment from roughly 165 to 280. But in 1991–92, in the face of declining numbers of adolescents in the population and a regional economy in recession, the school experienced more difficulty maintaining those numbers—especially in grades nine through twelve, where many girls were transferring out.

Out of fifteen students who were in eighth grade together in 1990 at Brimmer and May, only ten remained in the fall of their tenth-grade year. The parents of several who left said they wanted coed schools for their daughters. Others said they wanted a larger school that offered a wider variety of sports and extracurricular opportunities. Although almost all parents agreed that the school was academically rigorous and doing a fine job, they still thought their children could somehow "get more" at a bigger, coed school.

Brimmer and May's unique pedagogy and educational philosophy were not cited by most parents as reasons for choosing the school. "I'd like to think they choose us because we're a Coalition school," Anne Reenstierna said, "but not too many do—maybe one or two students in the Upper School this year."

How many parents visit classes when considering where to send their children to school? How many prospective Academy parents visited classes in the different houses at Cambridge Rindge and Latin? How many Brimmer and May parents have really compared the academic challenges in the classrooms of different independent schools? Few, if any. Academic rigor does not appear to be the major consideration of most parents in decisions about where to send their children. The size of the campus, the number of extracurricular, sports, and course offerings, and, above all, the school's social cachet or prestige (whether deserved or not) hold more sway with parents. This was true both at Brimmer and May and at the Academy.

While Brimmer and May teachers would like to go even further in implementing a curriculum and whole-school program based on the Coalition principle of "less is more," the educational marketplace demands that Brimmer and May do the opposite—try to be "all things to all people." The school is under constant pressure to offer more courses, extracurricular offerings, and sports programs in order to compete with larger, more well-endowed prep schools in the area. More serious still, the school has had to become coeducational—against the better judgment of many.

Improving the enrollment picture was the main reason for this decision, as we learned. It isn't necessarily the best *educational* decision. Many of the administrators, teachers, trustees, and alumnae believed in the value of an all-girls secondary day school, and there are numerous studies that suggest that girls do learn more when not competing with boys.

The result of this decision is that Brimmer and May's projected enrollment of 310 students for 1993–94 is the highest ever, but some parents still talk about sending their sons and daughters to other, more well-known schools for the last years of high school. In the summer of 1993, Anne told me that a number of eighth-graders had been accepted at other schools for ninth grade, and their parents wanted them to transfer, but the students refused to go.

So the pressure on Anne and on the teachers is unrelenting, and the school must continue to work very hard to keep costs down, maintain a quality program, and hold to high academic standards—all while trying to pay teachers better salaries. At the same time, other larger, more well-endowed (and in my observation, much less intellectually challenging) prep schools in the area have little difficulty attracting and retaining top-notch students and paying faculty closer to what teachers in public schools make.

Standardized Tests: Part of the Problem, Not the Solution

How do we determine whether or not a school is doing a good job? How can we really know whether "student as worker, teacher as coach" makes a difference in the quality of Brimmer and May students' work as compared with the work of students who are educated more conventionally? The problem is not just that many parents choose schools for reasons other than academic quality, it is also that even when academic excellence becomes the main criteria of parents for their choice of schools, they have no way of knowing which schools are the best.

An inability to define and measure true educational quality—the bottom line—in schools is another reason why the business model fails both as a metaphor and as a primary strategy for school reform. While the profit margin determines how well a company is doing, there is no comparable reliable way to measure a school's successes.

Students' average scores from standardized multiple-choice tests, such as the Scholastic Aptitude Test (SAT), are widely used by colleges, school boards, and the media—and therefore by educators and parents—as indicators of a school's quality. But these tests do not measure the more subtle and sophisticated skills that students need in adult life. Former Xerox CEO David Kearns, coauthor of *Winning the Brain Race*, and many other business leaders decry "the tyranny of the $20, machine scorable, true and false tests" and stress the need for future employees to learn how to be lifelong learners, risk-takers, problem-solvers, and tolerant, respectful team players.[4] These are the skills that Brimmer and May teachers (and many others) are trying to impart, but we have no tests to measure the results. While Anne and the teachers described improvements they had observed in the quality of students' work, Judy Guild and others worried about how the results of the school's efforts would be assessed. "Colleges are still emphasizing SATs heavily in admissions, and I don't know if what we're doing will make a difference on the test scores," she said.

This same concern surfaced at a parents' evening I attended in May 1989. After viewing a film about the Coalition, one parent asked, "How are the Coalition schools measuring success—are students getting into better colleges? Are their test scores improving?" And another parent asked whether the Brimmer and May courses "covered what students needed for SATs."

Teachers, too, worried about the problem of SATs and college admissions. Over and over again, I heard the most experienced Coalition teachers at Brimmer and May express the concern that they might be sacrificing too much coverage of content in order to allow more time for students to be workers. While the school can now point to an increasingly successful track record with regard to college admissions, the question of what students truly need to know in all the different subject areas in order to do well on the SATs and achievement tests, and in college, continues to trouble teachers.

Brimmer and May teachers are experimenting with evaluations of student work based on individual and group projects, and on the contents of accumulated portfolios, as well as other kinds of "exhibitions of mastery," as proposed by Theodore Sizer.[5] Most of the European national exams are essay-based, and the state of Vermont is now piloting the use of student portfolios to assess how well schools are doing. These means of assessment can show the degree to which students have achieved some of the thinking and problem-solving skills mentioned above. Grant Wiggins, educational researchers at the Coalition of Essential Schools, and faculty at some of the leading Coalition schools are also developing important new approaches for more qualitative and performance-based assessments.[6] However, such tests are very time-consuming to create and to administer.

Developing state and national assessment systems that use reliable, scorable data from more sophisticated, "performance-based" tests to compare graduates from different schools will take a great deal of time and money—if it's done at all. Until such tests of students' real academic achievement become available and are widely used by colleges and employers in place of SATs, educational consumers will have no quick or easy way of knowing whether Brimmer and May's or the Academy's products are truly better than the competition's—except by direct observation. And too few parents know enough to ask thoughtful questions about what students are learning.

The all-too-likely scenario is a quicker, cheaper fix—the development of a series of state and national "standards," and computer-scored tests to measure them, that are not very different from existing ones. Wider use of such tests would further institutionalize test scores as the benchmark for quality. And so long as high standardized test scores define a "good" school, legislation for school choice will strengthen the monopoly of those traditional public and private prep schools that have histories of producing high scorers on SATs and graduates who go on to name-brand colleges, no matter how inadequate their curricula.

Although many public and private prep schools get good results because they start by admitting only the most academically talented students, they are rarely examples of best practices in education; in fact, they often do our country's "best and brightest" a serious disservice. Teachers at elite private and public schools pride themselves on preparing the most gifted students for the Ivy League colleges, but their assumptions about what is needed to do well in college are frequently out of date, or just plain mistaken, and they rarely think about what competencies students will need beyond college, for a happy and productive life.

My eldest daughter was an honors student for seven years in an independent school reputed to be one of the very best in New England. Six months after she graduated, when I asked her how well the school had prepared her for the work she now had to do at an Ivy League college, she did not rate the education she had received there very highly. She felt she'd been taught to repeat teachers' opinions more than she had been to develop her own, and that she had not been taught to work as a part of a group or to explore the connections between issues and subjects—skills that were now essential.

There is no time to allow students to work together or explore connections, public and private prep school teachers argue, because so much material must be covered to prepare students for college. That's what prep schools are for, after all. Yet when I conducted a focus group with recent graduates from a leading public high school, all of whom had gone on to attend a range of

Ivy League colleges and state universities, these students said that there was no prior subject-specific content required to do well in any of their college courses, except for math. While teachers at both my daughter's school and the one these students attended continue to justify most of their curriculum as being what is necessary for college, their students had in fact discovered that a very different set of skills was needed for life in and beyond college classrooms. (Many teachers enjoy chatting with their former students—especially those who have gone on to be successful—but rarely do they, or their schools, ask more formally for essential feedback on the education their former "customers" received. In this respect, schools could, indeed, learn from what is becoming a common marketplace practice.)

Creating a system of national standards and SAT-type tests would not only bolster the admission applications—and arrogance—of those schools with high scores, it would make schooling in all of the nation's classrooms more focused on "drill and fill" exercises. Teachers around the country would be pressured to spend more time studying sample tests and coaching and cajoling recalcitrant students to do well on them. Teaching to the test will become, de facto, the new national curriculum—one that is very boring, time-consuming, and educationally regressive. Instead of learning to think—to pose questions and to solve problems—students would likely be taught only what was required to pass national or state exams, which do not measure such competencies.

Rather than getting into the business of regulating a new educational marketplace and administering a system of national tests, federal and state governments can best encourage systemic change in schools by

- collecting and disseminating the increasing number of studies about what students should know and be able to do for work, citizenship, and further study (some proposals are outlined later in this chapter);

- supporting further research and development efforts for performance-based systems of assessment;
- providing technical assistance and venture capital for a national network of laboratory schools;
- devising new formulas for equalizing school funding across districts and for providing supplemental support for schools serving at-risk students;
- sponsoring and promulgating more research, especially qualitative research, about how systemic change in schools really happens;
- promoting national and local forums for discussions of new educational goals.

More choices of schools and wider use of more sophisticated forms of assessment may be useful strategies as part of a comprehensive school reform effort, but only if we have first answered basic questions: What is the real purpose of educational change? What kind of high school education will best prepare students for the twenty-first century?

Theodore Sizer's idea that the purpose of high schools must be to develop thinking abilities—or what he calls habits of mind—is an important one, as is Howard Gardner's concept of "education for understanding."[7] It is these definitions of the purpose of a high school education that give the strategy of "student as worker, teacher as coach" its strength and coherence. We saw how having this clear focus gave the change efforts at Brimmer and May a significant boost. But even there, after four years teachers and administrators had just begun to talk about what they thought a diploma should stand for. And at Hull and in the Academy, the question of the purpose of a high school education had not even been addressed.

Educational Change: Creating a New Vision

We need to begin with a redefinition of the educational "problem." Our schools have not somehow suddenly "failed." They have simply become obsolete. The present American public high school curriculum and standards for a diploma are more than a hundred years old and hopelessly out of date. They were formulated at a time when America needed a minimally educated blue-collar labor force, when few students were expected to finish high school and go to college, when most of what a young "scholar" needed to know might reasonably be divided into so-called Carnegie units (a system for standardizing the high school curriculum developed in 1905) and "covered" over a four-year period, and when the skills needed for citizenship and personal growth were very different than they are now.

Living in the midst of them, it is very difficult for any of us to really see and understand the economic, political, and social changes that have taken place in the past three decades and how these changes, in turn, require a new definition of what it means to be an educated adult. And so, too, many teachers, business and community leaders, and parents rely on old ways of thinking about education, and their own experiences as adolescents as they try to determine how schools can best be improved.

If you ask teachers why we need school reform, some are likely to talk about how students don't respect teachers, watch too much TV, and don't do homework anymore. The absence of supportive parents in the home is the main problem, as most teachers see it, and they have no idea what to do.

Many parents, on the other hand, yearn for "the little red schoolhouse of the 19th century, with its emphasis on basic skills and traditional values," according to recent research by the Public Agenda Foundation. They tend to think teachers make things "too easy" for kids and want schools to teach respect for hard work and adult authority.

School administrators often define "the problem" as simply how to get more students to attend classes and graduate, and to raise SAT and other test scores. Pizza parties for the homerooms with the best attendance rates, academically diluted work-study internships for potential dropouts, and coaching kids for standardized tests are some currently popular strategies for achieving these goals. Most of these efforts, no matter how well-intentioned, will not teach students the skills that business and community leaders say are needed in the workplace now.

When thinking about school improvement, many educators pay little attention to the pronouncements of business leaders for several reasons. Some CEOs sound as though they are only concerned about developing students as "human resources" that will enable business to compete more effectively in the world marketplace. Also, business leaders do not speak with a clear or consistent voice about the skills they seek. CEOs are quoted in the media with increasing frequency about the need to improve schools in order to have a better-prepared work force, but few spell out what "better-prepared" might mean. For a persistent few it is still vocational training, for some it is simple mastery of "the basics," while for others it is proficiency in "higher order" skills.

One of the most startling and unexpected findings of my research in these three schools was that while most adults shared a commitment to educational change, they had never discussed *why* we need fundamental educational reform. Nor was there agreement about what most needs changing. In the epigraphs at the beginning of the Hull, Academy, and Brimmer and May chapters, Claire, Ruben, and Anne all describe the need for educational reform in terms of how both students and the world have changed, but the language of even these very thoughtful leaders is rather general.

In over thirty interviews that I conducted with adults for this study—including administrators, board of trustees and school committee members, teachers, and parents—the answers that I received to the questions of whether or not and why we need fundamental educational reform were even less clear. Changes in society, changes in kids, the need to motivate students, and greater respect for teachers were some recurring themes—but in none of these interviews were the *goals* of educational reform clear to the people who were most involved in trying to make it happen:

"Yes, we need reform. There's been so many changes in society so schools have to change. We need new approaches to education. But I'm not sure how we should go about it. It scares me to think that we might be going about it in the wrong way." (Hull teacher)

"Public education is in a mess. There's an internal problem in schools, as well as external problems—problems in the home and in lack of morals in our society. Internally, there's burnout. Staff has become flaccid." (Hull teacher)

"We absolutely need school reform. It just isn't working. Kids have a whole different agenda now. They lack the motivation, knowledge, and discipline that they used to have." (Hull teacher)

"Yes, we need school reform. We're using a model of education for a world that existed fifty years ago. I am struck by the statistic that in 1960 only 60 percent of the kids graduated from high school because most were going to work in a factory. Now that's not true."

(Hull school board member)

"The methods that we used over the years just aren't working with kids we're getting now—with all the problems they have, and the upheavals in their lives and in society." (Academy teacher)

"The rhetoric is that teachers are important. But the reality is that people don't care about teachers at this level. Everybody talks about how improving school climate starts with

the teacher—with teacher empowerment. But in reality teachers are not valued as they should be."
(Academy teacher)

"I'm not sure what you mean by school reform. I don't think our high school is perfect. Certainly we need change. But do we need reform? I'm not sure. Should we do away with the principal and have teachers run it? I do think we need to move toward more involvement of teachers but not tear the place down."
(Cambridge school committee member)

"I don't know if I'm qualified to answer that question. My gut feeling is that schools need to respond to the community they're in, to the different kinds of kids. In general, I think our society needs to put more emphasis on education." (Brimmer and May teacher)

"We need school reform for a lot of reasons. Every ed report that comes out, every time you pick up a paper, you find that school districts are in some terrible trouble. Our system of factory-style education doesn't fit the times. We're assuming that the same approach we used in the first half of the century will fit and it doesn't. I think we need to blow up the existing structures—the teacher ed programs, teacher standards, the bloated bureaucracies. We have to rethink everything: buildings, curriculum, tracking."
(Brimmer and May teacher)

"The first problem is the education of educators. We're not recruiting the right kind of people for the job. There's a shortfall of quality teachers." (Brimmer and May trustee)

These quotes suggest that in any school trying to undertake reform the first task is an intellectual one: to develop a broader and clearer understanding of the kinds of changes that have taken place in America and the world in the last quarter century. Developments in the world economy, the quickening pace of global social, technological, and environmental change, and the changing emotional needs of adolescents all must be considered.

Described below are four elements of an analytic framework for thinking about these issues, a framework which in turn suggests new and more sharply defined goals for education.

Education for a Changing Economy

Over the last twenty-five years, we have shifted from a society where most people earned their living with skilled hands to one in which more and more people must have and use a skilled intellect to earn a decent living. We have gone from a predominately industrial, blue-collar economy to one that is based on white-collar work related to services, information analysis, and technology. This fundamental change requires that we have a more highly educated labor force. Where in 1960 we only needed 20 percent of our work force to have completed high school and some college, today that figure is somewhere between 60 and 80 percent.

The high-tech, restructured workplace of the 1990s—both profit and nonprofit, white- and blue-collar—also requires new kinds of skills. According to David Kearns, former CEO of Xerox, "Today's successful companies bear little resemblance to the companies of ten or twenty years ago. . . . It's decentralized, relying on the know-how and professionalism of workers close to the problems. It's innovative in the deployment of personnel, no longer relying on limited and limiting job-classifications. . . . Indeed, the job descriptions for our technical and scientific employees—and our sales force, as well—sound much like the characteristics that make a good teacher: imagination, resourcefulness, energy, intelligence, mastery of a field, ability to communicate, and enthusiasm."[8]

And so the first skill that all high school graduates need is the ability to learn on their own. They must also learn how to work effectively in teams, as increasingly this is the way all work is organized in large organizations. Finally, well-prepared workers must know how to solve problems and take initiative—in a word, innovate. Many educators, preoccupied with teaching what they think is required to do well on standardized tests and in college, have not even begun to consider how to teach and assess these new and critical workplace skills.

Education for Continuing Learning

The new technology-based "information age" demands that we also rethink essential knowledge in the major subject-area disciplines. It is estimated that our culture's knowledge base doubles perhaps as often as every seven years. Neil Rudenstine, president of Harvard University, recently suggested that "the 'half life' of what is learned in the humanities is eight or ten years, and in math and the sciences, it is three or four."[9] Information-laden textbooks and curricula written only five or ten years ago are now badly out of date.

The essential skill for the information age is not how to memorize information, but how to use and make sense of it. Far more important than memorization of facts is the development of a breadth of understanding of central concepts and the ability to integrate knowledge within, as well as across, traditional disciplines. While E. D. Hirsch's call for "cultural literacy" deserves consideration in discussions about what high school graduates should know and be able to do,[10] the development of students' abilities to be lifelong learners and to use knowledge in new ways must be the overriding curriculum goal. Above all, students must learn to solve problems and to create new understandings. "Cultural literacy," or any other "content-specific" curriculum, is a useful tool, but only when seen as a means to achieving these competencies.

Education for World Citizenship

Social change—global change—is now the norm of our life. We take it for granted that the world is becoming smaller, more complex, more interdependent, and more seriously threatened by new technologies and the effects of industrial growth. Yet we have not taken the time to consider what these profound changes imply for the ways in which we prepare the young for their future. Meanwhile, it seems that fewer and fewer adolescents bother to vote or even to read a newspaper. While business leaders talk about creating a "world-class" work force, very few in the community are discussing the critical need to educate for active and informed world citizenship.

Educators must first consider how to help adolescents better understand and respect others from diverse cultural and ethnic backgrounds. This must be both communicated as a core value in schools and taught as an essential skill, not just for enlightened citizenship, but also for working in teams and doing business in an increasingly global marketplace. Young people must be taught how to sift through complex or contradictory information, understand divergent points of view, and think critically and creatively about a wide range of social problems. Finally, academic and extracurricular activities—such as internships and community service projects—must be developed to nurture a broader awareness of civic issues and the spirit of service. In my experience, these programs also help adolescents to know that social change is possible, and so to feel more hopeful about the future.[11]

Education for Personal Growth and Health

In our consumer-driven society, an increasingly seductive and distracting mass media culture subliminally promotes certain values and habits: passivity, the desire for instant gratification, and a kind of hungry self-centeredness. Increasingly, adolescents—and many of the rest of us, as well—too often want it all, want it now, and want it without effort, as we have discussed. Core values that promote individual growth and development are not by themselves enough to counteract these influences. Even when students wish to, many lack the *capacity* to sustain concentration on a difficult task or even to be alone without distractions for a period of time.

Yet without mastery of these skills, people cannot do serious intellectual or creative work. They cannot pursue individual interests or use their leisure time productively. Nor, it may be argued, will they have the emotional aliveness and inner discipline required to understand other people, remain committed in relationships over time, or be effective and loving parents. Community leaders, educators, and parents, too often distracted by mini-controversies such as whether or not to distribute condoms in high schools, have not begun to consider the deeper questions of how to both nurture the values and teach the skills necessary for personal growth and health in our society. Nor have we begun talking together about how we can respond to the increased stress and lack of emotional support in students' lives.

Drugs, alcohol, sex, and violence are more and more a part of the everyday life of adolescents—in both public and private schools. Adolescents experience enormous peer pressure to become involved in any or all of these activities at a younger and younger age. Lacking the active presence of concerned adults in their lives, many adolescents do not have the inner strength necessary to resist the pressure of peers or the motivation to do well in school. While they are generally scornful of one-day adult-dominated "drug and alcohol awareness programs," many long for opportunities to talk to peers and to caring, nonjudgmental adults about pressures in their lives and related larger questions of values, as we saw.

The high school curriculum of the future must focus both on new intellectual competencies and on new methods of teaching that develop the capacities and the motivation needed for productive work and more disciplined forms of adult play rooted in creating, not consuming. With opportunities to pursue their real interests, as well as the chance to master adult competencies, students will be far more motivated to acquire the capacities needed for both—curiosity and enthusiasm for learning, concentration, self-discipline, and the ability to work both collaboratively and independently.

* * *

Education for the twenty-first century, then, must develop adolescents' workplace skills, citizenship skills, and skills for personal growth and health. English, social studies, geography, math, science, the arts, and other traditional subject matter become the means or the content for the teaching of these skills.

Many of the competencies required for work and citizenship are congruent with some of the more traditional goals of an outstanding liberal arts education: a broad understanding of mathematical and scientific concepts, and of cultures and peoples; the ability to communicate clearly, to reason, to think critically, and to solve problems. However, the new curricula that reflect recent profound changes in the nature of work and knowledge—that redefine the meaning and content of a liberal arts education—remain to be developed.

Here are a few examples of the competencies we might expect of students before they leave high school.[12]

To be prepared for a changing economy, students should be able to

- formulate questions about difficult issues—questions that indicate understanding of the issues—and create an oral and written presentation about the problem and possible alternative solutions;
- discuss the implications of a mathematically expressed hypothesis;
- accurately critique and assess their own and group learning.

To be capable of continuing learning, they should know how to

- design independent research projects in mathematics, science, and humanities, using appropriate research tools and techniques;
- state a hypothesis and present supporting evidence in an organized and persuasive fashion orally and in writing in both humanities and science curriculum areas;

- analyze and describe a historical period from several different perspectives.

With regard to world citizenship, the goal should be students who

- exhibit tolerance for diversity of others' viewpoints, and recognize the contributions of differing opinions to a discussion;
- can carry out a community service project;
- can resolve conflicts when disagreement persists on an issue and action is needed.

For personal growth and health, students should be able to

- set realistic personal goals—as demonstrated by the articulation of a post-graduation work/education plan;
- sustain a long-term relationship with at least one adult outside their immediate family;
- pursue an individual, nonacademic interest or hobby on a regular basis outside of school.

Tools and Strategies for Building Consensus

If educational goals and core values are developed by a few educators in isolation from their communities, no matter how well thought out they may be they will not create the conditions needed for change. Unless there is a broader consensus, efforts to develop new programs will always be vulnerable to changes in the political winds.

Communities are daily torn apart by increasingly polarized and polemical debates about schools. We saw that this was true even in the school committee meeting of a "progressive" city like Cambridge. Around the country, programs for school-based management, school choice, and multicultural education are hotly contested, while school budgets are being slashed. Without a consensus about what the goals of school reform should be, we lack a framework for making intelligent decisions about strategies, educational and financial priorities, and the training needed for change. Nor will budgets or strategies for change be sustained over a period of years.

And so the first priority in communities must be to develop a broad-based consensus about the goals of high school reform, priorities for the curriculum, and the most effective ways to measure progress.

How do we begin building such a consensus? Governments, colleges and businesses, outside consultants, and the media all have important new work to do to support the efforts of local communities as they struggle with what their high school graduates should know and be able to do.

The Role of Government

Federal and state governments are in the best position to collect, analyze, and disseminate information from the growing proliferation of studies and reports about what high school graduates need to know and be able to do. Reports from various groups on job-related skills—such as the National Center on Education and the Economy's report, "America's Choice: High Skills or Low Wages," and the report of the Secretary's Commission of Achieving Necessary Skills (SCANS), "What Work Requires of Schools"—need to be studied and synthesized for use by local communities.[13]

The national reports of various organizations that have focused on more content-specific standards for high school graduates are also an important source of ideas. "Guidelines for Geographic Education," put out by the National Council for Geographic Education and the Association of American Geographers; the American Association for the Advancement of Science's blueprint for developing scientific literacy, "Science for All Americans"; and the report of the National Council of Teachers of Mathematics should all be analyzed, along with forthcoming reports from the National Council for the Social Studies, the National Council of Teachers of English, and others.[14]

However, these reports must be viewed skeptically. Subject

content experts, like many individual high school teachers, often outline what they think students should know in their subject area with the assumption that all students will do further work in that field and without considering everything else that students must learn. Communities will ultimately have to decide their own educational priorities.

Several organizations, such as the Center for Civic Education, have developed curricula related to citizenship skills.[15] Other groups have developed materials for health and parenting education and for teaching practical skills such as money management. These materials should also be reviewed.

It may also be useful for state governments to use these reports to create their own guidelines for what high school graduates should know and be able to do. I make this recommendation cautiously, because guidelines can often be interpreted as requirements—thus seriously restricting local control and autonomy. Nevertheless, California, Connecticut, Maine, New Hampshire, Pennsylvania, and Vermont are among the states that have recently developed guidelines for competencies which are worth considering. Pennsylvania has also become the first state to eliminate the acquisition of Carnegie units as the basis for granting a high school diploma.[16]

What Colleges and Local Employers Must Do

College and university admissions offices must wean themselves from the "numbers approach" to their decision making. The use of standardized test scores for college admissions purposes has only served to strengthen the American preoccupation with standardized tests and has spawned a whole new "test-prep" industry. Colleges can best promote high school improvement by paying more attention to students' portfolios of collected work and other more qualitative assessments of academic achievement, and by relying less on SATs. Admissions materials also need to emphasize citizenship and service as important qualities for both admission and success in college life. Finally, colleges can help to break down old myths about what's needed to do well in their courses by publishing materials which spell out the subject-area core knowledge and competencies needed for academic success.

Faculty in schools of education have an especially vital role in the change process. They can help redefine the new competencies educators will need to develop clear goals, core values, and collaboration in schools—and then prepare future educators for new roles. Through a more focused collaboration with public schools, they can also offer the training and technical assistance needed by teachers. Finally, education schools must take the lead in creating model lab school programs such as the one John Dewey created at the University of Chicago at the turn of the century. We need demonstration sites where new curricula are developed, present and future teachers get hands-on experience with new methods, and citizens can see new forms of teaching and learning in action.

Employers can also contribute to the development of consensus about what a high school education should be by publishing their own sets of standards and skill expectations for prospective employees.

With these kinds of assistance, local communities will be in a far better position to make some informed choices about curriculum priorities and expectations for high school graduates. What is needed next is a new methodology in schools and towns for considering this new information and promoting the development of consensus about educational goals among people with very different points of view.

Focus Groups and "Town Meetings for Learning"

In the past, many communities have set up committees to rewrite curriculum goals. Almost invariably, they have produced long lists of what high school students should learn. However, rarely do such committees engage in "reality checks"—that is, consideration of how much can be taught in four years, what the priorities should be, and what the implications are for new teaching strategies—or in discussions about how the community might know if any of its education goals were being met. So while the goals were distributed in nicely printed documents, they rarely effected change in schools.

If yet another committee were merely to collect all the new information from many sources about what should be taught to high school students, they would only be contributing to the problem of a curriculum already overburdened with add-ons of "things to cover." A high school curriculum cannot do it all—teach all the workplace skills that business leaders might want, cover all the content-specific materials that academics decree, prepare students to be competent citizens and parents, and encourage students to pursue individual interests and perform community service. Citizens in local communities—not academic experts and not the federal government—must make informed but difficult choices about priorities for their children's education.

We need new formats for discussions to consider the alternatives and work for consensus. Just as a growing number of businesses and political parties have done, so must schools move toward using qualitative research in order to understand what and how people think about education.

Focused group discussions with twelve or so people led by a trained moderator have been used very successfully for years by the Public Agenda Foundation, founded by public opinion analyst Daniel Yankelovich and former secretary of state Cyrus Vance, to understand how people think about complex social problems and policy questions, and to uncover significant areas of disagreement and agreement. Focus group results are a far better indicator of people's deepest concerns and priorities for change than are the more commonly used public opinion polls. For example, while surveys show strong general public support for "generic" school reform, focus group research conducted by Public Agenda in 1991 on the opinions of business and community leaders versus the public's perceptions of the educational "problem" revealed important differences in these two groups' priorities for change. "Although experts tend to stress the kinds of skills required for the 21st-century world of work—skills such as communications, problem-solving, a grasp of basic scientific and mathematical concepts, familiarity with computers, the ability to work as part of a team—much of the public seems to yearn for the little red schoolhouse of the 19th century, with its emphasis on basic skills and traditional values."[17]

Focus groups can also be used successfully to introduce new ways of viewing a problem. This latter use of focus groups is critical for the school change process. It is far easier to develop consensus on the problems and priorities for educational change among different groups when they are first presented with a common context for viewing the issues, a context such as the four-point framework for understanding change that I have proposed.

Serious efforts for systemic change in schools, then, might begin with a series of focus group sessions—including present and prospective parents, business and community leaders, educators, and present and former students—around questions related to the strengths, weaknesses, and priorities for change of a community's schools.

In one high school community where I recently conducted a series of two-hour focused discussions with representative groups, we considered the following questions: What significant changes have occurred in our society since you left high school? In light of these changes, what are some of the most important things for high school graduates to know and be able to do? How can we know if students have mastered these competencies? After considering these issues, what do you now see as our high school's strengths, weaknesses, and the priorities for change?

There were some startling findings—as well as significant rewards—for the courageous team of high school teachers and administrators who sponsored this focus group series. First, we found that business leaders, community members, and parents, when they stopped to think about all the changes that have taken place in our society, no longer put the blame on teachers for the problems that concerned them in schools; they were able to acknowledge that everyone must take more responsibility for the improvement of education. Second, after people had an opportunity to hear one another and to reflect on the challenges of preparing students for the twenty-first century, they were much more prepared to support profound curriculum changes—including a greater focus on competencies rather than coverage, more interdisciplinary and team teaching, and the development of alternative forms of assessment such as portfolios and projects—than teachers had assumed.

Focus group work with students in the same community revealed that they, too, believed they should take more responsibility for their own learning. But they also said their school was deeply divided into cliques and that they needed an improved school climate, one which promoted greater respect for students and adults alike. Students also wanted closer informal advisor relationships between teachers and students.

Finally, this process contributed to an increased sense of trust and respect for educators in the community. *Everyone* appreciated the invitation to become more involved and the opportunity to have a voice. Focus groups, then, offer a significant first step toward clarifying academic goals and core values, as well as a way to initiate greater collaboration.

This school's next step is to present these findings, as well as some possible priorities for change, to the larger community at what I call a "town meeting for learning," where all will try to understand and work through areas of agreement and disagreement.

Through such town meetings for learning, business and community leaders, academics, teachers, parents, and even older students can come together, first to hear data from focus groups as a starting point for discussion, and then to consider what skills and knowledge they think are most important for all graduates.

Such evenings are occasions for genuine dialogue and learning together, the goal being to create a public mandate for change which is broadly based and sustainable. An alternative to what has become an increasingly acrimonious and adversarial educational debate, town meetings for learning hold the promise of bringing together the diverse elements of communities on new common ground—a shared concern for all our children.

An impartial moderator for such meetings is essential and is among the new resources needed in the school change process. Many schools are beginning to discover that in addition to specific kinds of training and greater involvement of parents and community members, they need the help of an outsider, one whom Theodore Sizer would call a "critical friend." A consultant who has both an understanding of the research and broad experience in schools attempting change can lead focus group sessions; help educate the community about economic and social changes as they are related to education; facilitate the development of goals, priorities, and strategies; teach new skills; and critique the ongoing work of committees, individual teachers, and administrators. Many school people hang on to the notion that they ought to be able to manage change by themselves—for reasons of both pride and expense, but corporations, who routinely use long-term consultants to help facilitate change, have found that the additional expense is more than offset by substantial improvements in both the speed and effectiveness of their change process.

New Roles for the Media

Local and regional public media have an important role to play in helping to develop a new consensus about what a local town or community's high school diploma should really mean. Rather than focusing on controversies, which fuels an adversarial process, the media could participate in a public service campaign to inform everyone about research, the nature of the issues, and most importantly, the emerging common ground. In several such nonpartisan public education efforts, pioneered by the Public

Agenda Foundation, the general level of understanding and quality of discussion for even complex policy issues among citizens in large cities was greatly elevated. In areas where this strategy has been utilized, it has become significantly easier to develop and sustain broad and long-term public support for new policy directions.[18] Such long-term public support is crucial for new initiatives in education to continue.

Task Forces to Develop Goals and Methods of Assessment

Once there is a broader and more widely shared understanding of what a high school diploma should mean, task forces led by educators, but with community, parent, educator, and student representation could then begin to outline in more detail the kinds of workplace, citizenship, and personal growth skills—as well as core information in different academic subjects—all students might be expected to master. They can also begin to consider how these competencies would be best assessed. If a diploma is to certify that a student has learned both to work effectively in a team and carry out independent projects, for example, then the traditional standardized multiple-choice tests will not serve as an adequate means of assessment. Task forces can begin to look at true performance-based indicators of competencies, such as those described earlier in this chapter.

With the work of task forces in hand, educators can begin to break down broad goals and indicators into age- and subject-appropriate categories. And with appropriate skills and knowledge clearly identified for different points in the high school experience, entry requirements for high school—and thus the broad outline of curricula for elementary and middle schools—will also become clearer.

When there is a broad consensus and a shared understanding of new educational goals, change at all levels becomes much more possible in schools, and a variety of new strategies and partnerships emerges.

Teachers no longer feel bound by the mandate to cover an outdated, information-based curriculum. Encouraged to take risks and think of their work as action research, they can begin to try the new classroom strategies that are most likely to both engage students and teach specific skills. In such an environment of ongoing "R & D," experience shows that teachers are more motivated to seek out models of new programs in other communities, try new ideas, critique one another's efforts, and work more collaboratively with colleagues and parents. The kinds of additional training teachers and parents need then becomes more clear.

With consensus on clear goals, priorities for school budgets will be easier to determine and public support will be more readily sustained. There will also be a more rational framework for considering alternative school schedules and structures of the workplace for teachers. Finally, schools can develop new or improved models for school-business partnerships and school-based community social services that better meet the needs of students and parents.

Creating Learning Communities

All that we have discussed in this chapter points to a fundamental redefinition of teachers' roles in schools. They must, of course, be the architects of change—as the Carnegie Commission report *A Nation Prepared*[19] and other studies have suggested. But to do that work effectively, I argue, all educators must also become masters of two worlds: the intellectual and emotional world of students and the emerging world of newly redefined adult skills and competencies. Teachers and administrators must become anthropologists who study more closely students' individual and group life circumstances, needs, and interests, as well as what the adult world will require of them. This means maintaining a simultaneous focus on where students are coming from and where students are going—beyond college—and what they will need to get there. In the crucible of the curriculum, teachers must bring together these two constantly changing worlds.

However, teachers should no longer feel as though they can or must take on these challenges alone. With clearer goals and a better understanding of some of the new strategies to be used, everyone—educators, community members, parents, and the students themselves—can become more involved in a very different and dynamic process of systemic school change. New ways of changing schools require a greater involvement of the entire school community in an ongoing critical examination of goals and practices: going back and forth between setting goals, looking at best practices elsewhere, developing new programs, assessing results, further refining the goals, and then trying out still more new ideas. As I suggested in the Brimmer and May chapter, this means developing what some in business characterize as a "learning organization"—or, more appropriate for schools, "a learning community"—which calls upon the talents of many to help create continuous improvements.

Time: The Essential Resource

We must understand that even with greater consensus, collaboration, and outside help, change is neither quick nor easy. In my experience, the scarcest resource in the change process is time, even more than money. Time for teachers to meet to discuss students' needs, observe each other's classes, assess their work, design new curricula, visit other schools, and attend workshops. Time for teachers and students to get to know each other. Time for parents and community members to become involved in children's learning. Time for leaders at all levels to reflect and plan collaboratively. Time—perhaps five years—to rethink the purposes of education, reinvent teaching and learning, and create new school cultures.

No doubt many of the new goals and strategies that I have outlined here will strike some as not only time-consuming but also risky, even utopian, perhaps. But what are the alternatives? After more than a decade of national school reform efforts, high schools are more obsolete than ever, and some college educators claim the writing and thinking skills of entering freshmen are still getting worse every year.

More school choice may, at best, permit a few able students to attend marginally better schools, but such programs will not fundamentally improve the school experience for most American students, while an increased emphasis on national standards and multiple-choice tests will only further burden and "dumb down" a hopelessly out of date curriculum that tries to "cover" everything. At worst, these policies will increase the gap between those students who think themselves "winners" and those who know that, through no fault of their own, they have been labeled "losers." The potential social and economic costs of an increasing polarization of our young people are staggering.

What we need most in order to improve our nation's schools are not new policy gimmicks and tests, but rather some old-fashioned democratic virtues—thoughtful leadership, greater clarity and consensus about academic goals and core values, and new forms of collaboration at many levels. The high school of the future can and must be invented in many individual schools and towns by groups of active citizens working together to define and teach real adult competencies, to express more active caring for the next generation, and to re-create community.

Can educators make the case in their communities for taking the risks, as well as the time, needed to do this important work? Perhaps, but only by creating inclusive, thoughtful, compelling conversations about purposes and other important questions. And then by acting with urgency, discipline, and courage.

The dedicated people in Hull, in the Academy at Cambridge Rindge and Latin, and at Brimmer and May have made a significant beginning. Their work continues.

FIVE

Reflections at the Dawn of the Millennium

As I mention in the introduction to the second edition of this book, much has changed in the world since the completion of the book in 1993. In this chapter I review briefly the important educational policy changes that have taken place in the 1990s, both nationally and in Massachusetts. Without this background one cannot make sense of what has happened in the last seven years in Hull, Cambridge Rindge and Latin High School, and the Brimmer and May School. I also think the Massachusetts story is an invaluable case study about how educational reform actually takes place at the state level.

After telling the story of the evolution of educational reform efforts in Massachusetts, I go on to consider the impact of these changes on our three schools. Finally, at the end of the chapter, I reflect on some new lessons learned from these case studies about what will—and will not—contribute to improving all students' education.

"High Stakes"—A Fast-Changing Policy Context

The movement to introduce "choice" into the public education "market," primarily through the creation of charter schools, has swept the country with great speed in the last five years. While the enabling legislation—and thus the schools themselves—vary greatly from state to state, generally charter schools are publicly funded schools, which are organized and managed outside the confines of the public school district bureaucracy. Students and their families "choose" to go to these schools, and the state or district provides per-student funding to the charter school usually comparable to what other public schools receive in conventional districts.

Minnesota was the first state to pass charter school legislation in 1991. Currently 36 states and the District of Columbia have charter school legislation, and there are more than 1,600 charter school sites in operation, serving about 250,000 students or about 0.8 percent of the total public school population.[1]

The standards movement has moved through this country with equal speed and will likely have far greater impact than charter schools in the next few years. Between 1996 and 2000 the number of states that had established new achievement standards for public school students in core academic subjects leapt from 14 to 49. The number of states that provided some kind of public "report card" on individual school performance on standardized tests has gone from a handful to 36 in ten years, while states requiring passing grades on tests for promotion or graduation—so called high stakes tests—has jumped from 17 to 27 in only four years.[2]

With the passage of the Education Reform Act of 1993, Massachusetts has rapidly moved into the forefront of states pushing the twin strategies of giving families greater school choice, through the establishment of charter schools, and developing higher academic standards and high stakes tests. The history of the bill and its implementation by the state board of education is an interesting case study of increasing business involvement in education and the politicization of educational reform efforts.

Paul Reville, executive director of the Massachusetts Business Alliance for Education (MBAE) since its founding in 1988 and currently a lecturer at the Harvard Graduate School of Education, explained the origins and intent of the bill in a recent interview with me:

MBAE was founded by a number of business leaders in the state who realized that business had better do more in schools than form local partnerships if they wanted to have real impact on improving student achievement. There needed to be a state business voice.

We spent several years studying the issues and developed a plan for comprehensive change, *Every Child a Winner*, in 1991. Eighty percent of our plan was incorporated into the 1993 bill. It was the most significant school reform bill in decades, and yet it passed with relatively little grassroots support.

At its heart, the bill was a trade-off: more money for schools in return for significant reform and increased accountability. The state's education system had been ravaged by the effects of Proposition Two-and-a-Half [the impact of which on Hull I chronicled in chapter 1]. Essentially, the bill guaranteed financial adequacy, equity, and stability to school districts that were overly dependent on local real estate taxes for school finance.

Approximately $250 million of new money went to school districts every year for seven years, doubling the state's investment in education, through a complex formula that made sure every community did its part, with the state filling the gap in poorer communities. The bill ensured that every district would be funded at what we called a "foundation" level. We pulled together a group of superintendents to define "adequacy" for educational funding—what it would take to run a "Ford Taurus" district, and that became the "foundation level" of basic funding.

The provision creating charter schools was included in the bill at the last minute. Some leaders in the business community thought the only way to change public schools was through the pressure of charters and vouchers. It showed how the business community was, itself, divided on strategy.

The law provided for the creation of publicly funded charter schools, and 15 new schools came into existence in 1995. By 1999 there were 39 schools in operation, with a total enrollment of 9,673 students, about 1 percent of the state's total public school enrollment.[3]

> At first educators thought it was just a money bill, and they were very happy. But there was no way business leaders were going to provide educators with more money without real change and accountability. It took awhile for the understaffed State Department of Education to begin getting the word out.

In addition to his position at the Business Alliance, Paul also served on the Massachusetts State School Board from 1991 to 1996. He was both an observer and a participant in the state's efforts to implement the new reform law.

> In 1994 there were a series of high-profile hearings on the new Common Core of Learning—what every high school graduate should know and be able to do. Then we set to work on new "Curriculum Frameworks" and "Content and Learning Standards." [They prescribe what all students are supposed to know and be able to do in each subject at the end of the fourth, eighth, tenth, and twelfth grades.] It was a very inclusive process. The same was initially true of the "Curriculum Framework" development process. In fact, one reason why the standards are "a mile wide and an inch deep" is precisely because the process was so democratic. Everyone's point of view and priority got included.

While this may have been true, when it came to the assessment system as it was originally conceived, there was an obvious "progressive" educational slant that pleased many reform-minded educators. The State Department of Education's 1994

Five Year Plan had stated that "the new assessment system will strive towards a goal of authenticity by incorporating essay, problem solving, and other open ended questions in place of multiple choice." The plan went on to state that there is "a limit to how authentic an assessment can be if it focuses on how a student performs at a single sitting. Other, more authentic, approaches to student assessment will utilize techniques such as interdisciplinary projects and student portfolios to measure the development of students' skills in real life situations over an extended period of time."[4] However, this focus was soon lost, according to Paul, for both financial and political reasons.

> There was good language about "multiple forms of assessment" in the bill, but most of our [the state board's] focus was on the curriculum frameworks. It took a great deal of time to do all the hearings around the state. We got behind schedule. We met with Advanced Systems a few times [the firm that was awarded the contract to develop new statewide tests.] They explained what percent of the test had to be multiple choice, versus essay-based, but we decided to leave these technical matters to the Department of Education to work out with the test maker.
>
> Then John Silber was appointed chair of the school board by Weld in November 1995. [Silber is the former president of Boston University and was the democratic candidate for governor in 1994. He lost to Republican Bill Weld in a very hotly contested election, during which he earned a reputation for frequent bitter attacks on anyone who disagreed with him.]
>
> He demanded plenipotentiary powers and wanted to choose his own board. The legislature essentially gave him what he wanted. The board was reduced from sixteen to nine, and the new members were all very ideological. They were all outside critics who had never worked inside the system. All they knew how to do was lob grenades.

Paul knew his tenure with the reconstituted board would be short-lived. It turned to be even shorter than he had thought.

> The first thing Silber did at our initial meeting was attack a Department of Education document, which stated that all children can learn at high levels. He said it was a ridiculous proposition and went on and on about how everyone knows that not all children have the same abilities.
>
> I tried to explain that the department meant we could be doing a much better job for all kids, not that all children had the same IQ. The next day I received a phone call, informing me that Jim Peyser had been appointed to my slot. [Peyser is head of the Pioneer Institute, an organization that advocates for charter schools and school vouchers. He currently serves as chair of the state board.] Of course, Silber felt compelled to re-do everything, including the curriculum frameworks and content standards.

Silber is a strong advocate for a "back to basics" approach to curriculum and believes that memorization of factual information has an important role in the curriculum—and thus the state tests. I asked Paul about where things stand in the state now.

> With the confusion of constantly changing curriculum frameworks, the time line for the new tests is much too quick. And the consequences fall too much on kids, not the adults. It is a very tense time in the state, politically.

Paul is referring to the imposition of the new Massachusetts Comprehensive Assessment System tests (MCAS). In 1998 they were given to all public school students in fourth, eighth, and tenth grades, statewide, for the first time in three subject areas: English language arts, mathematics, and science and technology. Testing in a fourth subject area, history and social science, was added to the eighth grade battery in 1999.

The state board of education has decided that, beginning in 2003, students who do not pass the tenth grade MCAS tests will not be able to receive a high school diploma. The consequences could be dramatic—both for schools and for students.

In 1999, 32 percent of all the tenth grade students in the state failed the English language arts test, an increase of 4 percent from the percent failing in 1998. And 53 percent of the tenth graders failed the mathematics test, a 1 percent increase in the failure rate from the year before.[5]

The numbers are far worse for minorities. According to a recent University of Massachusetts study, if passing the MCAS had been a graduation requirement in 1999, 83 percent of Hispanic high school students would not have graduated. And 80 percent of the black students would not have received their diplomas.[6]

Some educators claim the tests are little more than an academic version of "Trivial Pursuit," and test memorization rather than real intellectual skills—a far cry from what the 1993 bill and Five Year Plan had originally called for. Others are more concerned with the potentially catastrophic consequences of large numbers of students being retained in grades 3, 7, and 9 in order to improve test scores, as well as the impact of denying large numbers of students a high school diploma. They cite research that shows a high correlation between grade retention and increased school dropout rates. This group also argues that substantial additional resources and more time will be required in order to significantly improve students' achievement levels—smaller classes, remedial instruction, and a longer school day and year.

As the policy debate swirls around the state house, the most important question, I think, is what the real impact of these reform efforts on schools and districts is? How do community leaders and practitioners perceive these policy initiatives, and what are they doing in response? To answer these questions, I returned to each of the three communities I initially researched for this book and spent time observing and interviewing.

The Hull High School

You will recall that Claire Sheff accepted a position as a superintendent in a New Jersey school district. John McLean succeeded Claire as Hull superintendent in July 1993. He served until 1999, when the school board voted not to renew his contract. There is a long story behind that decision, with several different points of view, as there usually is when a superintendent's contract is not renewed. But in this case, it may be more a story about a town awakening than a superintendent's departure. David Kellem, a prominent attorney in town, a school board member from 1989 to 1995, and a founder of the Hull Academic Support Committee (HASC), perhaps tells it best in a recent interview with me:

> When I was serving on the board, our biggest problem was that we didn't admit to our problems and confront them directly. We wanted to protect the schools and were disconnected from what was really happening in them. There would be a nice presentation by the superintendent at every board meeting.
>
> When I got off the board, I realized that none of it was true. On the soccer fields and in the coffee shops, the community complained, but they had no voice. The School Improvement Councils (SIPS) did nothing. They had no real authority to even understand the problem, let alone create a meaningful plan. The school board and superintendent weren't in touch with what was going on. So five of us formed the Hull Academic Support Committee (in 1996) to be a community/parent group that would have real input.
>
> Eighty people came to the first meeting. In the beginning, we saw ourselves as a sort of academic "booster club." We raised money for academic enrichment and tried to be a kind of watchdog group and to keep learning.

> In 1998 we presented an academic agenda to the board. A hundred and fifty people came to the meeting . . . but there was no response from either the board or the superintendent.

The HASC Academic Agenda is a tightly worded one-page document that calls for some sweeping, but common-sense changes, including:

- Developing a coordinated curriculum
- Establishing and enforcing student discipline codes
- Creating a more positive learning environment that celebrates academic success
- Raising academic expectations for all students
- Creating more effective parental involvement strategies
- Clarifying and publishing grade level learning objectives
- Ending social promotion
- Improving communications from administration to faculty and parents
- Encouraging students to think more about college and career opportunities.

> Over the next several years we worked to get HASC members and supporters elected to the school board. Now 100 percent of the board backs the HASC program. One of our founders and another member served on the hiring committee that finally chose our new superintendent, Kathleen Reynolds. Her focus is firmly on academics—especially literacy. And she communicates with people. When she started the job (in August 1999), she set up more than ninety half-hour sessions to listen to members of the community.

I asked David what had been the impact on the Hull community of the new South Shore Charter School, which was established in 1995 by another prominent school critic in town, Tim Anderson.

> I was in the midst of a war between Anderson and McLean. Tim wanted to work collaboratively, at first. He had a plan to take the best staff from the Hull for two years and then have them go back . . . but he had no plan to replace them. McLean wanted to drive the school out of existence.
>
> Tim wrote a $300,000 proposal for AmeriCorps funding for junior/senior high school project-based learning. It was very successful. The next year he and McLean submitted competing proposals, and nobody got funding.
>
> The only reason the charter school hasn't devastated us is because the state came to the rescue with the foundation budget. Our budget has increased with the state aid, and the charter school hasn't cost us a cent, but it has taken a lot of the most motivated parents. Word is that the parents love the primary school, and parents are required to be actively involved in the school.
>
> Currently attending South Shore are 174 children from Hull, which is about 12 percent of the public schools' total enrollment of 437. A much larger number of the town's students, 374, attended private or parochial schools in 1999.
>
> The staff and administration of our schools know their results are going to be measured against the charter school. And there's real competition for the motivated kids. But right now the charter school's MCAS scores are no better than the public schools' scores.

David's assessment of how the district's MCAS scores compare to the charter school's is essentially correct. In the 1999 test 23 percent of the Hull High School tenth graders failed the English test, an increase of 8 percent over the previous year; 51 percent failed the math portion, an increase of 9 percent; and 35 percent failed the science and technology test, an increase of 11 percent. (Compared to the state, Hull did better than average on the English test and about average in math and science and technology.) The percent failing the same tenth grade tests at South Shore Charter School are higher than Hull's in English (36 percent) and about the same in math (50 percent) and science and technology (32 percent).

However, perhaps because the charter school is getting the more motivated parents and students according to David, the percentage of students scoring in the advanced and proficient categories on the 1999 test are significantly higher than the Hull High School students: 32 percent in English, 32 percent in math, and 21 percent in science and technology in the charter school versus only 21 percent, 20 percent, and 15 percent scoring advanced and proficient in the respective subjects in the Hull High School tenth grade.

It was clear from this conversation that for David, as for a growing number of educators, school improvement has become a numbers game—but one with very serious consequences. Increasingly, test scores are how schools and communities rate their schools—and now it is also how the competition with new charter schools is scored. Realtors tell us that test scores even determine real estate values in a community—the higher the scores, the more desirable the community is perceived to be as a place to raise children. So I asked David his views on the new MCAS:

> As screwed up as they are, I'm thankful for the curriculum frameworks and MCAS. It has forced communities to raise standards. The "mile wide, inch deep" problem will sort itself out in time. The tests provide good information, which can benefit communities if they honestly look at the data, instead of sugarcoating the results—which is what we did for too long.
>
> I've learned a lot from our mistakes of the last ten years. The most important thing is open communication. We have to be honest with each other and ourselves about

> what the real problem is. We used to be afraid that if we acknowledged the problem then things would get worse. But the opposite is the case. The town would have excused the school committee and the superintendent if they'd just been honest. I'll tell you, though, the conversation continues around here on whether it's the community or the exam that needs adjusting!

Down the street, in a dilapidated former elementary school building, there is no debate. The conversation is totally focused on the data and on how to improve results. The cramped office walls of the new Hull superintendent, Kathleen Reynolds, are plastered with newsprint sheets charting Hull MCAS test scores, and outlines of strategic plans and priorities.

Kathleen, in office only five months, nevertheless conveys a powerful sense of urgency and focus about her work. "If the new graduation standards were in place now (instead of 2003), 55 percent of our current ninth graders would not graduate," Kathleen tells me early into our conversation.

> But it's not always easy to set priorities and focus on teaching and learning as we need to. This is a district that has been neglected and abused for too long. We have no science labs in the middle school, and the high school labs lack water and electricity. Engineers have told us that all our systems—heating, electrical—have outlived their lives. The feds are breathing down our necks because our school buildings are in such bad shape. It's going to take $10 million just to bring our buildings up to code, and there's no help from the state for this.
>
> Still, there are a lot of wonderful people in this district—highly motivated, caring, committed teachers and administrators who need significantly more support than they've received in the past.

I asked Kathleen what she meant by support, and she replied,

> We have individuals who know what good teaching is, but there is no process for sharing, and there is very little discussion or understanding of the student achievement data.
>
> I am trying to set clear priorities. The core question is: Why are we collecting data and what should it be used for? I want to make each individual student's achievement data available electronically so that it can be tracked over time and used as a basis for student individual education plans.
>
> Also, our curriculum is not aligned with state frameworks, and we have no common protocols for planning instruction. So I am trying to create an infrastructure for teachers to talk with curriculum coordinators about teaching and learning—monthly department meetings to talk about specifically identified tasks, and school improvement plans and professional development goals in each building that relate to improving student achievement. The key is putting an infrastructure in place.

Given that the stakes are so high, the time short, and the resources scarce, does Kathleen have qualms about the new tests, I wondered?

> I'm an MCAS supporter. At least MCAS makes explicit what's really going on. It's a wake-up call, a step in the right direction. And it's a useful tool; it helps focus and motivate teachers. Some people say it's not fair to test the poor kids, but those people want the tests for *their* kids. Tests are the gatekeepers.
>
> There are issues with MCAS. The content is not 100 percent right—but that's because educators have not come up with our own accountability process. And there are increased dropout rates in Texas and Florida [where high stakes tests have been in place for longer and where Kathleen served as a teacher and administrator for a number of years]. But here we should be smart enough to get it right.

* * *

Smart how? What will it take to raise standards for all students without increasing the dropout rate? Those were the questions that nagged me as I drove over to the high school.

The principal, Dr. Geoffrey Fanning, was out of the building at a conference for the day, so I met with assistant principal Bob Cochran, a long-time veteran of the school. We talked as we toured the building together. I asked him what changes there had been since I last spent time at the school nearly ten years ago.

"Bob McIntyre [former principal] left four years ago," he explained. "Dr. Fanning has put structure back into the school. People—teachers and kids—know what they're supposed to do and when. It's a very different climate than it used to be. Our daily attendance rate is 92 percent, up from 88 percent four years ago."

I asked about some of the innovations—ninth-grade teams and the environmental theme-based curriculum—that Claire had put into place.

> Teaming went the way of the lonesome buffalo. The new superintendent [Bob McLean] didn't feel strongly about teaming so teachers went back to teaching multiple grades.
>
> We have a modified block schedule now—academic classes have 93-minute periods every other day, and we've added 3 minutes to the school day. And we offer honors courses as electives, plus note-taking classes and SAT (Scholastic Achievement Test) prep classes. Our SAT scores have gone up, and more of our kids are taking the SATs and going to four-year colleges. [In 1999, 62.2 percent of Hull graduates stated that they planned to attend a four-year college and 10 percent a two-year college.]

Real, incremental improvements, no doubt. And, in walking around the building, there was a clear sense of order in the school. No kids in the halls, no student voices drifting from the classrooms. An almost eerie silence. As the last period of the day ended, students trudged dutifully out to waiting buses and cars with little animation or conversation.

Yes, SAT scores are up. The average score for the class of 1999 was 495 in verbal and 454 in math. But they are still below the state and national averages. (The state average was 511 in both.) And yes, the majority is going on to some kind of college, but how many end up with a degree? No one at the school knew—but in the new introduction to this book, I quoted Assistant Secretary of Education Patricia McNeil as saying that, nationally, fewer than a third of the kids starting out end up with any kind of degree. Worse still is the looming MCAS catastrophe that Kathleen mentioned at the beginning of our conversation—55 percent of this year's class wouldn't graduate if the test were in place today, she said.

Incremental improvements are significant, and the politicians and media should give educators at Hull and elsewhere the credit they deserve—instead of constantly castigating them. But, clearly, these changes are not enough, not by half. And I worry about the unintended consequences of the almost single-minded focus on test scores—kids becoming test-wise, but still lacking real skills, a deeper appreciation for learning, and a sense of core values and their roles as citizens. My own "high standards" for good schools—competencies, core values, and collaboration—seem more important than ever.

Kathleen knows more is needed. In our interview, she talked about needing to rethink high school—perhaps putting in some kind of career pathways. But that is a somewhat hazy vision, sort of reminiscent of Claire's environmental theme school, and in any event, it is years away from implementation. For now, Kathleen is totally focused on achieving higher levels of literacy for all kids.

So we are still left with the question: What will it take to enable all high school students to achieve at high levels? What kinds of fundamental, rather than incremental, change might be required? The Cambridge Rindge and Latin High School is about to implement a bold new plan that may provide one answer to this question.

The Cambridge Rindge and Latin High School

In the nearly ten years that have passed since I last spent time observing and interviewing in Cambridge, the educational "old guard" has all moved on. Long-term veteran of the system Superintendent Mary Lou McGrath left in 1997. She was replaced by Bobbie D'Alessandro after a national search—a search conducted by a younger, more "professional" school committee. The colorful but obstreperous "Al Vellucci's" of the committee are gone—much to the relief of many Cambridge citizens who had long ago tired of some school committee members' old-time politicking and occasional circus antics.

In 1998 the high school principal, Ed Sarason, also retired, which gave the new superintendent a chance to choose a leader who might take the school in a very different direction. Bobbie D'Alessandro graciously agreed to talk with me on a chilly January morning.

> When I came in, the system had too many goals. We created a strong mission statement and narrowed our goals down to eleven—but even that was too many. The test scores clearly showed that kids weren't reading, so literacy became our focus.
>
> Now 75 percent of our third graders are reading at an advanced or proficient level—an 11-point gain in one year, but we have too many kids in high school who are non-readers.

It remains to be seen whether gains made last year on another kind of standardized test in third grade will translate into improved MCAS scores in 2000. The 1999 Cambridge citywide fourth-grade MCAS tests, scored on a different scale, reported only 17 percent advanced or proficient in English language arts, up 3 percent from the previous year. The percentage of students failing the 1999 fourth-grade English test was 18 percent, only 1 percent better than in 1998.

Whatever the numbers for elementary, the tenth-grade MCAS scores certainly bear witness to Bobbie's sense of urgency about the high school literacy problem: 40 percent of the tenth-graders failed the English language arts test in 1999, an increase of 14 percent from the previous year! And 58 percent of the tenth-graders failed the math test—a 7-percent increase in the failure rate from 1998. Nearly as many, 51 percent, failed the science and technology test.

If the new state requirement that students must pass the MCAS in order to receive a diploma were in place this year, 58 percent of the Cambridge public schools' tenth-graders would not graduate. When broken down by race/ethnicity, the percentage of students who would not graduate shows a dramatic disparity. While 49 percent of the white students would not graduate, 71 percent of all African-American students, 73 percent of the Hispanic students, and 88 percent of other Black (predominantly Haitian) students would not receive a diploma.[7]

Given the high stakes, does Bobbie see the MCAS tests as unfair, I asked?

> A lot of people in this community don't like the MCAS and will boycott the tests, but it has helped me to look at student achievement. We have low test scores because there is no articulated or aligned curriculum, K-12. I say, let's not fight it. Let's add the alternative assessments that were originally called for.
>
> I was very concerned about the high school from the beginning. Despite the fact that we had created an after-school homework center and a mentoring program, 34 percent of the kids failed one or more subjects last year. There had been a lot of talk about restructuring, but there had been very little action. When Ed Sarason retired in 1998, I couldn't find the right person to replace

> him, so I had two people serve as interim coprincipals for a year."

Beginning in Sarason's last year, the faculty had, in fact, gone through an elaborate two-year planning process, which resulted in a proposal to restructure the high school into ten small "learning communities"—similar in concept to the original academy proposal, except with even smaller teacher-student units. In the end, however, the faculty voted not to adopt the proposal.

Different people suggest diverse reasons for the final outcome of the vote: lack of support from Superintendent D'Alessandro, lack of enthusiasm for change from a largely veteran faculty. But all agree that the effect on the school was quite demoralizing. The faculty seemed paralyzed—unable to act, despite the long-standing evidence that the high school simply wasn't working for a disproportionate number of minority students.

So the superintendent decided on a bold move. In August 1999 she hired Paula Evans as the new permanent principal. A former high school teacher, Paula has no experience as a school administrator. But she has worked in senior positions with Ted Sizer and other high school visionaries at the Coalition of Essential Schools and later at the Annennberg Institute for School Reform. "I gave Paula a mandate for fundamental change," Bobbie explained. "I told her I didn't think the school was addressing the needs of all kids and that the house system was inequitable."

In her new position only four months when I interviewed her, Paula has wasted no time in developing a proposal for fundamental restructuring of the high school. Paula explained:

> I made clear in the interview process that I wasn't interested in just managing the school. It's clear that the school doesn't work for a lot of kids.
>
> But because of the size of the school [now about two thousand students], complexity, and shopping mall qual-

> ity, you can't change anything with the present structure. There is a ninth-grade advisory program [where students meet regularly in small groups with a faculty advisor], but we're holding on by our fingers. The scheduling is just too difficult. It's the same problem with our houses—they're largely administrative units now. There's no guarantee that kids will have all their ninth-grade classes in their house.

The result of several months of work with a group of teachers, Paula's "Proposal for Organizational Redesign to Effectively Support Student Learning and Achievement" is a bold document that lays out a vision for a radically different high school. According to Paula, the plan is based on three fundamental principles.

> The first principle is that all kids will be intellectually challenged. This is not the same thing as being academically challenged. You don't have to take AP [advanced placement] courses to learn to use your mind well.
>
> The second principle is that all students will be well-known by at least one or two adults. Schools have to be more personalized. Kids need caring relationships with adults.
>
> The third principle is that kids will experience a sense of community and will learn the responsibilities of belonging to a community. [It's interesting to note that the formulation of these three principles and the organization of the schools into teams is very similar to the three that I have used as lenses for analysis throughout the book: competencies, core values, and collaboration.]

Structurally, the plan calls for a total reorganization of the school into five autonomous schools of similar size (about 375 students), which would share the same building. All students would take most of their courses in their "home school," and there would be an even demographic distribution of students and staff, common planning time for teacher teams, and teacher advisor groups in grades 9–12 for all five schools.

Paula's proposal to the school committee is substantiated with a rapid, but well-thought-out timeline and plan for implementation, as well as a review of the research on small schools, which summarizes their main advantages:

- Students at all grade levels learn more in small schools than in large schools
- At-risk students are much more likely to succeed in small schools than in large schools
- Small schools are far more likely to be violence-free than large schools
- The bonds created in small schools enable such schools to influence students' post high school behavior, including college attendance
- The success of small schools is attributable to various features, all of which seem to emerge from three key factors: 1) small size; 2) an unconventional organizational structure; 3) a setting that operates more like a community than a bureaucracy.[8]

What is interesting about the fierce opposition that developed in response to Paula's plan is that no one questioned the research or the rationale for the creation of the new small schools. What they objected to was the elimination of choice! This plan essentially does away with the high school choice program that has been in place since 1990.

No one talks about charter schools much in Cambridge. When I asked Bobbie D'Alessandro about the impact of charter schools in her district, she said, "There hasn't been much affect on us. We have a good relationship with them. My focus is on getting more people to say 'yes' to public education." The reason why charter schools aren't bigger news here is that having a choice of schools in Cambridge is nothing new. As I recounted in Chapter 2, Cambridge has had a program of "controlled choice" since 1979.

The problem with choice at the high school—Paula, Bobbie, and others believe—is that it has led to an inequitable distribution of resources and talents. In fact, the MCAS failure rate is very unevenly distributed across the six "houses" in the high school. The houses with the highest scores—House A and Pilot—had 40 percent and 35 percent of their students fail the math portion of the exam (the portion of the MCAS on which all students did least well, statewide). However, 88 percent of the students in Technical Arts and 77 percent of the students in Fundamental—the two lowest scoring houses—failed the math MCAS. There were similar disparities in the English language arts test, as well.[9]

"There are just too many stereotypes about the groups of faculty and the houses, which have at least a grain of truth to them," Paula explained.

Many teachers are understandably very upset at the prospect of change. The median age of the faculty at the school is 54, and a number have worked together in their houses or teams for years. Now Paula wants to break these teams up—so that the most successful teachers are more equitably distributed among the five new schools, rather than continuing to have a choice of programs within which to teach.

Paula's reform strategy is essentially top-down, mandated change and is reminiscent of Claire's effort to impose theme schools and teaming on the Hull teachers. Even Paula acknowledges that at least half the faculty is opposed. While her sense of urgency is certainly understandable and her plan to invest heavily in professional development for faculty a wise one, it remains to be seen whether a sufficient number of faculty will be motivated to do what is required to make the plan really work.

But it has been the middle-class white parents who have been the most opposed to the new plan. When the school committee held its first public meeting to consider the plan on January 12, 2000, more than five hundred people came, and fifty asked to speak. After listening to hours of statements, the school committee voted to approve the plan. I spoke with Paula the morning after the marathon meeting.

> I don't think Cambridge looked very pretty last night. There were very few people of color there—and the few who did speak were outraged at the elitist view of the school and the population it serves.
>
> But some of the students who spoke were incredible! Several said that the school isn't fair because people who scream the loudest get whatever they want.
>
> The most vocal parents feel that their students should, above all, have choice. They're worried that some of the AP classes might be scheduled at inconvenient times; they don't like the idea of heterogeneous grouping.
>
> I understand that parents are, first and foremost, advocates for their kids. But my responsibility is to look at the needs of the whole school. And it shouldn't be seen as a zero-sum game, where some group loses. I don't feel that even our brightest kids are intellectually challenged either.

With so many changes in the district's and school leadership over the last few years, I wondered what had become of the Academy—the program that Rubin Cabral and his colleagues established in 1990-91. I was surprised to find the program virtually unchanged—and thriving.

Al Weinstein, the Academy's codirector (and part-time teacher) was elected when Arnie Clayton and Nancy Burns stepped down in 1997 and then reelected, along with his colleague Eleanor Farinato, two years later. Having worked very hard for many years to make the Academy a model educational program, Al is understandably ambivalent about the proposed new high school structure—which would mean the end of the program, along with all the other houses.

"Choice isn't helping the school population as a whole," he acknowledged. "Some parents who get into the programs they want feel it's working—for their kids, anyway. I see it as causing unhealthy competition. Whenever the administrators from the different houses get together, we're always clobbering each other with soft pillows over perceived inequities in distribution of resources." (It sounds unchanged from when Rubin struggled to get and keep what he needed for the school.) "Besides, it makes me feel that I'm marketing all the time."

While Al might not like marketing, he apparently does it well. The Academy is the largest house in the school, with five hundred students enrolled. Last year there was a 50 percent increase in the number of families who listed the Academy as their first choice. Despite the fact that this house has never tracked students and is the designated program for bilingual and non-English-speaking students, 63 percent of its graduates go on to four-year colleges—an impressive achievement. Rubin would be proud.

At their meeting on February 2, 2000, the school committee voted unanimously to adopt the "Proposal for Organizational Redesign," thus effectively ending the choice program in Cambridge Rindge and Latin High School in September 2001. The question is: Will this restructuring effort really address the obstacles to improving achievement for all students? They were best summarized by Al:

> MCAS has added light to the problem of some students not achieving, but it didn't tell us anything we didn't already know. We made a choice a long time ago to retain [prevent from dropping out] a big percentage of students. Now we have to figure out how to make it work.
>
> Clearly, when kids fail, something is wrong. I'd like to see teachers banding together in ways that support each other and ways that support growth. We need to get parents involved so that they support learning. Some kids, you just wind them up and they'll go. But a lot of kids just don't care—don't care if they do well, don't care what happens when they leave school. We need to find ways to get these kids to care.

Are there schools where teachers collaborate, learn, and grow together? Places where parents are involved and where no student falls through the cracks? When I first spent time at Brimmer and May in the early 1990s I found it to be a school where all of these things were true to some degree. In January 2000 I set out to discover to what extent these qualities might still be in evidence.

The Brimmer and May School

Walking to the main office, Brimmer and May's growth is quickly evident: a new arts building is now a dominant feature of the campus, and the number of students rushing down the sidewalks to class appears to have multiplied considerably. In fact, Brimmer's total enrollment is now 400 students, grades nursery through 12, compared to only 260 students when I first visited the school ten years ago. And there are now 120 students in grades 9–12, versus 55 then.

The growth is partly the result of the school's decision to go coed in 1991. It is also a result of a surging economy, where more families can afford to send their children to a private school and may be driven to do so by the increasing worries about public school. Still, these changes don't account for all the growth. In fact, Brimmer and May has become a "hot" school in the education market. Last year, there were six openings in the high school and fifty applicants—a far cry from the time when the school could not begin to fill all the openings in the upper grades.

In the preceding chapter I described the "market" pressures on Brimmer and May to be "all things to all people" and a copy of other independent schools in order to maintain enrollment. But this has not happened—perhaps because of the increased demand for an independent school education. Other than the decision to admit boys, the school has remained true to its educational vision.

While favorable "market" conditions have no doubt helped, Brimmer and May has also enjoyed remarkably focused and consistent leadership. Anne Reenstierna is completing her fifteenth year as head of the school. And Judy Guild, who spent seven years away from the school raising a family and pursuing other careers, returned last year as associate head. I talked at length with the two of them about the school and their work.

The school is still an active member of the Coalition of Essential Schools. Brimmer is also a founding member of the National Center for Independent School Renewal, a group of twelve independent schools around the country dedicated to education reform and to Coalition principles. According to Judy, "We're still working on the ten common principles (one was added by the Coalition in 1997), portfolios, and exhibitions."

But it is the school's work on curriculum and commitment to a different approach to professional development that I found most impressive—and very different from public schools. In Massachusetts, and in other states around the country, independent and parochial schools are not required to take the new state tests or abide by the curriculum frameworks—a fact that is deeply resented by public school educators. Nevertheless, Brimmer and May has kept a careful eye on these developments. Said Judy:

> We've been looking at both the Massachusetts and New York state curriculum frameworks, as well as the new National Council of Teachers of Mathematics standards. And last year the whole faculty—nursery through twelfth grade—worked together to map the entire curriculum in content, skills, and assessments, month by month. Out of this process, we developed improvement goals by both grade level and subject area.
>
> For example, the curriculum review turned up the fact that we had a somewhat eclectic approach to writing—with different standards in different grades. So now we have developed a writing, research, and grammar manual that is used throughout the school. We also developed a

> new writing center, where students sign up to work one-on-one with a writing coach—or they can be assigned by a teacher to work on a revision of a specific paper.

Recall that both Kathleen Reynolds and Bobbie D'Alessandro talked about needing to review and align their district's curriculum to the new state curriculum standards in my interview with them. But they described the goal as a long-term one. Brimmer and May has done all this and more in only one year. Obviously this was somewhat easier for a smaller school to accomplish than it is for a district. Nevertheless the depth and breadth of curriculum work done is very rare in my school experience, even when districts take years to accomplish the task.

I mention this to Anne and she admits, "It was a lot of work. It sort of reminded me of the first year we joined the Coalition. And there was some resistance from teachers, too."

"It's different for each teacher, though," Judy offers. "Sometimes it comes down to individual insecurities. One teacher didn't want to put her curriculum on the computer (as a part of last year's review process) because she doesn't write well and isn't comfortable with computers. So we looked for a new software program that had a spell check and more user-friendly interface, and that made all the difference for her!"

Judy's description of efforts to help this individual teacher led to a discussion of the school's efforts to promote teacher growth—or what we call professional development. "Half of our teachers are involved with what the Coalition calls Critical Friends Groups," Judy tells me. "They are small groups that meet regularly around specific learning goals. Each has a trained coach. There's one group that's just for new teachers; another is for learning technology. Then there's an experienced teachers' group that visits and videotapes one another's classes. I think the Critical Friends Groups are an exciting model for setting professional development goals and lifelong learning for teachers."

In addition to these groups, the school invests in long-term onsite professional development around specific curriculum improvement objectives. For example, the school adopted a new interactive math program this year, which combines algebra, geometry, and so on with real-life problem solving and is based on the new national standards for teaching math referred to earlier. So all math teachers go through intensive training before they teach this program. Also, every teacher new to the school is assigned an experienced teacher who acts as a mentor.

Anne observes that the school's involvement with the National Center for Independent School Renewal has provided a great deal of ongoing professional development as well. "Twice a year, a large number of our teachers attend NCISR conferences and work with teachers from other schools on curriculum and community issues. These teachers often share ideas and solicit feedback from one another throughout the year. It is one of our most important professional development vehicles."

Judy describes the new position of the Learning Specialist as another example of the school's emphasis on site-based, continuous professional development. "In addition to doing individual student assessments, she trains teachers on how kids learn. She also runs workshops for teachers and parents on learning disabilities. It's so much better than sending teachers off to workshops because she can sit in on a class and be a real resource for teachers on a regular basis."

In part as a result of this training, Judy and Anne feel the school has gotten much better at identifying and dealing with individual student problems before they reach a crisis point. "We now have Early Intervention Teams for all three divisions of the school," Anne explains. The school psychologist, nurse, division head, learning specialist, and I meet every other week an hour and a half. We discuss individual students' issues in a confidential and professional manner—eating disorders, depression, academic, behavioral, or medical problems. This coordinated approach benefits students and their parents."

Not including the new faculty positions, Brimmer and May currently spends 1.5 percent of its budget on professional development, or $1,500 per teacher. By contrast, most districts spend less than 0.5 percent, and all too frequently even that small amount of money is not spent on programs that have any connection to priorities for improving student achievement.

Our discussion had focused mainly on what the school has done to continue to strengthen the academic program, so I asked what had become of the school's efforts to establish core values. Anne said:

> I've learned that you cannot discuss values once and think you're done. People come and go, and so the discussion has to be repeated. In fact, we spent all of last year reviewing our core values again—we wanted to establish some for the millennium and renew our agreements. We had films and discussions throughout the school. In grades 6–12, students met in small groups and brought back sheets of newsprint listing what they thought our values should be. Then we had to come to consensus. We ended up with the same values that we'd agreed on nearly ten years ago, but we added a new one—open-mindedness. It has to do with respecting others' beliefs and promoting equity.
>
> The other thing that has made a big difference in the school's climate is establishing the Judicial Board. Middle and high school students go before the board for any serious behavioral infractions. It's made up of three high school students, one middle school student, two teachers, a division head, and either Judy or myself, as a nonvoting member. Students are elected by faculty, and faculty are elected by the students—and it's not a popularity contest. They give speeches with real content.
>
> I tried to get something like this started ten years ago, but students said no, that they didn't want to judge their friends. But three years ago, they came back from a Coalition of Essential Schools cluster meeting saying they wanted to establish a Judicial Board.

> I've been so impressed with students' thoughtfulness, and there's never been a breach of confidentiality. This year they made the decision to expel a student who was very popular, and the student board members took a lot of flack, but they stood their ground.
>
> Something we didn't expect is how hard the adjustment is for teachers new to the school. They're surprised at how strong the student voice is here and struggle with what student-teacher respect means. It's not student silence!

I am impressed by all that Anne and Judy have accomplished just in the last year and ask if they've used a particular strategy. Anne's reply reflects her leadership philosophy: "Now there are so many strong leaders in the school that we don't have to do it all ourselves."

Lessons—Old and New

In the preceding chapter I introduced the concepts of free-market school choice and increased reliance on national standards and "high stakes" tests as strategies for school improvement. I also raised some fundamental questions about their value, but at the time these arguments were academic, as we had few real-life examples of either strategy being used on a large scale.

Now, however, they have become the preferred strategies of educational reformers in most states. What can we learn about the effectiveness of these strategies in promoting school improvement efforts from our three case studies? And what are some of the "side effects," or unintended consequences of their use? Finally, what else may be required to create meaningful change in our nation's schools? These are the questions to which I now turn.

I think a careful review of both school choice and an increased reliance on standards and high stakes tests in these three examples point to both real benefits and significant liabilities with each strategy. Let's look at each separately.

Choice

In my original analysis, I suggested that school choice provided opportunities and benefits to parents and teachers who wanted to create a different kind of school. At the time, I underestimated both the power and importance of these opportunities in creating laboratories for "educational research and development." (A year after the book was published, I wrote about the "R & D" potential of charter schools and then became involved in one as a founding board member.[10])

The existence of very different kinds of successful charter schools does help make the case that there may be more effective methods for educating students. In the same way, Brimmer and May's success provides a model for a very different kind of independent school. We need these living proofs to persuade the skeptics that there are better ways to organize schools. Most important, they provide real educational alternatives for families and for teachers.

We also learned in Hull that the competition with charter schools makes those in public schools pay at least some attention to what charters are doing. However, so far, there is no evidence whatsoever that charter schools are influencing public schools. Furthermore, both in Hull and nationally, there is no evidence that students in charter schools outperform comparable students in conventional public schools.[11]

My greatest concern with school choice back in 1993 had to do with issues of equity and, in fact, the Hull and Rindge and Latin stories suggest that increased inequity is a significant danger with school choice.

The growing inequity in Hull is one of social capital. The question there is, if most of the more motivated students and families leave the public schools, who will be the role models for those who remain?

The inequity that developed at Rindge and Latin was one of political and financial capital. In Cambridge, parents who know how to work the system have been more able to get what they want for their children; those that do not, get less. Apparently, it has been the same for house administrators. Some have been able to secure more financial resources than others. If this system had been allowed to continue, would some of the less desirable, less chosen high school houses have become like public housing or public health care—a minimum-standard safety net for those who cannot go elsewhere? Clearly, these were the concerns that led Paula and Bobbie to seek alternatives to the choice system at Cambridge Rindge and Latin.

In their new book, *When Schools Compete: A Cautionary Tale* (Washington, D.C.: Brookings, 2000), Edward Fiske and Helen Ladd describe research they conducted in New Zealand, where all parents have had public school choice since 1989. They, too, have found the kinds of inequities in those schools that I have described, and they report that the new Labor government is adding safeguards that limit free market choice in an attempt to ensure greater equity of opportunity. No one yet knows whether the new policies will work.

Nevertheless, I now believe that school choice is critical, but not just for the educational "R & D" value and certainly not because it is likely to drive bad schools out of business—an unlikely prospect for many reasons. Rather, we need choice because the act of choosing to associate with a school promotes the sense of commitment and community that lies at the heart of all good schools. Choice also allows students and families to pick programs that reflect their interests and values—critical motivational elements in improving student achievement. (These are themes that I will explore more fully in my forthcoming book.) While I understand why the leadership in Cambridge has chosen to do away with choice programs at Rindge, I fear they may lose more than they gain by creating identical new schools—significantly smaller, but all the same.

We need choice. We also need equity of opportunity for all students. A critical challenge for policy makers in the coming decade is to "invent" new forms of public school systems that integrate these seemingly opposing values. The work of Paul Hill at the

University of Washington and the recent report of the Education Commission of the States, *Governing America's Schools: Changing the Rules—Report of the National Commission on Governing America's Schools* (Denver, CO: ECS, 1999) point to some promising new policy directions that deserve consideration.

High Stakes Test

In my original analysis of the dangers of an overreliance on new national standards and standardized tests as a school reform strategy, I expressed two concerns: first, that the standardized tests used would not measure the skills that are most important; and second, that with "higher stakes tests" teachers would feel compelled to spend more time "teaching to the test." At the time, I did not think that sufficient time or money would be spent on creating tests worth teaching to.

I was both right and wrong. It is clear from all three case studies that the development of some national standards (notably the new NCTM math standards, in the case of Brimmer and May) and the existence of high stakes tests have created pressures for educational improvements. New state and national standards have led leaders in all three schools to review and improve curricula, and both Kathleen Reynolds and Bobbie D'Alessandro described the pressure of the MCAS tests as helping to focus the system on needed improvements in teaching and learning. They are also, unquestionably, a powerful tool for mandating greater equality of educational opportunity. Now, all students and all public schools in the state are expected to achieve a uniformly high achievement standard.

Nevertheless, there are fundamental issues about the nature and use of these tests, which are raised in the case studies. Three people whom I interviewed talked about the "mile wide, inch deep" problem. What they mean is that what some of the tests measure is primarily factual information, not skills. You will recall that, for both financial and political reasons, the intellectual sophistication of the MCAS tests has been substantially watered down, though portions of the tests do require students to demonstrate mastery of real competencies.

As I wrote back in 1993, it costs a lot of money to develop and score a good test and, thus far, Massachusetts and other states have been unwilling to make the required investment. This explains why there are fewer essay and more multiple-choice elements in the MCAS tests than many educators would like.

Even if states were willing to spend more money for a better test, the problem of getting agreement on what's most important to learn remains. Lacking consensus on what's most important, or even a discussion of the topic, we take the apparently easy way out and test anything that anyone with influence thinks is important, as Paul Reville explained earlier in this chapter.

Even many supporters of high stakes tests privately agree that there need to be some mid-course corrections. However, in Massachusetts and elsewhere, I do not see any leadership coming forward to initiate this process. Thus far, both educational and political leaders are reluctant to publicly criticize the tests for fear of appearing "soft" on standards and backtracking on a commitment to accountability. As Paul Reville said, "If you get rid of MCAS, you may lose all the increased funding for public education that we've been able to secure. Then we're headed for the 'brave new world' of privatization and vouchers."

A way out of this political standoff is for states, districts, and schools to focus, initially, on just one category of high stakes test: literacy. The ability to read thoughtfully, write clearly and analytically, make oral presentations, and do research—these are the foundation skills for lifelong learning, for citizenship, and increasingly for most work in our society. Let's figure out how to get all students to high levels of achievement with these skills first, and then worry about the other subjects.

Informally, that's exactly what some school leaders are doing. Both superintendents described their strategic focus on literacy.

They know, as experienced leaders, that you can't do everything at once. Having five priorities means having none at all.

Making the choice to focus on improving some skills and not others in the current political climate, however, is a real risk for educators. We need to take away the risk. We need to give them permission to focus on one thing at a time. Only then can we begin to have a meaningful dialogue on what it will really take to get the job done—a discussion that is, thus far, almost entirely missing in the debate about high stakes tests. Many decry students' poor performance on MCAS. No one seems to be talking about what must be done to ensure that all students reach higher levels of achievement.

Throughout this book, I have maintained that the key ingredients for a quality education are:

- A clear focus on intellectual competencies—such as the literacy skills just described—rather than coverage of academic content. What matters most is whether students can write, not their memorization of the parts of speech, for example.
- An emphasis on *core values*. Respect, tolerance, responsibility, and other similar values are universal ethical principles and are the foundation for a vibrant democracy. There are also the preconditions for a constructive learning environment.
- The importance of collaboration—within schools, between schools at different grade levels, and between schools and communities. Collaboration is essential to reach agreement on competencies and core values that should be taught and to track student progress. It is also the only way we can ensure that all students succeed. Educators cannot do the job alone.

All of the work that I have done in schools and districts over the past ten years, and all of the evidence from the most successful public, charter, and independent schools, continue to underscore the importance and centrality of these three principles.

Looking at our three case studies, they are clearly key ingredients in Brimmer and May's success, and now essentially similar principles will be the intellectual foundation for the creation of the five new high schools within Cambridge Rindge and Latin.

The first answer to the question of what must be done to ensure that all students succeed in school, then, is to take these principles very seriously as criteria for evaluating existing programs and as benchmarks for quality. Sadly, in my experience, a focus on intellectual competencies, living core values, and collaboration are still rarely in evidence in most schools.

However, my recent experiences in schools and the opportunity to revisit the three in this book suggest that while these "three C's" are necessary for success, they are not, by themselves, sufficient. To these three original principles, I would now add three new C's: improving the *conditions* of teaching and learning, developing teachers' *capacity*, and ensuring greater *constancy* of focus and leadership. Let me explain each briefly:

- Improving the *conditions* of teaching and learning: In speeches throughout the country, Coalition of Essential Schools founder Theodore Sizer makes one simple declaration, with which no one disagrees: "You can't motivate a student you do not know." A teacher can't know—and therefore cannot motivate—140 or more students in a semester, which is the average load of a typical public high school teacher. To know students, teachers have to work with fewer students over longer periods of time in smaller school units. This simple structural change in the conditions of teaching and learning is the "secret ingredient" of the success of many independent schools—which rarely have more than 100 students in a graduating class. It is why small schools have higher levels of student achievement than larger ones, and it is a significant factor in Paula's decision to create five small high schools at Rindge and Latin.

- Developing teachers' *capacity*: Brimmer and May's continuing success is partially a result of a substantial financial and time commitment to teachers' professional development. Curriculum review, Critical Friends Groups, mentoring, discussions of student work, and special on-site training—these are just some of the strategies Brimmer and May and other schools employ to develop teachers' capacity to improve teaching. In addition, successful schools have systems in place for peer supervision—as well as evaluation by supervisors.
- Ensuring greater *constancy* of focus and leadership: For too many years our public schools have practiced what has come to be called *reform de jour*. Educational fads and school leaders come and go at an ever-quickening pace. School boards decide on new priorities from year to year, or just keep adding to the already over-long list of "urgent" items. This is not how schools are improved. Once again, the case of Brimmer and May speaks clearly to the importance of focusing on a few important things and maintaining that focus over time. Obviously, consistent leadership is often at the heart of maintaining constancy of focus, though it is not a requirement. What is required is a consensus on what few things are most important in a school or a community.

These six principles are not hard to understand. Nor are they particularly controversial. When given an opportunity to discuss them, most educators and parents understand their importance. But they are rarely in evidence in American schools today for several reasons. First, they are, in fact, hard to put into practice. They take time and, more importantly, courageous and skillful leadership, as the case of Brimmer and May teaches us. They also require something more—community understanding, leadership, and support. It seems to me that most leaders in business and politics still do not really understand the first thing about these six principles and their importance for achieving success with all students. They still do not understand the real problem in American public education. And if we do not correctly perceive the problem, then we will never be clear about the appropriate solution.

Listen carefully to the language of "educational reform" in the United States today. It is a punitive language of blame. "Schools are failing," or so say most business and political leaders. And increased accountability—things like MCAS tests—will "reform" the schools—meaning students and teachers.

Paul Reville, former state school board member, suggests that the prevailing view, at least in Massachusetts, is one advocated by what he calls the "pricklies." "They think every problem in public education is the result of the excesses of the 1960s," he said. So, naturally, the solution is to re-create the schools of the 1950s.

Let me suggest an alternative view. The American system of public education was designed to be a sorting machine—ferreting out, through standardized tests, the few kids who would go on to college from the vast majority who would go to work on an assembly line and who only needed a sixth-grade education.

Now, however, all students need real intellectual skills such as the ability to analyze information, think critically, and solve problems to be employable and to be responsible citizens. The truth is that we don't know how to educate all students to these high academic standards. We never have. And so the system is not "failing." It is obsolete. It needs to be reinvented, not reformed.

Such an analysis leaves many questions unanswered. What are the principles of reinvention? How are schools going about this work? What strategies are most effective in helping schools and districts to reinvent themselves? What do meaningful high standards for all students look like, and how do we best motivate students to achieve them and teachers to want to work in new ways? What kinds of accountability systems might ensure that schools are doing an effective job and that students are learning real competencies without constant testing? And what are the roles of parents and business and community leaders in helping educators to achieve results? These are some of the critical questions that must be answered for the future of American education—questions which I will take up in my next book, now in progress.

If we do not find better answers to these questions soon, I fear that leaders' impatience and growing distrust of educators—understandable though ill-informed—will lead to the establishment of a minimally regulated free-market system of public education. We learned from the Hull and Cambridge case studies that such a choice system is likely to increase the educational disparities among different groups of students. And we know that fundamental inequities in educational opportunities lie at the heart of this country's racial and economic divisions. Sadly, family education and income levels remain highly accurate predictors of students' SAT scores. Thus, it may not be only the future of public education that is at stake, but the future of our democracy as well. Time is running short.

Notes

Introduction to the Second Edition

1. Address at the U.S. Department of Education Conference on the New American High School, May 23, 1996, Washington, D.C., as transcribed onto the website of the Office of Vocational and Adult Education, U.S. Department of Education: http://ed.gov/offices/OVAE/newam.html.
2. Ibid.

Introduction

1. U.S. National Commission on Excellence in Education, *A Nation at Risk* (Washington, D.C.: The Commission, 1983).
2. See Theodore R. Sizer, *Horace's Compromise: The Dilemma of the American High School* (Boston: Houghton Mifflin, 1984); John Goodlad, *A Place Called School* (New York: McGraw-Hill, 1983); and Ernest Boyer, *High School* (New York: Harper & Row, 1983). Albert Shanker has published numerous articles on the role of unions in the *American Educator,* a publication of the American Federation of Teachers. Finally, see the report of the Carnegie Forum on Education and the Economy, *A Nation Prepared: Teachers for the 21st Century* (New York: Carnegie Corporation, 1986).
3. See Theodore R. Sizer, *Horace's School: Redesigning the American High School* (Boston: Houghton Mifflin, 1992). For more information on the Coalition of Essential Schools (CES), see the appendix in *Horace's School* or write to CES, Box 1969, Providence, RI 02912.

4. The Coalition plans to publish its own case studies of several member schools in 1994. See also George Wood, *Schools That Work: America's Most Innovative Public Education Programs* (New York: NAL, 1992), which describes two prominent Coalition schools (Central Park East Secondary School and Thayer Academy) but does not explain how their work relates to the Coalition's principles or to Sizer's critique.
5. See Michael Maccoby, *The Gamesman* (New York: Simon & Schuster, 1976) and *Why Work: Leading the New Generation* (New York: Simon & Schuster, 1988).
6. Sara Lawrence Lightfoot, *The Good High School: Portraits of Character and Culture* (New York: Basic Books, 1983), 369.

1. The Hull Junior-Senior High School

1. Hull Council for Business and Cultural Development, "Hull Overview" (Hull, Mass.: The Council, 1989).
2. Statistics from the New England Association of Schools and Colleges, "Report of the Visiting Committee" (Boston: NEASC, April 1991), 7.
3. See Howard Gardner, *The Unschooled Mind: How Children Think and How Schools Should Teach* (New York: Basic Books, 1991); and Theodore R. Sizer, *Horace's Compromise: The Dilemma of the American High School* (Boston: Houghton Mifflin, 1984).
4. A recently released Massachusetts State Department of Education report revealed that in sixteen of the thirty-eight Boston-area school districts for which data was available, more than half of all eighth-graders reported watching four or more hours of TV and having less than one hour of homework a day (*Boston Globe*, 6 June 1993, 29–30).
5. See Sizer, *Horace's Compromise*; John Goodlad, *A Place Called School* (New York: McGraw-Hill, 1983); and Ernest Boyer, *High School* (New York: Harper & Row, 1983).
6. See Sizer, *Horace's School: Redesigning the American High School* (Boston: Houghton Mifflin, 1992).
7. It is my experience that the majority of male high school teachers tend to think of themselves as teachers of subject matter first, and only secondly as teachers of students. Because their primary focus

is usually on students' intellect, they often downplay or even disregard students' emotions. Carol Gilligan's important work about differences between men's and women's ways of perceiving the world sheds further light on this issue. See Carol Gilligan, *In a Different Voice: Psychological Theory and Women's Development* (Cambridge, Mass.: Harvard University Press, 1982).

8. See "The Challenge of Change: What the 1990 Census Tells Us about Children" (Washington, D.C.: Center for the Study of Social Policy, 1992).
9. See Juliet B. Schor, *The Overworked Americans* (New York: Basic Books, 1992).
10. As reported in the *Boston Globe,* 10 June 1993, 3.
11. See Douglas Coupland, *Generation X: Tales for an Accelerated Culture* (New York: St. Martin's Press, 1991).
12. See "Voices from the Inside: A Report on Schooling from Inside the Classroom" (Claremont, Calif.: Institute for Education in Transformation, (Claremont Graduate School, 1992), 11.
13. See James P. Comer, *Maggie's American Dream: The Life and Times of a Black Family* (New York: New American Library, 1988).
14. The speech was delivered at Teachers College, Columbia University, 22 May 1993.
15. Psychoanalyst Erich Fromm was one of the first social critics to recognize the serious psychological dangers of our consumer society, and his work has greatly influenced my thinking. See *The Sane Society* (New York: Holt, Rinehart & Winston, 1955); *The Revolution of Hope: Toward a Humanized Technology* (New York: Harper & Row, 1968); and *To Have or To Be* (New York: Harper & Row, 1976). See also Mihaly Csikzentmihalyi's provocative editorial in the *New York Times,* 12 August 1993, A25.
16. See Michael Maccoby, "Toward a Moral Education," *Independent School,* May 1977. Michael Maccoby, a student of Erich Fromm's, was also one of the first to suggest that students in our consumer society must be taught specific skills for growth and mental health, and I have drawn from his work for many valuable insights on this subject. See Maccoby, "The Three C's and Discipline for Freedom," *School Review,* vol. 79, no. 2 (February 1971), and "A Psychoanalytic View of Learning," *Change Magazine,* Winter 1971–72.

17. See Sizer, *Horace's Compromise*; Comer, *Maggie's American Dream*; and Sara Lawrence Lightfoot, *The Good High School: Portraits of Character and Culture* (New York: Basic Books, 1983).
18. Draft "Report of the Visiting Committee," New England Association of Secondary Schools and Colleges (Winchester, Mass., 1989, 39–40.
19. *The American Educator*, the journal of the American Federation of Teachers (555 New Jersey Avenue, N.W., Washington, D.C. 20001) has published numerous articles about these local efforts, as well as the views of Albert Shanker.
20. Susan Moore Johnson, *Teachers at Work* (New York: Basic Books, 1990).
21. Tony Wagner, "Carnegie School-Business Partnerships: A Report on the First Year" (Quincy, Mass.: Massachusetts State Department of Education, 1990).

2. The Academy at Cambridge Rindge and Latin

1. See Jonathan Kozol, *Savage Inequalities: Children in America's Schools* (New York: Crown Publishers, 1991).
2. See Theodore R. Sizer, *Horace's School: Redesigning the American High School* (Boston: Houghton Mifflin, 1992), chapter 4 and appendix A.
3. See Arthur Powell, Eleanor Farrar, and David Cohen, *The Shopping Mall High School* (Boston: Houghton Mifflin, 1985).
4. There are now many excellent books and articles on "process" writing. One of the first and most influential was one authored by Donald Graves, *Writing: Teachers and Children at Work* (Portsmouth, N.H.: Heinemann, 1983).
5. See Peter Senge, *The Fifth Discipline: The Art and Practice of the Learning Organization* (New York: Doubleday/Currency, 1990).
6. See Eliot Wigginton, *Sometimes a Shining Moment: The Foxfire Experience* (New York: Anchor Books, 1985).
7. Jeannie Oaks's book *Keeping Track: How Schools Structure Inequality* (New Haven: Yale University Press, 1985) is a fine summary of the important research and arguments against tracking.
8. See Anne Wheelock, *Crossing the Tracks: How Untracking Can Save America's Schools* (New York: New Press, 1992).
9. Sizer, *Horace's School,* 145.

10. For a fuller description of the combined seminar/independent study approach I used, see my article "Learning Democratically," *The English Journal,* vol. 99, no. 6 (September 1977).
11. See James Comer, *Maggie's American Dream: The Life and Times of a Black Family* (New York: New American Library, 1988).
12. See Nell Nodings, *The Challenge to Care in School: An Alternative Approach to Education* (New York: Teachers College Press, 1992).
13. For a description of strategies used in "Comer schools," see Edward B. Fiske, *Smart Schools, Smart Kids: Why Do Some Schools Work?* (New York: Simon & Schuster, 1991), 207–220.
14. See "Voices from the Inside: A Report on Schooling from Inside the Classroom" (Claremont, Calif.: Institute for Education in Transformation, Claremont Graduate School, 1992).
15. For a fuller discussion of the role of advisory groups in schools, see the quarterly newsletter of the Coalition of Essential Schools, *Horace,* vol. 7, no. 1 (September 1990).
16. *New York Times,* 14 July 1993, B8.
17. See Tony Wagner, "Straddling Two Cultures: Polaroid's Project Bridge and School Reform" (Cambridge, Mass.: Polaroid Corporation, 1991).
18. See James P. Comer, "Educating Poor Minority Children," *Scientific America,* vol. 259, no. 5 (November 1988).
19. Fiske, *Smart Schools, Smart Kids,* 212-214.
20. I am grateful to PJ Blankenhorn for first suggesting this idea to me.
21. For a summary of recent research and a description of new programs, see "Is Smaller Better? Educators Now Say Yes for High School," *New York Times,* 14 July 1993, A1.

3. The Brimmer and May School

1. These figures for independent school minority enrollments and tuition aid are taken from *NAIS Statistics 1992,* a publication of the National Association of Independent Schools (Boston: NAIS, 1992).
2. The coalition now requires that schools subscribe to all of the "nine common principles" in order to join. For a description of these and more information about the Coalition, see Theodore R.

Sizer, *Horace's School: Redesigning the American High School* (Boston: Houghton Mifflin, 1992), appendix A, or write Coalition of Essential Schools, Box 1969, Providence, R.I. 02912.

3. See John Goodlad, *A Place Called School* (New York: McGraw-Hill, 1983).
4. I describe this problem in more detail, as well as the efforts of another independent school, Sidwell Friends, to deal with it in my article "Educating for Character," *Independent School,* October 1979.
5. See Robert Coles, *Privileged Ones: The Well-off and the Rich in America* (Boston: Little, Brown, 1977).
6. Wagner, "Educating for Character."
7. Thomas Lickona, *Educating for Character: How Our Schools Can Teach Respect and Responsibility* (New York: Bantam, 1991), 401–402.
8. Erich Fromm's book *Man for Himself: An Inquiry into the Psychology of Ethics* (New York: Holt, Rinehart & Winston, 1947) is a classic study of universal core values that promote human development. Lickona's book, cited above, also makes the case for universal values, and describes both conceptual and practical classroom approaches to moral education; however, the majority of his examples come from elementary schools and are not readily applicable to high school. Lickona's discussion of teacher collaboration, and parental and community involvement is also much less well developed. A student of Erich Fromm's, Michael Maccoby, and the work we did together with educators at the Sidwell Friends School in 1975–77, taught me a great deal about the importance of a whole-school focus on universal values and educating the heart as well as the head. See Maccoby, "Towards a Moral Education," *Independent School,* May 1977; and Wagner, "Educating for Character."
9. The title for my talk was inspired, in part, by David Elkind's book *The Hurried Child: Growing Up Too Fast Too Soon* (Reading, Mass.: Addison-Wesley, 1981). Elkind's book also documents the pressures that children of middle- and upper-middle-income families face.
10. See Mary Field Blenky, Blythe McVicker Clindry, Mancy Rule Goldberger, and Jill Mattuck Tarule, *Women's Ways of Knowing:*

The Development of Self, Voice, and Mind (New York: Basic Books, 1986).

11. See Howard Gardner, *The Unschooled Mind: How Children Think and How Schools Should Teach* (New York: Basic Books, 1991).
12. See Dan C. Lortie, *Schoolteacher: A Sociological Study* (Chicago: University of Chicago Press, 1975).
13. See Susan Moore Johnson, *Teachers at Work: Achieving Success in Our Schools* (New York: Basic Books, 1990).
14. See Peter M. Senge, *The Fifth Discipline: The Art and Practice of the Learning Organization* (New York: Doubleday/Currency, 1990).
15. See Jane L. David, "Synthesis of Research on School-Based Management." *Educational Leadership,* vol. 45 (May 1989): 45–53.
16. See Paul Hill, Gail Foster, and Tamar Gendler, *High Schools with Character* (Santa Monica, Calif.: Rand Corporation, 1990).
17. *New York Times,* 14 July 1993, B8.
18. For a fuller description of Central Park East Secondary School, see George Wood, *Schools That Work* (New York: New American Library, 1992).

4. Some Lessons Learned

1. For a very thoughtful discussion of the myth of the golden educational past, see Deborah Meier, "Myths, Lies and Public Schools," *The Nation,* 21 September 1992. See also chapter 4, "Built to Fail," in Samuel G. Freedman's superb book, *Small Victories* (New York: Harper & Row, 1990).
2. See John Chubb and Terry Moe, *Politics, Markets, and America's Schools* (Washington, D.C.: Brookings Institution, 1990).
3. See the Carnegie Foundation for the Advancement of Teaching, *School Choice: A Special Report* (Princeton, N.J.: The Foundation, 1992).
4. David Kearns and Dennis Doyle, *Winning the Brain Race* (San Francisco: ICS Press, 1991), 90.
5. This is the phrase Theodore Sizer uses in *Horace's School: Redesigning the American High School* (Boston: Houghton

Mifflin, 1992), which contains numerous examples of "exhibitions" which students might be expected to perform.

6. Grant Wiggins has authored a number of excellent articles which are available from the Center on Learning, Assessment, and School Structure, 39 Main St., Genesco, N.Y. 14454. The Coalition of Essential Schools (Box 1969, Providence, RI 02912) also has a research project and a number of publications. See also Ruth Mitchell, *Testing for Learning: How New Approaches to Evaluation Can Improve Schools* (New York: Free Press, 1992).
7. See Howard Gardner, *The Unschooled Mind: How Children Think and How Schools Should Teach* (New York: Basic Books, 1991).
8. Kearns and Doyle, *Winning the Brain Race,* 140.
9. As quoted from a speech given at a Harvard Graduate School of Education symposium, April 1992.
10. See E. D. Hirsch, *Cultural Literacy: What Every American Needs to Know* (Boston: Houghton Mifflin, 1987).
11. See Tony Wagner, "Educating for Excellence on an Endangered Planet," in *Social Issues and Education: Challenge and Responsibility,* edited by Alex Molnar (Washington, D.C.: Association for Supervision and Curriculum Development, 1987).
12. Many items on this list of outcomes were developed by RMC president Everett Barnes, vice president Chris Dwyer, University of New Hampshire assistant professor Joseph Onosko and myself as a part of a New American Schools Development Corporation proposal we authored.
13. See the report of the Commission on the Skills of the American Workforce, "America's Choice: High Skills or Low Wages" (Rochester, N.Y.: National Center on Education and the Economy, 1990); and the Secretary's Commission on Achieving Necessary Skills, "What Work Requires of Schools" (Washington, D.C.: U.S. Department of Labor, 1991).
14. For a summary of these and other efforts to set subject-specific standards, and for addresses to obtain additional information, see *Education Week,* 16 June 1993.
15. Ibid.
16. *New York Times,* 21 July 1993, B10.
17. John Immerwahr, Jean Johnson, and Adam Kernan-Schloss, "Cross-Talk: The Public, the Experts, and Competitiveness"

(New York: Public Agenda Foundation, 1991), 13. See also Public Agenda Foundation's more recent reports, "Educational Reform: The Players and the Politics," and "Divided Within, Besieged Without: The Politics of Education in Four American School Districts." Both were prepared by Steve Farkas and were published by the Public Agenda Foundation in 1992 and 1993 respectively. For further information, contact Public Agenda Foundation, 6 East 39th St., New York, N.Y. 10016.

18. For a fuller description of these nonpartisan media campaigns and other forms of public education about complex policy issues, see Daniel Yankelovich, *Coming to Public Judgment: Making Democracy Work in a Complex World* (Syracuse, N.Y.: Syracuse University Press, 1991).
19. Carnegie Forum on Education and the Economy, *A National Prepared: Teachers of the 21st Century* (New York: Carnegie Corporation, 1986).

5. Reflections at the Dawn of the Millennium

1. United States Department of Education, *The State of Charter Schools 2000—Fourth-Year Report, January 2000* (Washington, D.C., 2000).
2. Achieve Inc., *1999 National Education Summit Briefing Book* (Washington, D.C., 1999).
3. United States Department of Education, *The State of Charter Schools 2000.*
4. Massachusetts State Department of Education, *Five Year Plan* (Malden, Mass., 1994).
5. These MCAS scores, and all others reported in this chapter except for Cambridge, Mass., data by race and house, are taken from the "Massachusetts Comprehensive Assessment System Summary of District Performance," Massachusetts State Department of Education, Malden, Mass., 1998, 1999.
6. As quoted by Drew Lindsay in "Call to Arms," *Teacher Magazine*, April 2000, p. 19.
7. Office of Development and Assessment, "1999 MCAS Report" (Cambridge Public Schools, 2000).
8. Mary Anne Raywid,"Small Schools: A Reform That Works," *Educational Leadership* 55, no. 4 (December 1997/January 1998).

9. Office of Development and Assessment, "1999 MCAS Report."
10. See Tony Wagner,"Why Charter Schools?" *Education Week*, Commentary, June 22, 1994.
11. United States Department of Education, *The State of Charter Schools 2000.*

Bibliography

Barth, Roland, *Improving Schools from Within.* San Francisco: Jossey-Bass, 1990.

Blenky, Mary Field, Blythe McVicker Clindry, Mancy Rule Goldberger, and Jill Mattuck Tarule. *Women's Ways of Knowing: The Development of Self, Voice, and Mind.* New York: Basic Books, 1986.

Boyer, Ernest. *High School.* New York: Harper & Row, 1983.

Carnegie Forum on Education and the Economy. *A Nation Prepared: Teachers for the 21st Century.* New York: Carnegie Corporation, 1986.

The Carnegie Foundation for the Advancement of Teaching. *School Choice: A Special Report*, foreword by Ernest L. Boyer, Princeton, N.J.: The Foundation, 1992.

Carnevale, Anthony P. *Workplace Basics: The Essential Skills Employers Want*, San Francisco: Jossey-Bass, 1990.

Chubb, John E., and Terry M. Moe. *Politics, Markets, and America's Schools.* Washington, D.C.: Brookings Institution, 1990.

Coles, Robert. *Privileged Ones: The Well-off and the Rich in America.* Boston: Little, Brown, 1977.

Comer, James P. "Educating Poor Minority Children." *Scientific American* 259, no. 5 (November 1988).

———. *Maggie's American Dream: The Life and Times of a Black Family.* New York: New American Library, 1988.

Dewey, John. *The Child and the Curriculum* and *The School and Society.* Chicago: University of Chicago Press, 1956.

Elkind, David. *The Hurried Child: Growing Up Too Fast Too Soon.* Reading, Mass.: Addison-Wesley, 1981.

Fiske, Edward B. *Smart Schools, Smart Kids: Why Do Some Schools Work?* New York: Simon & Schuster, 1991.

Freedman, Samuel G. *Small Victories.* New York: Harper & Row, 1990.

Fromm, Erich. *Man for Himself: An Inquiry into the Psychology of Ethics.* New York: Rinehart & Winston, 1947.

———. *The Sane Society.* New York: Holt, Rinehart & Winston, 1955.

———. *The Revolution of Hope: Toward a Humanized Technology.* New York: Harper & Row, 1968.

———. *To Have or To Be.* New York: Harper & Row, 1976.

Gardner, Howard. *Frames of Mind.* New York: Basic Books, 1983.

———. *The Unschooled Mind: How Children Think and How Schools Should Teach.* New York: Basic Books, 1991.

Gilligan, Carol. *In a Different Voice: Psychological Theory and Women's Development.* Cambridge, Mass.: Harvard University Press, 1982.

———, and Lyn Mikel Brown. *Meeting at the Crossroads: Women's Psychology and Girls' Development.* Cambridge, Mass.: Harvard University Press, 1992.

Goodlad, John I. *A Place Called School.* New York: McGraw-Hill, 1983.

Graves, Donald. *Writing: Teachers and Children at Work.* Portsmouth, N.H.: Heinemann, 1983.

Hill, Paul, Gail Foster, and Tamar Gendler. *High Schools with Character.* Santa Monica, Calif.: Rand Corporation, 1990.

Hirsch, E. D. *Cultural Literacy: What Every American Needs to Know.* Boston: Houghton Mifflin, 1987.

Institute for Education in Transformation. "Voices from the Inside: A Report on Schooling from Inside the Classroom." Claremont, Calif.: Claremont Graduate School, 1992.

Johnson, Susan Moore. *Teachers at Work.* New York: Basic Books, 1990.

Kearns, David T., and Dennis P. Doyle. *Winning the Brain Race.* San Francisco, Calif.: ICS Press, 1991.

Lickona, Thomas, *Educating for Character: How Our Schools Can Teach Respect and Responsibility.* New York: Bantam, 1991.

Lightfoot, Sara Lawrence. *The Good High School: Portraits of Character and Culture.* New York: Basic Books, 1983.

Lortie, Dan C. *Schoolteacher: A Sociological Study.* Chicago: University of Chicago Press, 1975.

Maccoby, Michael. "The Three C's and Discipline for Freedom." *School Review* 79, no. 2 (February 1971).

———. "A Psychoanalytic View of Learning." *Change Magazine*, Winter 1971–72.

———. "Toward a Moral Education." *Independent School*, May 1977.

———. *The Gamesman.* New York: Simon & Schuster, 1976.

———. *The Leader.*New York: Simon & Schuster, 1980.

———. *Why Work: Leading The New Generation.* New York: Simon & Schuster, 1988.

Mitchell, Ruth. *Testing for Learning: How New Approaches to Evaluation Can Improve Schools.* New York: Free Press, 1992.

Noddings, Nell. *The Challenge to Care in School: An Alternative Approach to Education.* New York: Teachers College Press, 1992.

Oaks, Jeannie. *Keeping Track: How Schools Structure Inequality.* New Haven: Yale University Press, 1985.

Peters, Thomas J., and Robert H. Waterman, Jr. *In Search of Excellence.* New York: Harper & Row, 1982.

Piaget, Jean. *To Understand Is to Invent.* New York: Viking Press, 1973.

Powell, Arthur, Eleanor Farrar, and David Cohen. *The Shopping Mall High School.* Boston: Houghton Mifflin, 1985.

Schor, Juliet B. *The Overworked Americans.* New York: Basic Books, 1992.

Senge, Peter M. *The Fifth Discipline: The Art and Practice of the Learning Organization.* New York: Doubleday/Currency, 1990.

Sizer, Theodore. *Horace's Compromise: The Dilemma of the American High School.* Boston: Houghton Mifflin, 1984.

———. *Horace's School: Redesigning the American High School.* Boston: Houghton Mifflin, 1992.

U.S. National Commission on Excellence in Education. *A Nation at Risk.* Washington, D.C.: The Commission, 1983.

Wagner, Tony. "All Is Quiet But Not All Is Well in Suburbia," *Phi Delta Kappan*, April 1976.

———. "Learning Democratically." *The English Journal*, September 1977.

———. "Teaching Writing as Self-Expression." *Maryland English Journal*, no. 1 (1978).

———. "Piaget on Moral Development." *Independent School*, October 1978.

———. "Educating for Character." *Independent School*, October 1979.

———. "Why Nuclear Education." *Educational Leadership*, May 1983.

———. "Educating for Responsibility in the Nuclear Age." *Media & Methods*, November 1983.

———. "New Ways of Teaching for the Nuclear Age." *Bulletin of Atomic Scientists*, December 1984.

———. "Educating for Excellence on an Endangered Planet." In *Social Issues and Education*, edited by Alex Molnar. Washington, D.C.: Association for Supervision and Curriculum Development, 1987.

———. "Carnegie School-Business Partnerships: A Report on the First Year" and "School-Based Management in Massachusetts." Massachusetts State Department of Education, 1990.

———. "Straddling Two Cultures: Polaroid's Project Bridge and School Reform." Cambridge, Mass.: Polaroid Corporation, 1991.

———. "Improving High Schools: The Case for New Goals and Strategies." *Phi Delta Kappan*, May 1993.

———. "Systemic Change: Rethinking the Purpose of School." *Educational Leadership*, September 1993.

Wheelock, Anne. *Crossing the Tracks: How Untracking Can Save America's Schools*. New York: New Press, 1992.

Wigginton, Eliot. *Sometimes a Shining Moment: The Foxfire Experience*. New York: Anchor Books, 1985.

Wood, George H. *Schools That Work: America's Most Innovative Public Education Programs*. New York: New American Library, 1992.

Yankelovich, Daniel. *Coming to Public Judgment: Making Democracy Work in a Complex World*. Syracuse, N.Y.: Syracuse University Press, 1991.

Index

Ability grouping, 50, 135
"Absent parent syndrome," 57–58
Activity periods, 69, 70, 73
Advising Program, 106
Advisory roles, for teachers, 139–42
Alcohol, pressures to experiment with, 200–201, 257
American Association for the Advancement of Science, report of, 260
American Federation of Teachers, 2, 76
Arts, emphasis on, in curriculum, 105, 106
Assessment, strong, 30
Association of American Geographers, report of, 260
Attendance, perfect, 71
Authority, challenges to, 57

Baltimore Country, 196
Basics Program, 103
Behavior, poor student, 53–56
Blenky, Mary Field, et al., *Women's Ways of Knowing*, 203
Boston Public Library, 189, 191
Boston Sunday Globe, 27
Boyer, Ernest, 1–2, 42
Brown, Neal, 192–93, 220
Brown University, 6, 173, 192
Budget, school, 25, 68, 84
Burns, Nancy, 89, 103–4, 117, 152, 153, 156; joint position of, at Academy, 164–68
Burwood, Bob, 42, 43, 44, 45
Bush, George, 239

Cabral, Ruben, 9, 81, 113, 162–63, 175, 251; achievements of at Academy, 117; and bureaucracy, 168–69; career of, 99–101; and collaboration, 147–50; and creation of Academy, 92, 93, 95–98; and faculty empowerment, 103–5; on gap between rhetoric and reality, 130–31; leadership of, 101–3, 152; resignation of, 150; struggle over replacement of, 151–53
Cambridge Teachers' Association (CTA), 152, 153, 157, 159, 161, 163
Caring, importance of, for development of children, 138–47
Carnegie Commission report (*A Nation Prepared*), 2, 268
Carnegie units, 250, 261

Census, U.S., 18
Center for Civic Education, 261
Center for the Study of Social Policy, 57
Central Park East Elementary School (New York City), 230
Central Park East Secondary School (New York City), 141, 223, 230, 238, 249
Change: creating new vision for educational, 249–59; limits of top-down, 78–80; tools for, 48. *See also* Collaboration; Core values; Goals
Charleton, Richard, 21
Chicago, University of, 262
Choice school, 6, 230–31, 239–44
Chubb, John, *Politics, Markets, and America's Schools* (with T. Moe), 239
Citizenship: core value of, 199, 202, 237; education for world, 255–56, 259
Claremont Graduate School, 140; Institute for Education in Transformation at, 60
Class and race, dealing with, 131–38
Class size, 84–85
Clayton, Arnie, 103, 117, 118, 152, 153, 156, 158; joint position of, at Academy, 164–68
Clindry, Blythe McVicker, et al., *Women's Ways of Knowing*, 203
Clinton, Bill, 239
Coalition of Essential Schools (CES), 9, 10, 23, 29, 141, 203; Brimmer and Mary's membership in, 6, 173–79, 190, 191–92, 205, 206–9; and interdisciplinary teaching, 220; principles of, 30, 177–78, 193, 206–7, 220, 243; and standardized tests, 245–46
Cochran, Richard, 21, 22, 27
Coeducation, 202, 203–5, 244
Cohen, David, et al., *The Shopping Mall High School*, 88, 89
Coles, Robert, *Privileged Ones*, 195
Collaboration, 11–12, 77, 78, 235, 237, 270; and Brimmer and May, 205–20, 222, 235–36; and Cambridge Rindge and Latin, 117, 147–64; and Hull High School, 48, 63–66, 75, 76
Colleges, role of, in building consensus, 261–62
Comer, James, 60, 63, 139, 144
Community and parental involvement in schools, 142–47
Community service, 30, 71, 72, 73, 256
Competency vs. curriculum, 120–31
Concerned Black Staff, 87, 88
"Connections," 189, 220
Consensus, tools and strategies for building, 259–62
Consultants, role of, in school change, 266
Consumption, addiction of students to passive, 56–57, 61
Cooper, Frances, 156
Cooperative learning, 48, 49 50, 51; at Cambridge Rindge and Latin, 104, 105, 106, 114, 117–18, 136–37; defined, 117
Core values, 11, 147, 230, 235, 270; and Brimmer and May, 195–205, 237; and Cambridge Rindge and Latin, 117, 131–38; and Hull High School, 24, 25, 48, 53–62, 76
Coupland, Douglas, 59
"Critical friend," 11; role of, 266
Cross-cultural education, 105, 106
Crowell, Eugene, 21

Curriculum Committee, 212, 214–15
Curriculum vs. competency, 120–31

Dade County, Florida, 2, 76, 228
David, Jane, 228–29
Davis Henrietta, 156–57
Decision making, shared, 105, 106
Dewey, John, 262
Dickson, David, 76
Diversity, celebrating, 105, 106, 134–35
Doble, John, 7
Dropout(s): prevention program (STRIDE), 26; programs to retain potential, 86; rate, 20, 86, 155, 156, 158–59, 238
Drugs, pressures to experiment with, 200–201, 257

Economy, education for changing, 254–55, 258
Edison Project, 241
Educational Leadership, 228
Employers, role of local, in building consensus, 261–62
Empowerment, leadership for faculty, 93–105
Enterprise Co-op, 86
Environmental studies, 50, 51–52
Equity, issues of, 203–5
Executive Educator, 22

"Face-to-face" high schools, 229–30
Faculty-Administrative Committee ("Ajax Committee"), 213–14, 216–19, 224–25
Faculty Council, 152–56, 160, 161, 162, 163
Faculty Senate, 70, 74
Farrar, Eleanor, et al., The Shopping Mall High School, 88, 89
Fernandez, Joseph, 76
Focus groups, 7; need for, 262–68
Foxfire, 130
Fundamental programs, 85, 86, 91, 93, 94, 148, 168

Gallup survey, 58
Galluzzo, Mary Lou, 20
Gardner, Howard, 37, 331, 249
Goals, clear academic, 11, 78, 147, 235, 270; and Brimmer and May, 189–95; and Cambridge Rindge and Latin, 117, 118, 120, 127, 131; and Hull High School, 48–53; need for dialogue about new, 237–39, steps for developing and implementing, 237; task forces to develop, 267–68
Goldberger, Mancy Rule, et al., *Women's Ways of Knowing*, 203
Goodlad, John, 1–2, 42, 190
Government, role of, in building consensus, 260–61
Gratification, addiction of students to instant, 56, 256
Growth and development: individual, 236, 256; social, 237
Growth and health, education for personal, 256–58, 259
Guidance counselors, 139–40
Guild, Judy, 9, 10, 174–75, 184–85, 197, 202; and Coalition of Essential Schools, 175, 176, 177–79, 191–92, 193, 206, 208, 210–12, 215; and Faculty-Administrative Committee, 213–214, 219; and interdisciplinary teaching, 220, 222–23; ninth-grade English class of, 179–82, 185–89; and SATs, 245

Hammond, Indiana, 76
Harvard University, 7, 83, 99, 130, 255

Heterogeneous grouping, 48, 49, 50, 51, 75
Hirsch, E. D., 225
Honesty, core value of, 199, 202, 237
Hope Essential High School (Providence), 192
Hull Council for Business and Cultural Development, 17–18
"Hull Public Schools—Now and in the Future," 23–24
Hull Teachers Association, 67, 72, 74
Hurst, Bill, 19

Interdisciplinary teaching, 29, 47, 48, 220–24
Internships, 256

John F. Kennedy High School (New York City), 89, 103
Johnson, Susan Moore, *Teachers at Work*, 77, 221–22

Kanter, Rosabeth Moss, 23–24
Kearnes, David, *Winning the Brain Race* (with D. P. Doyle), 245, 254
Key Results Committee, 87–91, 92, 103, 162
Kohlberg, Lawrence, 99
Kozol, Jonathan, 84

Leadership program, 92, 94
Learning: capacities for, 56–57; education for continuing, 255, 258–59; individualized, 135–38; town meetings for, 262–68; traditional incentives for, 57–58
Learning communities, creating, 268–69
Learning organization, creating, 224–27, 269
Lightfoot, Sara Lawrence, 7, 63; *The Good High School*, 7
Local control, at Brimmer and May, 227–29
Lortie, Dan, *Schoolteacher*, 221, 222
"Losers," students categorized as, 58, 59, 135, 196, 270

Maccoby, Michael, 7, 61
McGarth, Mary Lou, 97, 149
McIntyre, Bob, 18, 60, 64, 69, 70, 140
"McJobs," 59
McWalters, Peter, 76
"Marketplace," limits of educational, 239–44
Massachusetts Association of School Superintendents, 27
Massachusetts State Department of Education, 77
Math/science exam school, 87, 88, 93
Media, new roles for, in building consensus, 266-67
Meier, Deborah, 141, 238
Mentor programs, 144
Miss Brown's Classical (Boston), 174
Miss Folsom's (Boston), 174
MIT, 83
Moe, Terry, *Politics, Markets, and America's Schools* (With J. Chubb), 239
Monroe, Lorraine, 22
Moral issues, creating all-school conversations about, 197–203

National Center on Education and the Economy, Report of, 260
National Council for Geographic Education, report of, 260
National Council for the Social Studies, report of, 260

National Council of Teachers of English, report of, 260
National Council of Teachers of Mathematics, report of, 260
Nation at Risk, A, 1
Needs, attention to individual, in context of community, 105, 106
New England Association for Schools and Colleges (NEASC), 43, 64, 74, 88; report of, 64–66, 78
Ninth-grade academic classes, typical day of, 31–42
Noddings, Nell, 139

O'Rourke, Patrick, 76

Parents, involvement of, in children's schools, 30, 142–47
Park Service, 38–39
Performing arts, school for, 87, 88, 93
Peterkin, Robert, 87
Pilot program, 85, 86, 91, 93, 94, 148, 168
Portraiture, 7
Powell, Arthur, et al., *The Shopping Mall High School*, 88, 89
Prileson, Jenny, 193, 194, 214–15
Professional development, 30
Project America, 165
Proposition Two-and-a-Half, 19, 21, 22, 25, 84
Public Agenda Foundation, 7, 250, 263–64, 266–67

Race and class, dealing with, 131–38
Rafferty, James, 154, 155, 156
Rand Corporation, *High Schools with Character*, 229
Reagan, Ronald, 150
"Real world" experiences, allowing students', 138
Reenstierna, Anne, 9, 10, 171, 212, 243, 251; and board of trustees, 227–28; characterized, 175; and Coalition of Essential Schools, 175–76, 177–78, 192, 193–94; and coeducation, 203, 204–5; and core values, 202, 203; and Faculty-Administrative Committee, 213–14, 216, 217, 219; and faculty stress, 216; and interdisciplinary teaching, 220–21, 223–24; message from, 173–74; and moral issues, 197; pressure on, 244; and visitors' committee, 225–26
Respect, core value of, 199, 202, 237
Responsibility, core value of, 199, 202, 237
Rindge School of Technical Arts Program, 93, 94
Rindge Technical and Vocational program, 85, 91
Rochester, New York, 2, 76
Rudenstine, Neil, 255

Sarasin, Ed, 93–98, 147–48, 150–51, 154–55, 164
Scholarships, applying for college, 47
Scholastic Aptitude Test (SAT), 50, 168, 245–48, 250, 261; and Brimmer and May, 176, 194; and Cambridge Rindge and Latin, 194; and Hull High School, 20, 43, 45, 46, 48, 66, 68
School-based management (SBM), 2, 228–29; and Hull High School, 28, 29, 30, 48, 66–78
School-Within-a-School model, 94
Schor, Juliet, 57–58

Secretary's Commission of Achieving Necessary Skills (SCANS), report of, 260
Senge, Peter, 129–30; *The Fifth Discipline*, 224
Sex, pressures to experiment with, 200–201, 257
Shanker, Albert, 2, 76
Sheff, Claire, 15, 44, 78, 175, 219, 251; advisory committee chosen by, 24; budget cuts of, 25; characterized, 22–23, 24, 47; complaints about, 27–28; contract of, 79; departure of, from Hull, 80; grants secured by, 51; hiring of, for Hull superintendency, 21–22; and NEASC report, 64–66; her plan for change, 24–27, 28–31, 45, 47, 79–80, 97–98; priorities and strategies of, 23–24; 50; and school-based management, 66–67
"Shopping mall high school," 88, 89, 229
Sizer, Theodore, 1–2, 9, 42, 63, 184, 192; and Brimmer and May School, 174; Coalition of Essential Schools of, 6, 23, 29, 173; on "critical friend," 11, 266; on habits of mind, 37, 249; Horace's Compromise, 175, 203; Horace's School, 88; and "less is more," 207; and passiveness and docility, 190; on personalizing education, 85; on "student as worker, teacher as coach," 81, 95, 130, 178; on student "exhibitions of mastery," 45, 246; his suggestion about two diplomas, 137
Social values, nurturing, by schools, 62
Special education, improved, 30
Standardized tests, 239, 244–49
Stonehill College, 21
STRIDE (dropout prevention program), 26
"Student as worker, teacher as coach," 81, 95, 130, 177–79
Student Council, 161

Tarule, Jill Mattuck, et al., Women's Ways of Knowing, 203
Task forces, to develop goals and methods of assessment, 267–68
Teacher(s): advisory roles for, 139–42; attitudes, 63–64; full inclusion of, 29; team planning, 42–47
Team(s): interdisciplinary, 29, 47; meetings, 114–17; planning, teacher, 42–47, 50; teaching, 104, 105, 106, 113
Time, as essential resource in change process, 269–70
Tornillo, Pat, 76
"Total quality improvement" program, 2
Town meetings for learning, need for, 262–68
Tracking, 30, 135–37
Transitional Advisory Committee, 92
Triangulation, 8
TV, optimum use of cable, 30

Unions: at Cambridge Rindge and Latin, 76, 114, 152, 159; in Hull, 64, 72, 75, 76, 79
Upward Bound, 133
Urbanski, Adam, 76

Vance, Cyrus, 263
Vellucci, Alfred, 155, 156, 159, 160, 161–62, 163
Violence, 53, 257

Walnut Hill School, 178, 206
Wheaton College, 175
Wheelock, Anne, 137
Whittle, Christopher, 241
Wiggins, Grant, 246
Wigginton, Eliot, *Sometimes a Shining Moment*, 130
"Winners," students categorized as, 58, 196, 270
Winsor School, 174
Wolf, Alice, 154, 155, 156, 157, 161–62, 163

Xerox, 245, 254

Yale University, 60
Yankelovich, Daniel, 7, 263

RHODE ISLAND COLLEGE LIBRARY
3 1510 00455 6628

The first edition of ***How Schools Change*** chronicled the efforts of three very different high schools to improve teaching and learning in the early 1990's. The book—with its down-to-earth descriptions of the struggles of real teachers, parents, and students and insights into the change process—is widely considered a modern educational classic. Now, in a new second edition, Wagner concisely summarizes the decade-long history of education reform efforts and revisits the three communities at the beginning of a new century.

Advance Praise for the Second Edition

"Tony Wagner's fresh look at his three subject institutions in ***How Schools Change*** reveals sober and useful insights into contemporary educational reform. We must pay close attention to Wagner's conclusions."
—Theodore R. Sizer, Chairman of the Coalition of Essential Schools

Praise for *How Schools Change*

"In school reform, three careful case studies are worth 300 reports from blue-ribbon commissions. In ***How Schools Change***, Tony Wagner portrays the trials and the triumphs of three schools engaged in reinventing themselves."
—Howard Gardner, author of *Creating Minds*

"Weaving classroom scenes through a readable text of education data and interviews with faculty, students, and parents, [***How Schools Change*** is] a dedicated attempt to understand the struggle of education to survive."
—Pamela Ferdinand, *Boston Globe*

Tony Wagner is Co-Director of the recently created Change Leadership Group at the Harvard University Graduate School of Education. He also chairs the Harvard Seminar on Public Engagement, and consults to numerous school districts and foundations in the United States and internationally, and is currently senior consultant to the Bill and Melinda Gates Foundation.

RoutledgeFalmer will publish his second book, *The New Village School: Winning the Hearts and Minds of Kids and Teachers*, next year.

ROUTLEDGE / FALMER
Taylor & Francis Group

29 West 35th Street
New York, NY 10001
www.routledge-ny.com

11 New Fetter Lane
London EC4P 4EE
www.routledge.com

Printed in the U.S.A.

ISBN 0-415-92763-3

90000

9 780415 927635